# A Saint's Name

# A Comprensive Listing of Christian and Biblical Names

## Woodeene Koenig-Bricker

ACTA
ASSISTING CHRISTIANS TO ACT
PUBLICATIONS

*A Saint's Name*
*A Comprehensive Listing of Christian and Biblical Names*
by Woodeene Koenig-Bricker

Edited by Gregory F. Augustine Pierce
Cover design by Tom A. Wright
Page design and typesetting by Garrison Productions

Published by: ACTA Publications
           Assisting Christians To Act
           4848 N. Clark Street
           Chicago, IL 60640-4711
           800-397-2282
           e-mail: ACTApublications@aol.com

Library of Congress Catalog Number: 00-106103
ISBN: 0-87946-217-5
Year: 04 03 02
Printing: 8 7 6 5 4 3 2
Printed in the United States of America

# CONTENTS

# INTRODUCTION

Everyone in heaven is a saint. In faith, I believe my beloved grandfather John Patrick, your favorite Aunt Jean, and my boss's baby brother Tony may all be saints. But they are saints with a small "s." What we generally mean when we talk about the saints are those men and women who are saints with a capital "S," those individuals who were so extraordinarily holy here on earth the Church has officially recognized them as being in heaven.

The lengthy process by which a person becomes a capital "S" saint is called canonization. If a person has shown great holiness, he or she may be called "Venerable" after their death. Following intensive investigation of the person's virtue, writings, and life in general, and after one miracle attributed to him or her has been verified, he or she may be beatified and officially called "Blessed." (Names of some who have been officially named "Blessed" but are not yet canonized are included in this book.) Finally, after documentation of a second miracle performed by direct intercession of the blessed person, he or she may officially be declared "Saint" and given a feast day—usually the day of his or her death. The only exception to this canonization process is the martyr, who does not require documented miracles to be canonized.

The first formal canonization did not occur until 993 when Pope John XV proclaimed Bishop Ulric of Augsburg to be a saint. Prior to that time, men and women were acclaimed saints by popular sentiment, much the way Mother Teresa of Calcutta is already called a saint by the media and many of the faithful. However, even someone as obviously holy as Mother Teresa still has to go through the formal process before the Church will officially enter her in the roll call of canonized saints.

The practice of naming children after saints has a long and honorable history. Because the saints have "run the race, fought the good fight, kept the faith" as St. Paul says, the Church has long encouraged parents to name their child after a saint. Many people, Catholic and non-Catholic alike, believe that a Catholic child *must* be given a saint's name at Baptism. In fact, the only current requirement in the Code of Canon Law is that parents, sponsors and parish priests take care that the given name is not "foreign to Christian sentiment" (Canon 855). Thus, a Catholic child should not be named Hitler, Judas, Satan, or Lucifer. However, a baby can be named after anyone who has exhibited virtue or holiness.

The misconception regarding the Catholic requirement of giving children saints' names arose from the Code of Canon Law which was promulgated in 1917 and remained in force until it was revised in 1983. Under the "old code," parents were *required* to give their children a "Christian" name. If they did not do so, then the pastor was obligated to add a saint's name. So parents who wanted to call their daughter "Sunshine" might find the name "Edburga" added to the baptismal certificate because Edburga was the baptizing priest's favorite saint (as well as his mother's name!)

In order to prevent children being stuck with unwelcome monikers, it became customary for parents to choose a saint's name themselves. This practice gradually became fixed in many people's minds as the "requirement" to have a saint's name, but in fact this is not the law, even in the Catholic Church.

So, because even Catholic parents can select any name not against Christian sentiment, you can call your child almost anything you want. But choosing a saint's name for your child can still be an excellent idea. Not only will you provide your child with a heavenly role model, but you will give him or her a special protector and patron.

As you consider the names in this book, be sure to check out the different saints who share the same name. If you like the name "Peter" for your son, for example, you will find that there have been many Saint Peters—not to mention the Pierres and Piers—over the centuries. Pick one who may have special significance to your ethnic background or may have his feast day on your child's birthday. Or, simply choose the name and let your son (when he is old enough) pore over the various Peters who have become saints.

The custom of taking a saint's name is also important in the sacrament of Confirmation. This is an opportunity for a person to reestablish his or her connection with the saint's name given at birth or to choose another saint to honor by taking his or her name as a Confirmation name.

It isn't necessary to stick to the tried and true when it comes to a saint's name. Hundreds of names and variations of names are linked to saints. You may be surprised to discover just how many are listed in this book. And since saints come from *every* ethnic background and *every* continent (except Antarctica), it's possible to find a saint's name that has specific meaning for you.

One way to enlarge the number of possibilities, especially with ethnic names, is to consider using a saint's middle or last name. Adolphus Ludigo-Mkasa and Maria Clementine Anuarite Nengapete are African martyrs, for example. Using Mkasa or Nengapete as a first or middle name is an ideal way to incorporate an interesting and meaningful saint into your child's name.

Another way to choose a saint's name is to consider a patron saint. There are patrons for almost every occupation and state of life. A selected list of popular patron saints is given on pages 183-184. You may also want to consider a biblical name. While these holy men and women were never formally declared saints, their names certainly are appropriate choices. Appropriate biblical names are listed throughout the book alongside the saint names, and lists of the biblical names contained in this work can be found on pages 185 and 187.

Finally, not every saint's name in the history of the world is included in this collection. Some names just didn't seem appropriate to give to a modern child. In making judgment calls on which names to include, I may have omitted one of your family's favorites. If so, write or e-mail me and I'll try to include it in future editions. If you are looking for some suggestions for a particular ethnic group, you are welcome to write me or e-mail me c/o ACTA Publications at the address given on the copyright page of this book.

Choosing a name for your child is one of the most important decisions you will ever make. As author Bulwer Lytton says, "Some names stimulate and encourage the owner, others deject and paralyze him (or her)." As you peruse these pages for a name, remember that just as each child is a miracle fresh from the hands of God, so too there is one name that seems to fit each person perfectly.

May the saints themselves guide you as you locate *the* perfect name for yourself or another.

P.S. For all of you who are wondering what my saint's name is, it's Gertrude. My baptismal name is Woodeene Lynda Gertrude.

# HOW TO USE THIS BOOK

There are thousands of names and variations listed in this book. To make it easier to find a name, they are divided alphabetically into boys' and girls' names. Saints' names are then listed in the following manner (see samples on opposite page):

1. Main name is listed in bold.

2. The meaning of the name is given (where known).

3. Entries are presented for many (but not all) of the individual saints who share a particular name, with date of their death (Abbreviations: d. = died; d.c. = died circa or approximately.)

   For a pope who has been canonized, the years of his papacy are listed instead of his death date, although it is usually the same.

4. If a name is from the Scriptures, it is listed as "biblical," along with a scriptural reference.

5. If a last or middle name or a title of a saint is known, this is listed before his or her date of death.

6. A short description of each saint is given, followed by his or her feast day. (Some saints do not have formal feast days, and a few have more than one. Some traditional feast days are no longer celebrated on the Church calendar, but are still celebrated in particular areas or among specific groups and are given where known.)

7. Main names are followed by some (but not all) popular variations of the name.

8. Many girls' names are variations of a boy's name, such as Michelle or Micheala for Micheal. Some (but not all) of these variations are listed under the appropriate girls' section, with the meaning given as "feminine form" of the saint's name.

9. If a variation of a name (such as Zachary for Zachariah) is also the name of a saint, that variation is given its own listing, usually without variations.

10. If a variation has a much different spelling (such as Zak for Isaac, or Drew for Andrew), a separate listing is given with instructions to "see" the saint's name.

1 —— **Mark**

2 —— Meaning: from Latin "Mars" or "the god of war"

4 —— + (biblical): Companion of Sts. Peter and Paul, evangelist (Gospel of Mark). Feast day: April 25.

5 —— + Mark of Galilee (d. 92): Galilean by birth, missionary to Italy. Feast day: April 28.

## Michaela, Michelle —— 8
Meaning: feminine form of Michael

## Zachariah
Meaning: Hebrew "God has remembered"

+ (biblical): Father of St. John the Baptist (Luke 1:5-25, 57-79). Feast day: November 15.

7 —— *(Zacariah, Zacarias, Zachary, Zachery, Zackery, Zak, Zechariah)* —— 9

## Zachary
Meaning: Hebrew "God has remembered"

+ (date unknown): Martyr in Nicomedia (in modern Turkey). Feast day: June 10. —— 6

3 —— + (d.c. 106): French bishop and martyr. Feast day: May 26.

+ Zachary, Pope (served from 741-752): Rescued slaves from the Roman markets, supported St. Boniface's mission to the Germans. Feast day: March 15.

## Zak —— 10
See Isaac, Zachariah

# Saints' Names

# BOYS

# A

## Aaron

Meaning: Hebrew "light" or "mountain"

+ (biblical): Brother of Moses. (Exodus 4:14).

+ (d. 305): British martyr under the Emperor Diocletian. Feast day: July 1.

+ (d. 543 or 544): French abbot. Feast day: June 22

*(Aaran, Aaren, Aarin, Aaronn, Aaron, Aron, Arran, Arron, Ari, Arin, Aron, Arron)*

## Abban

Meaning: unknown

+ (date unknown): Irish hermit. Feast day: May 13.

+ (d. fifth century): Abbot and missionary. Feast day: October 27.

+ (d. 620): Abbot and Irish prince. Feast day: March 16.

*(Ewin, Evin, Neville, Nevin)*

## Abel

Meaning: Hebrew "breath"

+ (biblical): Second son of Adam and Eve (Genesis 4:2).

+ (d.c. 751): Archbishop and Benedictine abbot. Feast day: August 5.

*(Abell)*

## Abraham

Meaning: Hebrew "father of the nations"

+ (biblical): First Hebrew patriarch (Genesis 17:5).

+ (d.c. 345): Assyrian bishop. Feast day: February 5.

+ (d. 367): Egyptian hermit. Feast day: October 27.

+ Abraham of Carrhae (d.c. 422): Hermit, bishop, and missionary. Feast day: February 14.

+ (d.c. 480): Hermit and confessor from Iraq. Feast day: June 15.

+ (d. sixth century): Archbishop of Ephesus, Greece. Feast day: October 28.

+ Abraham Kidunaia (d. sixth century): Hermit. Feast day: March 16.

+ Abraham of Kratia (d.c. 558) Bishop and hermit in present-day Turkey. Feast day: December 6.

+ Abraham of Rostov (d. twelfth century): Apostle to the Russian people. Feast day: October 29.

+ Abraham of Smolensk (d. 1221): Biblical scholar and Russian monk. Feast day: August 21.

*(Abe, Abrahim, Abram, Avraham, Avram)*

## Absalom

Meaning: Hebrew "my father is peace"

+ (biblical): King David's son (2 Sam 14:25).

## Achillas

Meaning: unknown

+ (d. 313): Bishop of Alexandria, Egypt. Feast day: November 7.

+ (d.c. 330): Greek bishop. Feast day: May 15.

+ (d. fourth century): Egyptian hermit. Feast day: January 17.

*(Achilles, Achillius)*

# Achilleus

Meaning: probably derived from "the silent one"

+ Achilleus Kewanuka (d. 1886): One of the Martyrs of Uganda. Feast day: June 3.

# Adalar

Meaning: unknown

+ (d. 755): Priest and martyr. Feast day: June 5.

# Adam

Meaning: Hebrew "red earth" or "mankind"

+ (biblical): the first man (Genesis 2:7)

+ (d.c. 1210): Italian hermit and abbot. Feast day: May 16.

*(Addam, Adem)*

# Adolf

Meaning: Old German "noble wolf"

+ Adolf of Osnabrück (d. 1224): German monk and bishop. Feast day: February 11.

*(Adolfo, Adolphe, Adolphe, Adolphus)*

# Adolphus

Meaning: derived from "noble"

+ Adolphus Ludigo-Mkasa (d. 1885): Martyr of Uganda. Feast day: June 3.

# Adrian

Meaning: Latin "from the city of Adria"

+ (d. 304): Roman soldier and martyr. Feast day: September 8.

+ (d. 309): Missionary and martyr. Feast day: March 5 and March 7.

+ (d. 668): Dutch martyr. Feast day: March 19.

+ Adrian of Canterbury (d. 710): African abbot and scholar. Feast day: January 9.

+ Adrian III, Pope (served from 884-885): Feast day: July 8 and September 7.

+ Adrian, Blessed (d. thirteenth century): Dominican martyr in Yugoslavia. Feast day: December 21.

+ Adrian Fortescue, Blessed (d. 1539): English martyr. Feast day: July 9.

+ Adrian van Hilvarenbeek (d. 1572): Martyr. Feast day: July 9.

*(Adrayn, Adreaian, Adreian, Adreyan, Adrien, Adrion, Adryon)*

# Aemilio

See Emilian

# Aibert

Meaning: unknown

+ (d. 1140): Benedictine ascetic and recluse. Feast day: April 7.

*(Aybert)*

# Aidan

Meaning: Gaelic "fire"

+ (d. 626): Bishop known for his kindness to animals. Feast day: January 31.

+ Aidan of Ferns (d. 632): Irish bishop and missionary. Feast day: January 31.

+ Aidan of Lindisfarne (d. 642 or 651): Bishop and founder of monastery. Feast day: August 31.

# Aizan

Meaning: unknown

+ (d.c. 400): Martyr from Abyssinia (modern Ethiopia). Feast day: October 1.

# Alan

See Alanus, Elian

# Alanus

Meaning: Gaelic "rock"

+ Alanus de Solminihaec, Blessed (d. 1659): Former French aristocrat and priest.

*(Alan, Allan, Allen)*

# Alban

Meaning: Latin "from the city on the white hill"

+ (d.c. 304): The first victim of the persecutions conducted in England by Emperor Diocletian. Feast day: June 20.

+ Alban of Mainz (d.c. 400): Greek or Albanian priest. Feast day: June 21.

+ Alban Bartholomew Roe (d. 1642): One of the Forty Martyrs of England and Wales. Feast day: January 21.

*(Albain, Albany, Albein, Albin)*

# Alvis

See Elvis

# Alberic

Meaning: Old German "noble one"

+ (d. 784): Bishop and missionary. Feast day: November 14.

+ (d. 1050): Camaldolese monk and hermit. Feast day: August 29.

+ (d. 1109): Co-founder of the Cistercian Order. Feast day: January 26.

+ Alberic Crescitelli, Blessed (d. 1900): Missionary to China and martyr. Feast day: July 9.

# Albert

Meaning: Old German "noble"

+ Albert of Louvain (d. 1193 or 1202): French Cardinal and knight. Feast day: November 21.

+ Albert of Jerusalem (d.c. 1215): Patron of the Carmelite Order. Feast day: September 25.

+ Albert of Bergamo, Blessed (d. 1279): Farmer. Feast day: May 11.

+ Albert the Great (d. 1280): Doctor of the Church, also called Albertus Magnus. Feast day: November 15.

+ Albert Hurtado Cruchaga (d. 1952): Jesuit priest who served the poor in Chile.

*(Al, Alberto, Bert, Elbert)*

# Aldric

Meaning: Old English "wise counselor"

+ (d. 856): French bishop and court diplomat. Feast day: January 7.

*(Aldric, Aldrick, Aldridge)*

# Aldwin

See Ouen

# Alexander

Meaning: Greek "defender of humanity"

+ Alexander I, Pope (served from 105-115): Feast day: May 3.

+ (d.c. 165): Martyr with St. Felicity during the reign of Emperor Antoninus Pius.

+ Alexander of Jerusalem (d. 251): Bishop and martyr. Feast day: March 18.

+ Alexander of Constantinople (d. 340): Bishop. Feast day: August 28.

+ Alexander Akimetes (d.c. 403): Hermit. Feast day: February 23.

+ Alexander Briant, Blessed (d. 1581): English martyr. Feast day: December 1.

+ Alexander Sauli (d. 1592): Bishop of Corsica. Feast day: October 11.

+ Alexander Rawlins, Blessed (d. 1595): English martyr. Feast day: April 7.

*(Alax, Alec, Aleck, Aleesandro, Alejandro, Aleksandar, Aleksander, Alesandro, Alex, Alexandar, Alexandros, Alexious, Alic, Alixander, Allax, Allex, Sandy)*

## Alexis

Meaning: Greek "protector of men"

+ Alexis Falconieri (d. 1310): Feast day: February 17.

## Alfred

Meaning: Old English "benevolent ruler"

+ Alfred the Great (d. 899): King of Wessex, scholar, and renowned Christian monarch. Feast day: October 26.

*(Alf, Alfredo)*

## Aloysius

Meaning: Latin form of Louis

+ Aloysius Gonzaga (d. 1591): Scholar and patron of youth. Feast day: June 21.

## Alphonsus

Meaning: Old German "battle ready"

+ Alphonsus de Orozco, Blessed (d. 1591): Mystic and court chaplain. Feast day: September 19.

+ Alphonsus Navarrete, Blessed (d. 1617): Dominican martyr of Japan. Feast day: June 1.

+ Alphonsus Rodriguez (d. 1617): Confessor and lay brother. Feast day: October 30.

+ Alphonsus de Mena, Blessed (d. 1622): Dominican martyr of Japan. Feast day: June 1.

+ Alphonsus Marie Liguori (d. 1787): Bishop, Doctor of the Church and the founder of the Redemptorist Congregation. Feast day: August 1.

*(Alfonso, Alfonzo, Alphanso, Alphonse, Alphonzo)*

## Amadeus

Meaning: Latin "lover of God"

+ Amadeus of Lausanne, Blessed (d. 1159): Bishop and official in the French courts. Feast day: January 28.

+ Amadeus IX of Savoy, Blessed (d. 1472): Duke of Savoy, a model of charity. Feast day: March 30.

*(Amadeaus, Amado, Amador, Amadeo, Amedeus)*

## Amandus

Meaning: unknown

+ (d. 675): Bishop and missionary to Flanders. Feast day: February 6.

*(Amand)*

## Ambrose

Meaning: Greek "immortal"

+ (d.c. 250): Confessor and friend of Origen. Feast day: March 17.

+ (d.c. 303): Roman centurion and martyr. Feast day: August 16.

+ Ambrose of Milan (d. 397): Bishop and Doctor of the Church. Fought the Arian heresy, baptized St. Augustine. Feast day: December 7.

+ Ambrose Fernandez, Blessed (d.

1620): Martyr of Japan. Feast day: March 14.

+ Ambrose Edward Barlow (d. 1641): One of the Forty Martyrs of England and Wales. Feast day: September 11.

+ Ambrose Kibuka (d. 1886): Martyr of Uganda. Feast day: June 3.

*(Ambros, Ambrus)*

## Amos

Meaning: Hebrew "born by God"

+ (biblical): One of the Hebrew prophets (Book of Amos).

## Anatolius

Meaning: Greek "east"

+ (d.c. 283): Bishop, noted philosopher and scientist from Alexandria, Egypt. Feast day: July 3.

*(Anatole)*

## Andre

Meaning: French form of Andrew

+ Andre Bessette, Blessed (d. 1937): "The Miracle Worker of Montreal."

## Andreas

Meaning: Latin form of Andrew

+ Andreas Carol Ferrari, Blessed (d. 1921): Italian cardinal.

## Andrew

Meaning: Greek "courageous or virile"

+ (biblical): Apostle and martyr, the brother of St. Peter (Mark 1:16-18). Feast day: November 30.

+ Andrew the Tribune (d.c. 300): The "Great Martyr," the leader of converts in the Roman army. Feast day: August 19.

+ Andrew Corsini (d. 1373): Carmelite miracle worker and papal legate. Feast day: February 4.

+ Andrew Avellino (d. 1608): Theologian, founder, and friend of St. Charles Borromeo. Feast day: November 10.

+ Andrew Sushinda, Blessed (d. 1617): Native-born Japanese martyr. Feast day: June 1.

+ Andrew Tokuan, Blessed (d. 1619): Native-born Japanese martyr. Feast day: June 1.

+ Andrew Chakichi, Blessed (d. 1622): Eight-year-old martyr of Japan. Feast day: October 2.

+ Andrew Bobola (d. 1657): Jesuit missionary and martyr. Feast day: May 16.

+ Andrew Dung Lac (d. 1839): Native-born Vietnamese martyr. Feast day: December 21.

+ Andrew Kim (d. 1846): The first native-born Korean priest, martyr. Feast day: September 20.

+ Andrew Nam-Thuong (d. 1855): Native-born Vietnamese martyr. Feast day: July 15.

+ Andrew Kagwa (d. 1886): Martyr of Uganda. Feast day: June 3.

*(Anders, Anderson, Andras, Andre, André, Adreai, Andreas, Andrei, Andres, Andy, Aundré, Drew)*

## Angelico

Meaning: Italian or Latin "of the angels"

+ Fra Angelico (d. 1455): Dominican, one of the greatest religious painters of all time.

## Anselm

Meaning: Old German "god's helmet"

+ (d.c. 750): Benedictine abbot in France. Feast day: November 18.

+ Anselm of Nonantola (d. 803): Italian abbot and duke. Feast day: March 3.

+ Anselm of Lucca (d. 1086): Bishop and nephew of Pope Alexander II. Feast day: March 18.

+ Anselm Polanco Fontecha, Blessed (d. 1939): Victim of the Spanish civil war.

*(Ansel, Anselmo)*

# Anthony

Meaning: Latin "praiseworthy"

+ Anthony of Egypt (d. 356): One of the founders of monasticism, also called Anthony the Hermit. Feast day: January 17.

+ Anthony of Padua (d. 1231): Doctor of the Church and patron saint of lost objects. Feast day: June 13.

+ Anthony Mary Zaccaria (d. 1538): Co-founder of the Barnabites (the regular Order of St. Paul). Feast day: July 5.

+ Anthony Dainan (d. 1597): Thirteen-year-old Japanese martyr. Feast day: February 6.

+ Anthony Kimura, Blessed (d. 1619): Native-born Japanese martyr. Feast day: November 27.

+ Anthony Kiun, Blessed (d. 1622): Jesuit martyr of Japan. Feast day: September 10.

+ Anthony of Korea, Blessed (d. 1622): A Korean martyred in Japan. Feast day: September 10.

+ Anthony Sanga, Blessed (d. 1622): Native-born Japanese martyr. Feast day: September 10.

+ Anthony of Tuy, Blessed (d. 1628): Franciscan martyr of Japan. Feast day: June 1.

+ Anthony, Blessed (d. 1632): Native-born Japanese. Feast day: August 19.

+ Anthony Ishida and Companions (d. 1632): Japanese Jesuit martyrs. Feast day: September 3.

+ Anthony Daniel (d. 1648): Martyred Jesuit missionary slain in North America. Feast Day: October 19.

+ Anthony Lucci, Blessed (d. 1752): Bishop and papal aide.

+ Anthony Nam-Quynh (1840): Vietnamese physician and martyr. Feast day: November 24.

+ Anthony Mary Claret (d. 1870): Founder of the Claretians. Feast day: October 24.

+ Anthony Chevrier, Blessed (d. 1879): Priest.

*(Anfernee, Anthoney, Anthonie, Antoine, Antony, Antonio, Tony)*

# Anton

Meaning: Russian form of Anthony

+ Anton Maria Schwartz, Blessed (d. 1929): Patron of tailors and shoemakers.

# Apollo

Meaning: Greek "sun god" or "beautiful man"

+ (biblical): Early Christian teacher (Acts 18: 24).

+ (d. 395): Egyptian hermit, founder, and miracle worker. Feast day: January 25.

*(Apollus)*

# Aquila

Meaning: Latin "eagle"

+ (biblical): Husband of Priscilla (Acts 18:2).

## Aquinas

See Thomas

## Ardo

Meaning: may be derived from Latin "industrious"

+ (d. 843): Benedictine abbot from France. Feast day: March 7.

## Aric, Arik, Arick

See Eric

## Armand

See Ormond

## Arnold

Meaning: Old German "eagle power"

+ (d.c. 800): Confessor in the court of Charlemagne. Feast day: July 8.

+ Arnold Réche, Blessed (d. 1890): Christian Brother.

+ Arnold Jansen, Blessed (d. 1909): Founder of the Society of the Divine Word. Feast day: January 15.

*(Arne, Arney, Arni, Arnie)*

## Arnulf

Meaning: unknown

+ (d.c. 640): Bishop. Feast day: July 18.

## Arsenius

Meaning: Greek "masculine"

+ (d.c. 450): Confessor and hermit on the Nile. Feast day: July 19.

*(Arsenius, Arsinio)*

## Athanasuis

Meaning: unknown

+ (d. 373) Doctor of the Church, fought Arian heresy. Feast day: May 2.

## Athelm

Meaning: unknown

+ (d. 923): Archbishop of Canterbury. Feast day: January 8.

## Augustine

Meaning: Latin "venerable, revered or exalted"

+ Augustine of Hippo (d. 430): Doctor of the Church, author of *The Confessions*. Feast day: August 28.

+ Augustine of Canterbury (d. 604): Benedictine and first bishop of Canterbury, England. Feast day: May 27.

+ Augustine Chow, Blessed (d. 1815): Martyr of China. Feast day: July 9.

+ Augustine Moi (d. 1839): Vietnamese martyr. Feast day: December 19.

+ Augustine of Huy (d. 1839): Native-born Vietnamese martyr. Feast day: June 13.

+ Augustine Ota, Blessed (d. 1622): Native-born Japanese martyr. Feast day: September 25.

+ Augustine Roscelli, Blessed (d. 1902): Founder of the Institute of Sisters of the Immaculata.

*(August, Augustus, Austin, Gus)*

## Azadanes and Azades

Meaning: unknown

+ (d.c. 342): Martyrs of Persia. Feast day: April 22.

# B

## Bademus

Meaning: unknown

+ (d.c. 380): Martyr from Persia (modern Iran). Feast day: April 10.

# Baglan

Meaning: unknown

+ (d. fifth century): Name of two Welsh saints.

# Bagne

Meaning: unknown

+ (d.c. 710): Missionary in the area of modern Calais, France. Feast day: June 20.

*(Bain, Bagnus)*

# Bain

See Bagne

# Baithin

Meaning: unknown

+ (d.c. 598): Abbot and cousin of St. Columba. Feast day: June 9.

# Balderic

Meaning: probably Old German "bold"

+ (d. seventh century): Abbot and prince of Austrasia (parts of present-day Germany and France). Feast day: October 16.

# Baldomerus

Meaning: unknown

+ (d.c. 650): Patron saint of locksmiths. Feast day: February 27.

# Baldred

Meaning: unknown

+ (d. eighth century): Bishop of Scotland. Feast day: March 6.

# Baldwin

Meaning: German "bold friend"

+ (d.c. 680): Martyr and son of St. Salaberga. Feast day: October 16.

+ (d. 1140): Benedictine abbot and disciple of St. Bernard of Clairvaux. Feast day: July 15.

*(Baldwyn)*

# Balin

Meaning: unknown

+ (d. seventh century): Son of an Anglo-Saxon king. Feast day: September 3.

# Balthasar

Meaning: possibly Old German "king" or "battle"

+ (biblical): Traditional name of one of the Three Wise Men (Matthew 2).

+ Balthasar de Torres, Blessed (d. 1626): Missionary and martyr in Japan. Feast day: June 20.

*(Balthazar)*

# Bandaridus

Meaning: unknown

+ (d. 566): French bishop who became a gardener in England. Feast day: August 9.

*(Bandarinus, Banderik, Bandery)*

# Bardo

Meaning: unknown

+ (d. 1053): Benedictine archbishop and official of the Holy Roman Empire. Feast day: June 10.

# Barlaam

Meaning: unknown

+ (d.c. 304): Martyr of Caesarea, in

Cappadocia in modern Turkey. Feast day: November 19.

+ (d. 1193): Hermit of Russia who was christened Alexis. Feast day: November 6.

## Barnabas

Meaning: Hebrew "son of consolation"

+ (biblical): Companion of Saint Paul (Acts 11:25). Feast day: August 24.

*(Barney)*

## Barnard

Meaning: Old German "bear-brave"

+ (d. 841): Benedictine archbishop and member of the court of Charlemagne. Feast day: January 23.

*(Barnaby, Barney, Barnie)*

## Barry

See Finbar

## Bartholomew

Meaning: Hebrew "son of the furrow"

+ (biblical): One of the Twelve Apostles, missionary to Armenia and India, martyr. (Matthew 10:3).

+ Bartholomew of Rossano (d. 1050): Hymn-writer and advisor to Pope Benedict IX. Feast day: November 11.

+ Bartholomew of Farne (d.c. 1193): English hermit and miracle worker. Feast day: June 24.

+ Bartholomew Buonpedoni (d. 1300): Priest and leper. Feast day: December: 14.

+ Bartholomew Sheki, Blessed (d. 1619): Member of the royal family of Firando, Japan. Feast day: November 27.

+ Bartholomew Monfiore, Blessed (d. 1622): A martyr from Japan. Feast day: August 19.

+ Bartholomew Shikiemon, Blessed (d. 1622): A Japanese layman who died with Blessed Charles Spinola. Feast day: September 10.

+ Bartholomew Laurel (d. 1627): Medical student martyred with St. Paul Miki. Feast day: February 6.

+ Bartholomew Gutierrez, Blessed (d. 1632): Augustinian priest martyred in Japan. Feast day: September 3.

+ Bartholomew Alvarez, Blessed (d. 1737): Portuguese priest martyred in Vietnam. Feast day: January 12.

+ Bartholomew Maria dal Monte, Blessed (d. 1778): Priest famous for his parish missions.

+ Bartholomew Longo, Blessed (d. 1926): Founder of Marian devotion "Our Lady of Pompeii".

*(Bart, Bartlet)*

## Basil

Meaning: Greek "kingly"

+ Basil and Companions (d. fourth century): Martyred bishop and friends. Feast day: March 4.

+ (d. 335): Bishop of Bologna, Italy, ordained by Pope St. Sylvester. Feast day: March 6.

+ Basil of Ancyra (d. 362): Martyr in Galatia (modern Turkey). Feast day: March 22.

+ (d.c. 370): Father of St. Basil the Great, St. Gregory of Nyssa, St. Peter of Sebaste, and St. Macrina the Younger. Feast day: May 30.

+ Basil the Great (d. 379): Doctor of the Church. Feast day: January 2.

+ (d.c. 475): Bishop of Aix, in Provence, France. Feast day: January 1.

+ (d.c. 750): Defender of the veneration of images. Feast day: February 27.

+ Basil the Younger (d. 952): Hermit with gifts of prophecy. Feast day: March 26.

*(Bazil, Bazyli, Vassilij, Vassily)*

## Bassian

Meaning: unknown

+ (d. 413): Sicilian by birth, friend of St. Ambrose of Milan. Feast day: January 19.

## Bean

Meaning: unknown

+ (d.c. 1012): Scottish bishop. Feast day: October 26.

## Beatus

Meaning: Latin "blessed"

+ (d.c. 112): Apostle of Switzerland. Feast day: May 9.

+ Beatus of Vendôme (d. third century): Missionary who traveled through regions of France. Feast day: May 9.

## Bede

Meaning: Old English "prayer"

+ Bede the Venerable (d. 735): Doctor of the Church and the Father of English History. Feast day: May 25.

+ Bede the Younger (d. 883): Benedictine monk of the abbey of Gavello in northern Italy. Feast day: April 10.

## Benedict

Meaning: Latin "blessed"

+ Benedict of Nursia (d. 550): Founder of Western monasticism and brother of St. Scholastica.

+ Benedict Biscop (d. 690): Benedictine abbot from Northumbria, England. Feast day: January 12.

+ Benedict II, Pope (served from 684-685): Expert in Scriptures and sacred music. Feast day: May 8.

+ Benedict Crispus (d. 725): Archbishop of Milan, Italy. Feast day: March 11.

+ (d.c. 820): Bishop of Angers, France. Feast day: July 15.

+ Benedict of Aniane (d. 821): Cupbearer of Charlemagne, called "the Second Benedict" for his work in restoring Western monasteries. Feast day: February 11.

+ (d. 1184): Shepherd of Avignon, France, also called Benezet—"the Bridge Builder." Feast day: April 14.

+ Benedict the Moor (d. 1589): Black slave who is patron of African-Americans. Feast day: April 4.

+ Benedict Joseph Labré (d. 1783): Called "the Beggar of Rome," a homeless man who lived near the Coliseum. Feast day: April 16.

+ Benedict Menni, Blessed (d. 1914): Member of the Order of the Hospitallers of St. John of God.

*(Bennet, Bennett, Bennitt, Bennison, Benedick, Bent, Bengt)*

## Benilde

Meaning: Latin "good"

+ (d. 1862): Christian Brother schoolteacher. Feast day: August 13.

## Benjamin

Meaning: Hebrew "son of my right hand:

+ (biblical): Son of Rachel and Jacob (Genesis 35:18).

+ (d.c. 421): Martyr of Persia (modern Iran). Feast day: March 31.

*(Ben, Benn, Benny, Benjaman,*
*Benjii, Bennie, Benyamin, Jamie)*

## Berach

Meaning: unknown

+ (d. sixth century): Patron saint of Kilbarry, County Dublin. Feast day: February 15.

## Berard

Meaning: unknown

+ (d. 1220): Franciscan martyr, slain by the Moors. Feast day: January 16.

## Bernard

Meaning: Old German "bear-brave"

+ Bernard of Montjoux (d. 1081): Patron of mountaineers. Feast day: May 28.

+ Bernard of Carinola (d. 1109): Bishop and patron of Carinola. Feast day: March 12.

+ Bernard degli Uberti (d. 1133): Cardinal and papal legate. Feast day: December 4.

+ Bernard of Clairvaux (d. 1153): Cistercian Abbot and Doctor of the Church. Feast day: August 20.

+ Bernard of Calvo (d. 1243): Cistercian bishop in Spain. Feast day: October 24.

+ Bernard Maria Silvestrelli, Blessed (d. 1911): Called the "Second St. Paul of the Cross."

+ Bernard Lichtenburg, Blessed (d. 1943): Died on his way to Dachau.

*(Barnard, Bernardo, Berndt, Berney,*
*Bernhard, Bernie, Berni, Birnee,*
*Birney, Burney)*

## Berno

Meaning: unknown

+ (d. 927): The first abbot of Cluny. Feast day: January 13.

## Bernward

Meaning: unknown

+ (d. 1022): Bishop, architect, painter, sculptor, and metalsmith. Feast day: November 20.

*(Berward)*

## Bert

See Albert

## Berthold

Meaning: Old German "bright power"

+ (d. 1111): Benedictine lay brother. Feast day: October 21.

+ (d.c. 1195): Some believe him to be one of the founders of the Carmelite Order. Feast day: March 29.

## Bertrand

Meaning: "bright shield"

+ (d. 623): Founder of a church, a monastery and a hospice. Feast day: June 30.

+ Bertrand of Comminges (d. 1123): French miracle worker. Feast day: October 16.

+ (d. 1350): French bishop and martyr. Feast day: June 6.

## Betto

Meaning: unknown

+ (d. 918): Benedictine bishop of Auxerre. Feast day: February 24.

## Bill

See William

## Blaise

Meaning: Latin "crippled, stuttering"

+ (d.c. 316): Bishop and physician, martyr, patron saint of throat ailments. Feast day: February 3.

*(Blaize, Blayze, Blaze)*

## Blane

Meaning: Old Scottish "servant of the saint"

+ (d.c. 590): Scottish bishop. Feast day: August 10.

*(Blaine, Blain)*

## Bob

See Robert

## Bolcan

Meaning: unknown

+ (d.c. 840): Bishop and disciple of St. Patrick. Feast day: February 20.

## Bonaventure

Meaning: unknown

+ (d. 1274): Franciscan and Doctor of the Church.

+ Bonaventure of Miako, Blessed (d. 1597): Martyr of Japan. Feast day: February 6.

## Bond

Meaning: unknown

+ (d. seventh century): French hermit. Feast day: October 29.

## Boniface

Meaning: Latin "of good fate"

+ (d.c. 287): Martyr of Trier, Germany. Feast day: October 5.

+ Boniface I, Pope (served from 418-422): Supported St. Augustine against the Pelagian heresy. Feast day: September 4.

+ Boniface IV, Pope (served from 608-615): Turned the Pantheon in Rome into a Christian church. Feast day: May 8.

+ Boniface Curitan (d.c. 660): Evangelist to the Picts and Scots. Feast day: March 14.

+ (d. 754): Bishop and missionary to Germans, destroyed the Oak of Thor, the sacred tree of the Saxons. Feast day: June 5.

+ Boniface of Lausanne (d. 1265): Swiss bishop. Feast day: February 19.

## Boris

Meaning: Slavonic "battle, fight"

+ (d. 1010): Patron saint of Moscow. Feast day: July 24.

*(Boriss, Borriss)*

## Boswell

Meaning: unknown

+ (d.c. 661): English abbot with a gift of prophecy. Feast day: February 23.

## Brandan

Meaning: English "hill covered with broom"

+ (d. fifth century): Irish monk, missionary to England. Feast day: January 11.

## Brannock

Meaning: unknown

+ (date unknown): Welsh monk who migrated to Devon, England. Feast day: January 7.

## Brendan

Meaning: Irish "stinking hair"

+ Brendan of Birr (d.c. 573): Friend of St. Brendan the Voyager. Feast day: November 29.

+ (d. 575 or d.c. 583): One of the most famous saints of Ireland, called "the Voyager" or "the Navigator." Feast day: May 16.

*(Brandon, Brandyn, Brandin, Brannan, Brendon)*

## Brian

Meaning: traditional "honor"

+ Brian Lacey, Blessed (d. 1582): Martyr of England. Feast day: December 10.

*(Brien, Brient, Brion, Bryan, Bryen, Bryent, Bryon)*

## Brice

Meaning: Celtic "quick one'

+ (d. 444): Bishop of Tours, France, and disciple of St. Martin. Feast day: November 13.

*(Bryce)*

## Brocard

Meaning: unknown

+ (d. 1231): Carmelite prior of Mount Carmel monastery. Feast day: September 2.

*(Burchard)*

## Bron

Meaning: Welsh "breast:

+ (d.c. 511): Bishop and disciple of St. Patrick. Feast day: June 8.

*(Bronson, Bronnson, Bronsen, Bronsin, Bronsson)*

## Bruno

Meaning: Old German "brown or bear-like"

+ Bruno the Great (d. 965): Archbishop of Cologne. Feast day: October 11.

+ Bruno of Querfurt (d. 1009): Martyred archbishop, called "the Second Apostle to the Prussians." Feast day: June 19 and October 15.

+ (d. 1045): Bishop of Würzburg, Germany, scholar and author. Feast day: May 27.

+ (d. 1101): Founder of the Carthusian Order. Feast day: October 6

+ Bruno of Segni (d. 1123): Vatican librarian. Feast day: July 18.

+ Bruno Seronkuma (d. 1885): Martyr of Uganda. Feast day: June 3.

## Burchard

Meaning: unknown

+ (d.c. 754): Disciple of St. Boniface and missionary to Germany. Feast day: October 14.

# C

## Cachie

See Casimir

## Cadroe

Meaning: unknown

+ (d. 976): Scottish prince and Benedictine abbot. Feast day: March 6.

## Cadvael

Meaning: unknown

+ (d.c. 580): Welsh bishop and martyr. Feast day: January 24.

## Caedmon

Meaning: unknown

+ (d. 680): Benedictine monk and poet. Feast day: February 11.

## Caesarius

Meaning: Latin "leader"

+ Caesarius of Arles (d. 543): Monk, scholar, bishop. Fought Arian and Pelagian heresies. Feast day: August 27.

*(Ceasar, Cesar, Cesare)*

## Cagnoald

Meaning: unknown

+ (d.c. 635): Bishop of Leon, France, and companion of St. Columban. Feast day: September 6.

## Caius

See Gaius

## Caleb

Meaning: Hebrew "dog"

+ (biblical): One of the leaders of Israel after Moses (Numbers 13:6).

*(Caeleb, Cale, Kaleb)*

## Caillin

Meaning: unknown

+ (d. seventh century): Irish bishop. Feast day: November 13.

## Cairlon

Meaning: unknown

+ (d. sixth century): Archbishop of Cashel, Ireland. Feast day: March 24.

## Cajetan

Meaning: unknown

+ (d. 1547): Priest and founder of the Theatine order. Patron of domestic animals. Feast day: August 7.

## Callisto

Meaning: Greek "beautiful"

+ Callisto Caravario, Blessed (d. 1930): Missionary in China.

## Callistus

Meaning: Greek "most lovely"

+ Callistus I, Pope (served from 217-222): Roman slave who became pope. Feast day: October 14.

## Camillus

Meaning: perhaps from Italian "evergreen"

+ Camillus Constanzi, Blessed (d. 1622): Martyr of Japan. Feast day: October 12.

+ Camillus de Lellis (d. 1614): Patron saint, along with St. John of God, of the sick, and patron of nurses and nursing groups. Feast day: July 14.

## Candres

Meaning: Latin "shining"

+ (d. fifth century): French missionary to the Netherlands. Feast day: December 1.

## Canice

Meaning: Welsh "gentle to children"

+ (d.c. 599): Popular Irish saint. Feast day: October 11.

## Cannen

See Kanten

## Canute

Meaning: Old Norse "knot"

+ Canute Lavard (d. 1131): Son of King Eric the Good of Denmark. Feast day: January 7.

+ Canute IV (d. 1086): Martyred king

of Denmark Feast day: January 19.

*(Knute)*

# Caradoc
Meaning: Welsh "love"

+ (d. 1124): Welsh hermit and harpist. Feast day: April 13.

# Carl
See Karl

# Carthach
Meaning: unknown

+ (d.c. 540): Irish bishop. Feast day: March 5.

+ Carthach the Younger (d.c. 637): Irish hermit and bishop. Feast day: May 14.

# Casimir
Meaning: Old Slavic "commands"

+ Casimir of Poland (d. 1483): Patron saint of Poland and Lithuania. Feast day: March 4.

*(Cachie, Cash, Cashmere, Cashmir, Kashmere, Kasimer, Kasmir, Kasmira, Kazmir)*

# Caspar
Meaning: Persian "treasure holder"

+ (biblical): Traditional name of one of the Three Wise Men (Matthew 2).

+ Caspar Fisogiro, Blessed (d. 1617): Martyr of Japan. Feast day: October 1.

+ Caspar Kotenda, Blessed (d. 1622): Member of Japanese royal house, martyr. Feast day: September 11.

+ Caspar Sadamazu, Blessed (d. 1626): Japanese martyr.

+ Caspar Vaz, Blessed (d. 1627): Mar-

tyr of Japan with his wife Mary. Feast day: August 17.

+ Caspar del Bufalo (d. 1836): Founder of the Missionaries of the Most Precious Blood. Feast day: December 28.

*(Casper, Gaspar, Kaspar)*

# Cassian, Cassius
Meaning: perhaps Latin "vain" or Greek "cinnamon"

+ Cassian of Imola (d.c. 250): Teacher martyred for being a Christian. Feast day: August 13.

+ Cassian (d. 298): Patron of modern stenographers. Feast day: December 3.

+ Cassian of Autun (d.c. 350): Egyptian famed for miracles. Feast day: August 5.

+ Cassius (d. 558): Bishop of Narni, Italy. Feast day: June 29.

# Castor
Meaning: Greek "beaver"

+ (d.c. 420): French bishop. Feast day: September 2.

# Cathan
Meaning: unknown

+ (d. sixth or seventh century): Scottish bishop. Feast day: May 17.

# Cearan
Meaning: probably derived from "spear"

+ (d. 870): Irish abbot, called "the Devout." Feast day: June 14.

# Ceferino
Meaning: unknown

+ Ceferino Jimenez Molla, Blessed (d.

1936): First Roma person to be beatified.

## Celestine

Meaning: Latin "heavenly"

+ Celestine I, Pope (served from 422-432): Opposed the twin heresies of Pelagianism and Nestorianism. Feast day: July 27.

+ Celestine V, Pope (served 1294): Famed hermit, elected pope at age eighty-four and served only five months. Feast day: May 19.

## Cellach

Meaning: unknown

+ (d. ninth century): Scottish abbot and Irish archbishop. Feast day: April 1.

+ (d. 1129): Last hereditary archbishop of Armagh, Ireland. Feast day: April 1.

*(Ceilach, Keilach)*

## Ceolfrid

Meaning: unknown

+ (d. 716): Benedictine abbot, ordered production of the oldest known copy of the Vulgate (Latin) Bible in one volume. Feast day: September 25.

## Cettin

Meaning: unknown

+ (d. fifth century): Bishop and disciple of St. Patrick. Feast day: June 16.

## Chad

Meaning: Celtic "warrior"

+ (d. 673): Irish archbishop, brother of St. Cedd. Feast day: March 2.

*(Chadd, Chadley, Chadrick, Chadron, Chadwyck)*

## Charbel

Meaning: unknown

+ Charbel Makhlouf (d. 1898): Mystic and Maronite hermit. Feast day: December 24.

## Charlemagne

Meaning: Old English "great man"

+ Charlemagne, Blessed (d. 814): First Holy Roman Emperor. Feast day: January 28.

## Charles

Meaning: Old English "man"

+ Charles Borromeo (d. 1584): Cardinal and preeminent figure in the Catholic Reformation. Feast day: November 4.

+ Charles of Sezze (d. 1670): Franciscan mystic whose heart was pierced by a light from the Sacred Host. Feast day: January 6.

+ Charles Lwanga (d. 1885): Martyr of Uganda. Feast day: June 3.

+ Charles of Mount Argus Houben, Blessed (d. 1893): Passionist missionary.

*(Charle, Charley, Charlie, Chuck)*

## Christian

Meaning: Greek "anointed"

+ (d. 1138): Irish bishop. Feast day: June 12.

+ Christian, Blessed (d. 1186): Founder of the Cistercians in Ireland. Feast day: March 18.

*(Christiaan, Christianos, Christion, Christon, Christos, Chrystan, Chrystian, Cristian, Cristón, Kristar, Krister, Kristian, Kristjan)*

# Christopher

Meaning: Greek "one who carries Christ"

+ (d.c. 251): Legendary patron of travelers. Feast day: July 25.

+ Christopher of Guardia (d.c. 1490): Patron saint of Guardia, Spain. Feast day: September 25.

+ Christopher, Blessed (d.c. 1527 or 1529): Mexican child martyr, one of first martyrs of the Americas.

+ Christopher Bales, Blessed (d. 1590): English martyr. Feast day: March 4.

+ Christopher Magallanes and Companions, Blesseds (d.c. 1937): Mexican martyrs.

*(Chris, Chriss, Christepher, Christobal, Christofer, Christoff, Christopheror, Chrys, Cris, Khris, Khriss, Khristophe, Kris, Kristopher, Kristofer, Krys)*

# Cian

Meaning: Irish-Gaelic "ancient"

+ Cian (d. sixth century): Welsh hermit. Feast day: December 11.

*(Cianan, Ciannan)*

# Clarus

Meaning: perhaps "clear" or "bright"

+ (d. 397): Hermit and disciple of St. Martin. Feast day: November 8.

+ (d.c. 660): Benedictine abbot of St. Marcellus Monastery at Vienne, France. Feast day: January 1.

# Claude

Meaning: Latin "lame"

+ Claude de la Colombière, Blessed (d. 1682): Confessor to St. Margaret Mary Alacoque. He helped spread the devotion to the Sacred Heart. Feast day: February 15.

# Claudius

Meaning: Latin "lame"

+ (d. 283): Roman martyr with his wife, Hilaria, and sons, Jason and Maurus. Feast day: December 3.

+ Claudius of Besançon (d.c. 699): Benedictine abbot and bishop. Feast day: June 6.

+ Claudius Granzotto, Blessed (d. 1947): Franciscan artist.

*(Claude, Claudell, Claudio)*

# Clement

Meaning: Latin "merciful"

+ Clement I, Pope (served from 88-97): One of the Fathers of the Church, martyr. Feast day: November 23 (in the West), November 24 or 25 (in the East).

+ Clement of Alexandria (d.c. 217): Confessor and teacher of Origen. Feast day: December 4.

+ (d.c. 298): Martyr of Córdoba, Spain. Feast day: June 27.

+ (d. 308): Martyred bishop of Galatia (in modern Turkey). Feast day: January 23.

+ Clement of Okhrida (d. 916): First Slav to become a bishop. Feast day: July 17.

+ Clement Kingemon, Blessed (d. 1622): Japanese martyr. Feast day: November 1.

+ Clement Vom, Blessed (d. 1622): Japanese martyr. Feast day: September 10.

+ Clement Maria Hofbauer (d. 1830): Redemptorist preacher and reformer in Austria and Germany. Feast day: March 15.

+ Clement Marchisio, Blessed (d. 1903): Italian priest.

*(Clem, Clemens, Clément, Clemente, Klement)*

## Colgan

Meaning: unknown

+ (d.c. 796): Irish abbot. Feast day: February 20.

## Colin

See Nicholas, Gollen

## Colman

Meaning: Irish "dove"

+ Colman of Dromore (d. sixth century): Bishop and mentor of St. Finnian of Clonard. Feast day: June 7.

+ Colman McRhoi (d. sixth century): Abbot and disciple of St. Columba. Feast day: June 16.

+ Colman of Cloyne (d.c. 600): Bishop, poet, and royal bard. Feast day: November 24.

+ Colman of Elo (d. 612): Author of the Alphabet of Devotion. Feast day: September 26.

+ Colman of Kilmacduagh (d.c. 623): Abbot and bishop, son of the Irish chieftain, Duac. Feast day: October 29.

+ Colman of Lindisfarne (d. 676): Irish bishop. Feast day: February 18.

+ Colman of Stockerau (d. 1012): An Irish or Scottish pilgrim martyred in Austria. Feast day: October 13.

*(Coleman)*

## Columba

Meaning: Irish "dove"

+ (d. 597): One of the most famous Scottish-Irish saints, called "the Pilgrim of Christ." Feast day: June 9.

## Conall

Meaning: unknown

+ (d. seventh century): Irish abbot. Feast day: May 22.

*(Conal, Connel, Connell)*

## Conan

Meaning: Celtic "intelligence"

+ (d.c. 648): Irish bishop. Feast day: January 26.

*(Connan)*

## Conleth

Meaning: unknown

+ (d.c. 519): Irish metal worker and hermit. Feast day: May 4.

## Conon

Meaning: unknown

+ (d. 250): Gardener at Carmel in Turkey. Feast day: March 6.

+ (d. 275): Father and son killed on the rack. Feast day: May 29.

## Conrad

Meaning: Germanic "brave counsel"

+ Conrad of Constance (d. 975): Bishop and companion of Emperor Otto I. Feast day: November 26.

+ Conrad of Trier (d. 1066): Bishop and martyr. Feast day: June 1.

+ Conrad of Piacenza (d. 1354): Franciscan tertiary and hermit. Feast day: February 19.

+ Conrad of Parzham (d. 1894): Franciscan mystic and lay brother. Feast day: April 21.

*(Conrade, Conrid, Konrad)*

## Constantine

Meaning: Latin "firm or constant"

+ (d. 576): Scotland's first martyr. Feast day: March 9.

## Conwall

Meaning: unknown

+ (d.c. 630): Scottish priest. Feast day: September 28.

## Corbinian

Meaning: Latin "raven"

+ (d. 730): Evangelist to Germany. Feast day: September 8.

*(Corbin, Corban, Corben, Korban, Korbin)*

## Cormac

Meaning: Irish-Gaelic "charioteer"

+ (d. sixth century): Irish abbot who was a friend of St. Columba. Feast day: December 12.

+ (d. 908): King of Munster, Ireland. Feast day: September 14.

*(Cormack)*

## Cornelius

Meaning: Latin "a horn"

+ (biblical): Roman official baptized by St. Peter (Acts 10). Feast day: February 2.

+ Cornelius, Pope (served from 251-253): Roman priest, fought first antipope. Feast day: September 16.

+ (d. 1176): Irish Archbishop. Feast day: June 4.

+ (d. 1572): Dutch martyr. Feast day: July 9.

## Cosmas

Meaning: Greek "order:

+ Cosmas and Damian (d.c. 303): Martyred Arab brothers and physicians. Patrons of physicians, along with St. Luke, and patrons of Florence, chemists, grocers, dentists, and physicists. Feast day: September 27.

+ Cosmas Takeya (d. 1597): Japanese martyr. Feast day: February 6.

+ Cosmas Takuea, Blessed (d. 1619): Korean martyr in Japan. Feast day: June 1.

*(Cosmo, Cozma, Kosma, Kosmo)*

## Craton

Meaning: English "from the rocky place"

+ (d.c. 273): Martyr, converted by St. Valentine. Feast day: February 15.

*(Cray, Creighton)*

## Crispin

Meaning: Latin "curly haired"

+ Crispin and Crispinian (d.c. 285): Brothers, patrons of shoemakers and cobblers. Feast day: October 25.

+ (d. fourth century): Bishop and martyr. Feast day: November 19.

+ Crispin of Viterbo (d. 1750): Franciscan lay brother noted for miracles. Feast day: May 23.

## Cuthbert

Meaning: Old English "famous bright"

+ (d. 687): One of England's most famous saints, also known as Cuthbert of Lindisfarne. Feast day: March 20.

+ (d. 758): Benedictine archbishop of Canterbury. Feast day: October 26.

+ Cuthbert Mayne (d. 1577): English convert and martyr. Feast day: November 29.

## Cyd
See Sidney

## Cyprian
Meaning: Latin "man from Cyprus"

+ (d. 258): Famous early church theologian. Feast day: September 16.

+ (d. 582): Bishop of Brescia in Lombardy, Italy. Feast day: April 21.

+ (d. 586): French hermit. Feast day: December 9.

+ (d. sixth century): Bishop of Toulon, France. Feast day: October 3.

## Cyriac
Meaning: may be derived from "Cyril"

+ Cyriac Elias Chavara, Blessed (d. 1871): Carmelist priest and native of India.

## Cyril
Meaning: Greek "lord or ruler"

+ (date unknown): African martyr. Feast day: March 8.

+ (d. 251): Martyred as a boy. Feast day: May 29.

+ (d.c. 362): Deacon martyred in the persecution of Emperor Julian the Apostate. Feast day: March 29.

+ Cyril of Jerusalem (d. 386): Bishop of Jerusalem and Doctor of the Church. Feast day: March 18.

+ Cyril of Alexandria (d. 444): Patriarch of Alexandria and Doctor of the Church. Feast day: June 9 in the East; February 9 in the West.

+ Cyril and Methodius (d. 869 and 885): Apostles of the Slavs and co-patrons of Europe with St. Benedict. Feast day: February 14.

+ (d. 1182): One of the foremost biblical scholars in Russia. Feast day: April 28.

+ Cyril of Constantinople (d. 1235): Carmelite prior-general in Palestine. Feast day: March 6.

*(Cyrill, Cyrille)*

# D

## Daig
Meaning: unknown

+ Daig Maccairaill (d. 586): Irish bishop. Feast day: August 18.

## Dallan
Meaning: English "from the dale"

+ Dallan Forgaill (d. 598): Martyred poet. Feast day: January 29.

*(Daelan, Daelen, Daelin, Dalian, Daylan, Daylen, Daylin)*

## Damasus
Meaning: unknown

+ Damasus I, Pope (served from 366-384): Asked St. Jerome to translate the Bible into the vernacular, resulting in the Latin Vulgate. Feast day: December 11.

## Damian
Meaning: Greek "to tame" or Russian "one who comforts"

+ (dates unknown): Name of two saints, one a martyred soldier in Africa and the other a Roman martyr. Feast day: February 12.

+ (d. 168): Italian martyr. Feast day: January 3.

+ (d. 303): Brother of Cosmas, martyr. Feast day: September 27.

+ (d. 710): Italian bishop. Feast day: April 12.

+ Damien Yamiki, Blessed (d. 1622): Martyr of Japan. Feast day: September 10.

+ Damien Joseph de Veuster, Blessed (d. 1889): Patron of the lepers on Molokai, Hawaii.

*(Daemien, Daimyan, Dameion, Dameon, Damien, Damion, Damon, Daymon)*

## Daniel

Meaning: Hebrew "God is my judge"

+ (biblical): Survived the lions' den. (Book of Daniel).

+ (d. 344): Persian martyr. Feast day: February 21.

+ Daniel the Stylite (d.c. 493): Ascetic who lived on a pillar, knows as "the oracle of Constantinople." Feast day: December 11.

+ (d.c. 584): Welsh bishop. Feast day: September 11.

+ (d. ninth century): Hermit and martyr. Feast day: April 29.

+ (d. 1221): Franciscan martyr of Morocco. Feast day: October 10.

+ (d. 1411): A Camaldolese hermit, originally a German merchant. Feast day: March 31.

+ Daniel Comboni, Blessed (d. 1881): First bishop of Central Africa.

+ Daniel Brottier, Blessed (d. 1936): French missionary and chaplain.

*(Dan, Dániel, Daniyel, Danny, Dannie, Donyel, Donyelle)*

## Darius

Meaning: Greek "one who upholds the good"

+ (biblical): King of Persia who allowed the Hebrews to rebuild the Temple in Jerusalem after the Babylonian exile (Ezra 6).

*(Darian, Dariann, Darias, Darien, Darion)*

## Dasius

Meaning: unknown

+ (d.c. 300): Martyred Roman soldier. Feast day: November 20.

+ (d.c. 303): Martyr. Feast day: October 21.

## Dathus

Meaning: unknown

+ (d. 190): Bishop of Ravenna, Italy, who was elected when a dove appeared miraculously over his head. Feast day: July 3.

## Datius

Meaning: unknown

+ (date unknown): African martyr. Feast day: January 27.

+ (d. 552): Bishop of Milan. Feast day: January 14.

## David

Meaning: Hebrew "beloved friend"

+ (biblical): Great King of the Jewish people. (1 Samuel).

+ (d. fifth century): Greek hermit. Feast day: June 26.

+ (d.c. 600): Patron saint of Wales. Feast day: March 1.

+ David of Sweden (d.c. 1080): Benedictine bishop and missionary to Sweden. Feast day: July 15.

+ David I (d. 1153): King of Scotland. Feast day: May 24.

+ David Gonson, Blessed (d. 1541): Martyred English knight of St. John. Feast day: July 12.

+ David Lewis (d. 1679): One of the Forty Martyrs of England and Wales. Feast day: August 27.

*(Dave, Davey, Dayvid, Daved, Davy)*

## Day

Meaning: unknown

+ (date unknown): Cornish saint. Feast day: January 18.

## Declan

Meaning: unknown

+ (d. fifth century): English bishop. Feast day: July 24.

## Demetrian

Meaning: Latin "belonging to Demeter (the goddess of agriculture)"

+ (d.c. 912): Cypriot bishop. Feast day: November 6.

## Demetrius

Meaning: Latin "belonging to Demeter (the goddess of agriculture)"

+ (date unknown): Martyr. Feast day: April 9.

+ (date unknown): Martyred bishop. Feast day: November 10.

+ (d.c. 231): Bishop of Alexandria, Egypt. Feast day: October 9.

*(Deimitrios, Demeter, Demetrais, Demetreus, Demetrian, Dimitri, Demetrik)*

## Denis

Meaning: French form of Dionysius.

+ (d.c. 250): First bishop of Paris, patron of France. Feast day: October 9.

*(Denies, Dennis, Dennison, Dennes, Denny, Dennys, Denzil, Denzel)*

## Dentlin

Meaning: unknown

+ (d. seventh century): Seven-year-old saint. Feast day: March 16.

## Dermot

Meaning: Irish "envy-free"

+ (d. sixth century): Irish abbot. Feast day: January 10.

## Desideratus

Meaning: unknown

+ (d. sixth century): French bishop. Feast day: February 10 and 11.

+ (d. sixth century): French bishop famous for miracles. Feast day: May 8.

## Dichu

Meaning: unknown

+ (d. fifth century): First convert of St. Patrick in Ulster, Ireland. Feast day: April 29.

## Dick

See Richard

## Didacus

Meaning: unknown

+ (d. 1463): Noted healer and miracle worker. Feast day: November 13.

+ Didacus Carvalho, Blessed (d. 1624): Martyr of Japan. Feast day: February 25.

## Diego

Meaning: Spanish form of John

+ Diego Aloysius de San Vitores (d. 1672): Missionary and martyr in Guam.

# Dietrich

See Theodore

# Digain

Meaning: unknown

+ (d. fifth century): Prince of Cornwall, England. Feast day: November 21.

# Dionysius

Meaning: "god of wine"

+ (biblical): Man converted by St. Paul (Acts 17:34). Feast day: October 9.

+ Dionysius of Corinth (d.c. 170): Bishop famed for his letters. Feast day: April 8.

+ (d.c. 193): French bishop. Feast day: May 8.

+ (d. 257): Martyr of Alexandria, Egypt. Feast day: October 3.

+ Dionysius of Alexandria (d. 265): Called "the Great" by St. Basil. Feast day: November 17.

+ Dionysius, Pope (served from 259-268): The first pope not to be martyred. Feast day: December 26.

+ (d. 304): Martyr. Feast day: May 12.

+ Dionysius of Milan (d.c. 359): Bishop of Milan, Italy. Feast day: May 25.

+ Dionysius Fugishima, Blessed (d. 1622): Martyr of Japan. Feast day: March 5.

+ Dionysius, Blessed (d. 1638): A Carmelite martyr, formerly a trader and ship master. Feast day: November 29.

+ Dionysius Sebuggwao (d. 1885): Martyr of Uganda, Africa. Feast day: June 3.

# Dismas

Meaning: unknown

+ (biblical): Traditional name of the Good Thief who was crucified with Christ (Luke 23: 39-43). Feast day: March 25.

# Dominic

Meaning: Latin "the lord"

+ (date unknown): African martyr. Feast day: December 29.

+ Dominic of Brescia (d.c. 612): Italian bishop. Feast day: December 20.

+ Dominic Loricatus (d. 1060): Benedictine monk who wore a coat of mail under his clothes. Feast day: October 14.

+ Dominic of Silos (d. 1073): Benedictine abbot and defender of the faith. Feast day: December 20.

+ Dominic de la Calzada (d.c. 1109): Hermit who aided pilgrims to Compostela, the famed shrine in Spain. Feast day: May 12.

+ (d. 1221): Founder of the Order of Preachers, the Dominicans. Feast day: August 8.

+ Dominic Jorjes, Blessed (d. 1619): A martyr of Japan. Feast day: March 14.

+ Dominic Nakano, Blessed (d. 1622): Martyr of Japan. Feast day: September 10.

+ Dominic of Fiunga, Blessed (d. 1622): Japanese martyr. Feast day: June 1.

+ Dominic Shamada (d. 1622): Martyr of Japan, with wife, Clare. Feast day: September 10.

+ Dominic Castellet, Blessed (d. 1628): Martyr of Japan, Dominican vicar provincial of the mission in that country. Feast day: June 1.

+ Dominic Nifaki, Blessed (d. 1628): A two-year-old martyr of Japan. Feast day: June 1.

+ Dominic of Nagasaki, Blessed (d. 1628): Japanese martyr. Feast day: September 8.

+ Dominic Shibioge, Blessed (d. 1628): Japanese martyr. Feast day: June 1.

+ Dominic Tomaki, Blessed (d. 1628): Japanese martyr. Feast day: June 1.

+ Dominic Lentini (d. 1828): Priest.

+ Dominic Henares (d. 1838): Bishop martyr of Vietnam. Feast day: June 25.

+ Dominic Van Honh Dieu (d. 1838): Native Vietnamese martyr. Feast day: August 1.

+ Dominic Doan Xuyen (d. 1839): Martyr of Vietnam. Feast day: November 26.

+ Dominic Nicholas Dat (d. 1839): Vietnamese soldier and martyr. Feast day: July 18.

+ Dominic Tuoc (d. 1839): Dominican martyr of Vietnam. Feast day: April 2.

+ Dominic Uy (d. 1839): Vietnamese martyr. Feast day: December 19.

+ Dominic Trach (d. 1842): Vietnamese martyr. Feast day: September 18.

+ Dominic Savio (d. 1857): Mystic and the youngest non-martyr to be canonized. Feast day: March 9.

+ Dominic Iturrate Zuberto (d. 1927): Member of the Trinitarian religious order.

*(Dom, Domenick, Dominick, Dominik, Domingo)*

## Donald

Meaning: Gaelic "world mighty"

+ (d. eighth century): Scottish holy man. Feast day: July 15.

*(Don, Donal, Donn, Donny, Donnie)*

## Donat

Meaning: possibly Latin "gift"

+ (date unknown): Welsh saint. Feast day: August 7.

## Donnan

Meaning: unknown

+ (d. 618): Irish monk. Feast day: April 17.

## Drew

See Andrew

## Drostan

Meaning: unknown

+ (d.c. 610): Irish born abbot. Feast day: July 11.

## Dunstan

Meaning: English "stony hill"

+ (d. 988): Abbot of Glastonbury, archbishop of Canterbury. Feast day: May 19.

*(Dunsten)*

## Duthlac

Meaning: unknown

+ (d. 1065): Bishop of Ross, Scotland. Feast day: March 8.

# E

## Eberhard

Meaning: Old German "wild-boar brave"

+ (d.c. 1164): Archbishop of Salzburg, Austria. Feast day: June 22.

*(Eberhart, Everard, Evered, Everett, Everhart, Evers)*

# Edbert

Meaning: Anglo-Saxon "generous"

+ (d. 960): King of Northumbria, England. Feast day: August 20.

# Edgar

Meaning: Old English "prosperous spear"

+ Edgar the Peaceful (d. 975): English king. Feast day: July 8.

*(Ed)*

# Edmund

Meaning: Old English "rich protector"

+ Edmund the Martyr (d.c. 869): Martyred English king. Feast day: November 20.

+ Edmund Rich (d. 1242): Archbishop of Canterbury, England. Feast day: November 20.

+ Edmund Campion (d. 1581): Jesuit priest and one of the Forty Martyrs of England and Wales. Feast day: December 1.

+ Edmund Genings (d. 1591): One of the Forty Martyrs of England and Wales. Feast day: December 10.

+ Edmund Arrowsmith (d. 1628): One of the Forty Martyrs of England and Wales. Feast day: August 28.

+ Edmund Ignatius Rice, Blessed (d. 1844): The founder of the Congregation of the Brothers of the Christian Schools, often called the Irish Christian Brothers. Feast Day: May 5.

*(Eamon, Eamonn, Ed, Edmond, Edmondson, Ned, Ted, Teddy)*

# Edward

Meaning: Old English "property guardian"

+ Edward the Martyr (d.c. 978): King of England. Feast day: March 18.

+ Edward the Confessor (d. 1066): King of England. Feast day: October 13.

+ Edward Powell, Blessed (d. 1540): English martyr, a counselor to Queen Catherine of Aragon, wife of King Henry VIII. Feast day: July 30.

+ Edward Stransham, Blessed (d. 1586): English martyr. Feast day: January 21.

+ Edward James, Blessed (d. 1588): English martyr. Feast day: October 1.

+ Edward Shelley, Blessed (d. 1588): English martyr. Feast day: August 30.

+ Edward Campion, Blessed (d. 1588): English martyr. Feast day: October 1.

+ Edward Jones, Blessed (d. 1590): Welsh martyr. Feast day: May 6.

+ Edward Waterson, Blessed (d. 1593): English convert and martyr. Feast day: January 7.

+ Edward Fulthrop, Blessed (d. 1597): English martyr at Yorkshire. Feast day: July 4.

+ Edward Oldcorne, Blessed (d. 1606): English martyr allegedly involved in the Gunpowder Plot. Feast day: April 7.

+ Edward Catherick, Blessed (d. 1642): English martyr. Feast day: April 13.

+ Edward Coleman, Blessed (d. 1678): English martyr and secretary to the duchess of York. Feast day: December 3.

+ Edward Josephy Rosaz (d. 1903): Founder of the Sisters of the Third Order of St. Francis of Susa.

*(Ed, Eddie, Eduardo, Edwardo, Ned, Ted, Teddy, Ward)*

## Edwin
Meaning: Old English "prosperity" and "friend"

+ (d.c. 632): King and martyr of England. Feast day: October 12.

*(Edwyn, Edwy)*

## Egbert
Meaning: Old English "bright sword"

+ (d.c. 720): English Benedictine monk. Feast day: March 18.

+ (d.c. 729): English monk at Lindisfarne, Ireland. Feast day: April 24.

## Egwin
Meaning: Old English "brilliant"

+ (d. 717): English bishop who had a vision of Mary. Feast day: December 30.

## Eigil
Meaning: unknown

+ (d. 822): German Benedictine abbot. Feast day: December 17.

## Elbert
See Albert

## Elerius
Meaning: unknown

+ (d. sixth century): Welsh saint. Feast day: November 3.

## Elgar
Meaning: unknown

+ (d.c. 1100): Hermit who lived off the coast of Wales. Feast day: June 14.

## Elian
Meaning: unknown

+ (d. sixth century): Cornish saint. Feast day: January 13.

*(Alan, Eilan)*

## Elias
Meaning: Greek form of the Hebrew Elijah "The Lord is God"

+ (biblical): One of the great Hebrew prophets (2 Kings 1).

+ Elias and Companions (d. 309): Egyptian martyred with Daniel, Isaiah, Jeremiah, and Samuel. Feast day: February 16.

+ (d. 660): Benedictine bishop of Syracuse, Italy. Feast day: August 26.

+ (d. 856): Spanish martyr. Feast day: April 17.

+ Elias del Socorro Nieves, Blessed (d. 1928): Mexican martyr.

*(Elijah, Ellis)*

## Elijah
See Elias

## Elmo
See Erasmus

## Elsiar
Meaning: unknown

+ (d.c. 1015): Benedictine monk. Feast day: June 4.

## Elstan
Meaning: Old English "from the farm"

+ (d. 981): English Benedictine bishop. Feast day: April 6.

*(Ellston)*

# Elvan

Meaning: unknown

+ (d. second century): Briton sent to Pope St. Eleutherius to ask for missionaries. Feast day: January 1.

# Elvis

Meaning: possibly from Alvis, the suitor of the Norse god Thor's daughter, or a Scottish place name

+ (d. sixth century): Irish saint. Feast day: February 22.

*(Alvis, Elwin)*

# Ely

Meaning: unknown

+ (biblical): High priest in the time of Samuel (1 Samuel 1:19).

# Emeric

Meaning: German "leader"

+ (d. 1031): Son of St. Stephen, Hungary's first Christian king. Feast day: November 4.

*(Emerick, Emery, Emmory, Emory)*

# Emilian

Meaning: Polish "eager"

+ (d. 362): Bulgarian martyr. Feast day: July 18.

+ (d. 520): Italian bishop. Feast day: September 11.

+ Emilian Cucullatus (d. 574): One of the patron saints of Spain. Feast day: November 12.

+ (d. 675): Irish-born abbot of Lagny, France. Feast day: March 10.

+ (d. 767): Recluse of Bordeaux, France. Feast day: January 7.

+ (d.c. 820): Turkish bishop. Feast day: August 8.

*(Aemilio, Eminian, Emille, Emils, Imelin)*

# Emmanuel

Meaning: Hebrew "God is with us"

+ Emmanuel d' Abreu, Blessed (d. 1737): Martyr of China. Feast day: January 12.

+ Emmanuel Trieu (d. 1798): Native-born martyr of Vietnam. Feast day: September 17.

+ Emmanuel Ruiz, Blessed (d. 1860): Martyred with eleven companions in Lebanon. Feast day: July 10.

+ Emmanuel Domingo y Sol (d. 1909): Patron of youth.

*(Emanuel, Manuel, Manny)*

# Eneco

Meaning: unknown

+ (d. 1057): Benedictine abbot. Feast day: June 1.

*(Inigo)*

# Engelbert

Meaning: Old German "angel"

+ Archbishop of Cologne, Germany. Feast day: November 7.

*(Engelberth, Ingelbert, Ingelberth)*

# Enrico

Meaning: Italian form of Henry

+ Enrico Rebuschini, Blessed (d. 1938): Italian priest, called "the mystic of the streets."

# Enrique

See Henry

# Ephraem

Meaning: Hebrew "fruitful"

+ Ephraem the Syrian (d.c. 373): Doctor of the Church, credited with introducing hymns into public worship. Feast day: June 9.

*(Efraim, Efrayim, Ephraim, Ephrem)*

## Erasmus

Meaning: Greek "beloved"

+ (d.c. 303): Bishop, patron of sailors, commonly known as St. Elmo. Feast day: June 2.

*(Elmo)*

## Erhard

Meaning: Old German "resolute"

+ (d. 686): Bishop and missionary to Bavaria. Feast day: January 8.

*(Erhardt, Erhart)*

## Eric

Meaning: Old Norse "rule of all"

+ Eric IX of Sweden (d. 1160): Martyred king of Sweden. Feast day: May 18.

*(Aric, Arik, Arick, Erick, Erik, Eryk, Rick)*

## Ernest

Meaning: German "vigor"

+ (d. 1148): Benedictine abbot who went on the Crusades. Feast day: November 7.

*(Earnest, Ernie, Ernst)*

## Eskill

Meaning: Scandinavian "protester"

+ (d.c. 1080): English missionary to Sweden. Feast day: June 12.

## Esteban, Estevan

See Stephen

## Ethan

Meaning: Hebrew "firmness"

+ (biblical): Son of Zerah (2 Chronicles 2:6).

*(Eathen, Ethen, Eythan)*

## Ethelbert

Meaning: unknown

+ Ethelbert of Kent (d. 616): King of Kent, England, converted by St. Augustine. Feast day: February 25.

+ (d. 794): Martyred king of East Anglia, England. Feast day: May 20.

## Eugene

Meaning: Greek "well-born"

+ (date unknown): Bishop and martyr, companion of St. Denis. Feast day: November 15.

+ (d. 422): Disciple of St. Ambrose of Milan. Feast day: November 17.

+ (d. sixth century): Irish missionary to England. Feast day: August 23.

+ Eugene I, Pope (served from 654-657): Roman known for his charity and sanctity. Feast day: June 2.

+ Eugene II of Toledo (d. 657): Noted poet and musician. Feast day: November 13.

+ Eugene III, Pope, Blessed (served from 1145-1153): Abbot of the Cistercian monastery, Tre Fontane. Feast day: July 8.

+ Eugene de Mazenod (d. 1861): Founder of the Missionary Oblates of Mary Immaculate (the Oblates). Feast day: December 3.

*(Ewan, Euan, Euen, Ewhen, Gene)*

## Eusebius

Meaning: unknown

+ (d.c. 192): Martyr. Feast day: August 25.

+ Eusebius, Pope (served from April to August 309 or 310): Son of a Greek physician, exiled and died in Sicily five months after being elected pope. Feast day: August 17.

+ (d.c. 256): Roman martyr. Feast day: December 2.

+ (d. 362): Martyr with two brothers, Nestabus and Zeno. Feast day: September 8.

+ (d. fourth century): Roman priest. Feast day: August 14.

+ (d. fourth century): Syrian hermit. Feast day: January 23.

+ Eusebius of Vercelli (d. 371): Bishop and martyr. Feast day: August 2.

+ Eusebius of Samosata (d.c. 380): Bishop in Syria. Feast day: June 21.

+ Eusebius of Bologna (d.c. 400): Bishop of Bologna, Italy. Feast day: September 26.

+ Eusebius of Cremona (d.c. 423): Abbot of Bethlehem in ancient Palestine, a friend of Sts. Jerome and Paula. Feast day: March 5.

+ Eusebius of Milan (d. 465): Bishop of Milan, Italy. Feast day: August 12.

+ (d. 884): Martyred Irish Benedictine. Feast day: January 31.

## Eustace

Meaning: Greek "fruitful"

+ (d. 118): Roman military officer. Feast day September 20.

*(Eustasius, Eustis, Stacey, Stacy)*

## Euan

See Eugene

## Eval

Meaning: unknown

+ (d. sixth century): Bishop of Cornwall, England. Feast day: November 20.

## Evan

Meaning: Welsh for John "God has been gracious"

+ (d. ninth century): Scottish hermit. Feast day: August 18.

*(Evans, Eveann, Evin, Evyn)*

## Everard

Meaning: Old German "hard boar"

+ Everard Hanse, Blessed (d. 1581): Martyr of England. Feast day: July 30.

## Everett, Everhart, Evers

See Eberhard

## Ewin, Evin

See Abban

## Ewen

See Hywyn

## Eystein

Meaning: unknown

+ Eystein Eralndsson (d. 1188): Archbishop of Norway.

## Ezekiel

Meaning: Hebrew "God will strengthen"

+ (biblical): One of the great Hebrew prophets (Book of Ezekiel).

*(Zeik, Zeke)*

## Ezra

Meaning: Hebrew "helper"

+ (biblical): Priest who led return from Babylonian captivity (Book of Ezra).

*(Esra, Ezri)*

# F

## Fabian

Meaning: Latin "bean"

+ Fabian, Pope (served from 236-250): A dove reportedly landed on his head during the papal election. Martyr. Feast day: January 20.

*(Fabayan, Fabiano, Fabien, Fabio, Faybian)*

## Fachanan

Meaning: Latin "enterprising"

+ (d. sixth century): First bishop of Ross, Ireland. Feast day: August 14.

## Falco

Meaning: unknown

+ (d. 512): Dutch Bishop. Feast day: February 20.

## Fantinus

Meaning: unknown

+ (d. 980): Basilian monk famous for his prophecies. Feast day: August 30.

## Faro

Meaning: Latin "well"

+ (d.c. 675): French Bishop. Feast day: October 28.

## Faustus

Meaning: Latin "lucky"

+ (d.c. 190): Martyred soldier who suffered in Milan, Italy. Feast day: August 7.

+ (d. 250): Martyr caught in the persecution of Emperor Trajanus Decius. Feast day: July 16.

+ (d. 250): Egyptian martyr. Feast day: September 6.

+ (d. 304): Spanish martyr. Feast day: October 13.

+ (d. 490): French Bishop. Feast day: September 28.

## Fazzio

Meaning: unknown

+ (d. 1272): Goldsmith. Feast day: January 18

*(Facius, Fatius, Fazius)*

## Felician

Meaning: Latin "happy"

+ (d. 251): Martyred bishop of Foligno, Italy. Feast day: January 24 and October 20.

## Felipe

See Philip

## Felix

Meaning: Latin "happy"

+ (d. 303): Martyr. Feast day: October 24.

+ (d.c. 484): Martyred bishop of Abbir, Africa. Feast day: October 12.

+ Felix of Nantes (d.c. 584): Bishop known for the cathedral he erected in Nantes, France. Feast day: July 7.

+ (d. seventh century): Martyred Englishman sold into slavery in France.

Feast day: September 6.

+ Felix of Dunwich (d. 647): Bishop and an apostle of the East Angles of England. Feast day: March 8.

+ Felix of Valois (d.c. 1212): Hermit and co-founder of the Trinitarians with St. John of Matha. Feast day: November 20.

+ Felix of Cantalice (d. 1587): First Capuchin Franciscan monk to be canonized. Feast day: May 18.

*(Felician, Feliks)*

# Ferdinand

Meaning: Gothic or German either "peaceful traveler" or "bold traveler"

+ Ferdinand III (d. 1252): King of Castile, Spain, who ousted the Moors. Feast day: May 30.

+ Ferdinand Ayala, Blessed (d. 1617): Martyr of Japan. Feast day: June 1.

*(Fernado, Fernand, Ferrant, Hernando)*

# Fergus

Meaning: Gaelic "supreme choice:

+ (d.c. sixth century): Irish Bishop. Feast day: March 30.

+ (d.c. 721): Irish bishop, called "the Pict." Feast day: November 27.

*(Ferguson)*

# Fiace

Meaning: unknown

+ (d. fifth century): Irish bishop. Feast day: October 12.

# Fiacre

Meaning: unknown

+ (d.c. 670): Patron saint of the cab drivers and gardeners. Feast day: August 30.

*(Fevre, Fiacrius, Fiaker)*

# Fidelis

Meaning: Latin "faithful"

+ Fidelis of Como (d.c. 304): Roman soldier. Feast day: October 28.

+ (d.c. 570): Bishop of Merida, Spain. Feast day: February 7.

+ Fidelis of Sigmaringen (d. 1622): Franciscan Capuchin martyr. Feast day: April 24.

# Filippo

Meaning: Italian form of Philip

+ Filippo Smaldone, Blessed (d. 1923): Minister to the deaf, blind and abandoned.

+ Filippo Rinaldi, Blessed (d. 1931): Successor of St. Don Bosco.

# Finan

Meaning: possibly from Latin "light friend"

+ (d. sixth century): Disciple of St. Brendan. Feast day: April 7.

+ (d. 661): Bishop of Lindisfarne, in present-day England. Feast day: February 17.

# Finbar

Meaning: Irish "fair-haired"

+ (d. sixth century): Irish abbot. Feast day: July 4.

+ (d.c. 633): Irish miracle worker. Feast day: September 25.

*(Barry, Finbur)*

# Findan

Meaning: unknown

+ (d. 879): Benedictine hermit. Feast day: November 15.

# Finian

Meaning: unknown

+ Finian of Clonard (d.c. 549): Known as the "Teacher of the Irish Saints." Feast day: December 12.

+ (d. 579): Irish abbot who fought with St. Columba over a copy of St. Jerome's Psalter. Finian won. Feast day: September 10.

# Fintan

Meaning: unknown

+ (d. sixth century): Abbot and patron saint of Doon, in Limerick, Ireland. Feast day: January 3.

+ (d. 603): Abbot and disciple of St. Columba. Feast day: February 17.

# Flannan

Meaning: possibly Irish "haired" or Latin "blond"

+ (d. seventh century): Irish Bishop. Feast day: December 18.

# Flavian

Meaning: Latin "yellow-haired"

+ Flavius Clemens (d.c. 96): Roman martyr, the brother of Emperor Vespasian and uncle of Emperors Titus and Domitian. Feast day: June 22.

+ (d. 362): Prefect of Rome arrested for being a Christian. Feast day: December 22.

+ Flavian of Constantinople (d. 449): Patriarch of Constantinople (now Istanbul, Turkey). Feast day: February 18.

*(Flaviar, Flavio)*

# Florian

Meaning: Latin "flowery"

+ (d. 304): Martyr and patron of Poland and Upper Austria. Feast day: May 4.

*(Florien, Florrian)*

# Florentino

Meaning: Latin "blooming"

+ Florentino Asensio Barroso, Blessed (d. 1936): Martyr in the Spanish Civil War.

# Fort

Meaning: Latin "strong"

+ (d. first century): Bishop of Bordeaux, France, a martyr. Feast day: May 16.

# Foster

See Vedast

# Francis

Meaning: Latin "a Frenchman"

+ Francis of Assisi (d. 1226): Founder of the Franciscan Order. Feast day: October 4.

+ Francis of Paola (d. 1507): Patron of seafarers. Feast day: April 2.

+ Francis Xavier (d. 1552): Jesuit, one of the world's greatest missionaries, patron of foreign missions. Feast day: December 3.

+ Francis Borgia (d. 1572): Sometimes called "the Second Founder of the Jesuits." Feast day: October 10.

+ Francis Rod (d. 1572): Franciscan martyr, hanged in Holland by the Calvinists. Feast day: July 9.

+ Francis Dickenson, Blessed (d. 1590): English martyr. Feast day: April 30.

+ Francis Blanco (d. 1597): Franciscan martyr of Japan. Feast day: February 6.

+ Francis of Nagasaki (1597): Native Japanese, a physician and martyr. Feast day: February 6.

+ Francis of St. Michael (d. 1597): Martyr of Japan. Feast day: February 6.

+ Francis Page, Blessed (d. 1602): Jesuit martyr of England. Feast day: April 20.

+ Francis Caracciolo (d. 1608): Founder, with St. John Augustine Adorno, of the Minor Clerks Regular. Feast day: June 4.

+ Francis Solano (d. 1610): Franciscan missionary in Lima, Peru. Feast day: July 14.

+ Francis Chakichi, Blessed (d. 1622): Four-year-old martyr of Japan. Feast day: October 2.

+ Francis de Morales (d. 1622): Dominican martyr of Japan. Feast day: September 10.

+ Francis de Sales (d. 1622): Doctor of the Church and patron of the Catholic press. Feast day: January 24.

+ Francis of St. Bonaventure (d. 1622): Native-born martyr of Japan. Feast day: September 12.

+ Francis Takea, Blessed (d. 1622): Twelve-year-old martyr of Japan. Feast day: September 11.

+ Francis Galvez (d. 1623): Martyr of Japan. Feast day: December 4.

+ Francis Pacheco, Blessed (d. 1626): Jesuit martyr in Japan. Feast day: June 20.

+ Francis Kuloi, Blessed (d. 1627): Native Japanese martyr. Feast day: August 17.

+ Francis Kurobioye, Blessed (d. 1627): Native Japanese martyr. Feast day: August 17.

+ Francis of St. Mary (d. 1627): Martyr of Japan. Feast day: August 1.

+ Francis Nifaki, Blessed (d. 1628): Five-year-old martyr of Japan. Feast day: September 8.

+ Francis of Jesus Ortega, Blessed (d. 1632): Martyr of Japan. Feast day: September 3.

+ Francis de Capillas, Blessed (d. 1648): Dominican missionary and martyr in China. Feast day: January 15.

+ Francis de Montmorecy Laval, Blessed (d. 1708): Missionary to the Americas.

+ Francis Jerome (d. 1716): Famous Jesuit preacher. Feast day: May 11.

+ Francis Fasani (d. 1742): Franciscan mystic. Feast day: December 9.

+ Francis Gil de Frederich (d. 1745): Dominican martyr who worked in Vietnam. Feast day: January 22.

+ Francis Diaz (d. 1748): Dominican martyr of China. Feast day: October 20.

+ Francis Serrano, Blessed (d. 1748): Dominican martyr of China. Feast day: October 20.

+ Francis Regis Clet, Blessed (d. 1820): Martyr of China. Feast day: February 17.

+ Francis Isidore Gagelin (d. 1833): Martyr of Vietnam. Feast day: October 17.

+ Francis Chieu (d. 1833): Martyr of Vietnam. Feast day: October 17.

+ Francis Xavier Can (d. 1837): Martyr of Vietnam. Feast day: November 20.

+ Francis Jaccard (d. 1838): Martyr of Vietnam. Feast day: September 21.

+ Francis Mau, Blessed (d. 1839): A martyr of Vietnam. Feast day: December 19.

+ Francis Xavier Mau (d. 1839): Native-born martyr of Vietnam. Feast day: December 19.

+ Francis Trung (d. 1858): Native-born Vietnamese martyr. Feast day: October 6.

+ Francis of Camporossa (d. 1866): Capuchin brother, famous as a miracle worker and as a seer. Feast day: September 16.

+ Francis Palau y Quer, Blessed (d. 1872): Carmelite missionary.

+ Francis Coll, Blessed (d. 1875): Preacher.

+ Francis Fa'a di Bruno, Blessed (d, 1876): Mathematician, astronomer, priest.

+ Francis Spinelli, Blessed (d. 1909): Founder of the Sisters of the Perpetual Adoration of the Blessed Sacrament.

+ Francis Garate, Blessed (d. 1929): Doorkeeper, called "Brother Courtesy."

*(Fran, Francesco, Franchot, Francisco, Franco, Francois, Frank, Franz)*

# Franco

Meaning: Spanish form of Francis

+ (d.c. 1275): Benedictine hermit. Feast day: June 5.

# Frederick

Meaning: Old German "peaceful ruler"

+ (d. 838): Bishop and martyr. Feast day: July 18.

+ (d. 1121): Bishop of Liège, Belgium. Feast day: May 27.

+ Frederick Albert, Blessed (d. 1876): Founder of the Vincentian Sisters of Mary Immaculate (the Albertines).

*(Fred, Freddi, Frederico, Frederic, Fred, Frederich, Fredric, Fredrick, Fredrik, Friderich, Fritz, Rick, Rickey)*

# Frediano

Meaning: unknown

+ (d. 588): Irish bishop. Feast day: March 18.

*(Fred)*

# Fremund

Meaning: possibly Anglo-Saxon "free"

+ (d. 866): Martyred Anglo-Saxon hermit. Feast day: May 11.

*(Freedman, Freeman, Freemon)*

# Fulbert

Meaning: Old German "bright"

+ (d. 1028): Bishop of Chartres, France, and a poet. Feast day: April 10.

# Fulk

Meaning: unknown

+ (d.c. 600): Pilgrim who died helping plague victims. Feast day: May 22.

+ (d. 1229): Scottish Bishop of Pavia, Italy. Feast day: October 26.

# Fulrad

Meaning: unknown

+ (d. 784): Counselor of Kings Pepin and Charlemagne. Feast day: July 16.

# Fursey

Meaning: unknown

+ (d.c. 648): Irish monk. Feast day: January 16.

# G

## Gabinus

Meaning: unknown

+ (d.c. 295): Martyr of Rome, the brother of Pope St. Gaius. Feast day: February 19.

*(Gabby)*

## Gabriel

Meaning: Hebrew "hero of God"

+ (biblical): Archangel, the "Angel of the Annunciation" (Luke 1:26-38). Feast day: September 29.

+ Gabriel Jusuke (d. 1597): Native Japanese martyr. Feast day: February 6.

+ Gabriel of St. Magdalen, Blessed (d. 1632): Franciscan martyr of Japan. Feast day: September 3.

+ Gabriel Lalement (d. 1649): Martyr of North America. Feast day: October 19.

+ Gabriel du-Fresse, Blessed (d. 1815): Martyr of China. Feast day: September 14.

+ Gabriel Francis of Our Lady of Sorrows (d. 1862): Passionist monk. Feast day: February 27.

*(Gab, Gabe, Gabriell, Gabriello, Gabrielli, Gibbie)*

## Gaius

Meaning: Latin "to rejoice"

+ Gaius of Milan (d. first century): Italian bishop. Feast day: September 27.

+ (d. third century): Martyr of Alexandria, Egypt. Feast day: October 4.

+ (d.c. 259): Martyr at Nicomedia (in modern Turkey). Feast day: March 4.

+ Gaius Francis (d. 1597): Martyr of Japan. Feast day: February 6.

+ Gaius of Korea, Blessed (d. 1627): Korean Buddhist monk, martyred in Japan. Feast day: November 15.

+ Gaius Sheymon, Blessed (d. 1627): Native Japanese martyr. Feast day: June 1.

*(Caius, Cai, Caio, Caw)*

## Galation

Meaning: Greek "ivory"

+ (d. 251): Martyr with his wife Episteme. Feast day: November 5.

## Gall

Meaning: Irish "stranger"

+ (d.c. 554): French bishop. Feast day: July 1.

+ (d.c. 645): Irish missionary and companion of St. Columban. Feast day: October 16.

## Gamaliel

Meaning: Hebrew "God is recompensor"

+ (biblical): Rabbi and teacher of St. Paul (Acts 22:3). Feast day: August 3.

## Gamo

Meaning: unknown

+ (d. eighth century): Benedictine abbot and a staunch patron of the arts. Feast day: May 30.

## Garcia

Meaning: unknown

+ (d.c. 1073): Benedictine abbot and

military adviser to King Ferdinand I of Spain. Feast day: September 29.

## Garrat, Garrett
See Gerard

## Gaspar
Meaning: Persian "treasure holder"

+ Gaspar Stangassinger, Blessed (d. 1899): Priest and religious.

## Gaston
See Vedast

## Gatian
Meaning: Hebrew "family"

+ (d.c. 337): First bishop of Tours, France. Feast day: December 18.

## Gebhard
Meaning: unknown

+ (d. 995): French bishop. Feast day: August 27.

## Gebizo
+ (d.c. 1087): Benedictine monk who crowned King Zwoinimir of Croatia. Feast day: October 21.

## Gelasius
Meaning: Latin "bright"

+ Gelasius I, Pope (served from 492-496): Roman-born son of an African father. Feast day: November 21.

+ Gelasius II, Pope (served from 1118-1119). Deacon who was secretly elected pope and fought against Emperor Henry V. Feast day: June 29.

## Genesius
Meaning: Latin "bright"

+ Genesius of Arles (d.c. 300): Patron of actors. Feast day: August 25.

+ (d.c. 303): Martyred catechumen who was a notary in the court at Arles, France. Feast day: November 1.

## Gene
See Eugene

## Gennard
Meaning: unknown

+ (d. 720): Benedictine abbot. Feast day: April 6.

## Gennaro
See Januarius

## Geoffrey
See Godfrey

## George
Meaning: Greek "earthworker" or "farmer"

+ (d.c. 300): Martyr and patron saint of England, Portugal, Germany, Aragon, Spain, Genoa, and Venice. Feast day: April 23.

+ George Limniotes (d.c. 730): Hermit martyr on Mount Olympus. Feast day: August 24.

+ George of Antioch (d. 814): Bishop of Antioch, in present-day Turkey. Feast day: April 19.

+ George the Younger (d.c. 816): Bishop of Mytilene, the capital of Lesbos Island, Greece. Feast day: April 7.

+ George of Amastris (d.c. 825): Bishop of Amastris, on the Black Sea in modern Turkey. Feast day: February 21.

+ (d.c. 852): Spanish martyr. Feast day: July 27.

+ George Haydock, Blessed (d. 1584): One of eighty-five martyrs in England, Wales, and Scotland. Feast day: May 4.

+ George Swallowell, Blessed (d. 1594): English martyr who became a Protestant minister but then returned to the Catholic faith. Feast day: July 26.

+ George Gervase, Blessed (d. 1608): Benedictine martyr of England. Feast day: April 11.

+ George Napper, Blessed (d. 1610): English martyr. Feast day: May 4.

*(Georges, Georgio, Gheorghe, Giorgio, Giorgios, Jorge)*

# Gerald

Meaning: Old German "spear-ruler"

+ (d. 732): Abbot and disciple of St. Colman. Feast day: March 13.

+ (d. 896): Benedictine bishop, formerly a courtier of Charlemagne. Feast day: June 14.

+ Gerald of Aurillac (d. 909): Member of the French court and founder of a church and abbey. Feast day: October 13.

+ (d. 1077): Benedictine bishop. Feast day: February 6.

+ (d. 1095): Benedictine monk. Feast day: April 5.

+ (d. 1109): Benedictine archbishop of Portugal. Feast day: December 5.

*(Geraldo, Gerrald, Gerrold, Gerry, Jerald, Jerold, Jerry)*

# Gerard

Meaning: Old German "spear-brave"

+ (d.c. 639): English pilgrim-martyr. Feast day: April 28.

+ Gerard of Toul (d. 994): Bishop of Toul, France. Feast day: April 23.

+ Gerard of Brogne (d. 959): Benedictine monastic reformer. Feast day: October 3.

+ Gerard de Lunel (d. 1298): Patron saint of Monte Santo, near Ancona, Italy. Feast day: May 24.

+ Gerard Miles, Blessed (d. 1590): Martyr of England. Feast day: April 30.

+ Gerard Majella (d. 1755): Mystic known for bilocation, prophecies, visions, and other spiritual phenomena. He is patron of childbirth. Feast day: October 16.

*(Garrard, Garrat, Garrett, Gerry, Jerry)*

# Gerbold

Meaning: Old German "bold"

+ (d.c. 690): Benedictine bishop. Feast day: December 5.

# Gerlac

Meaning: Dutch "knight"

+ (d. 1170): Hermit and correspondent with St. Hildegard. Feast day: January 5.

# Gerland

Meaning: unknown

+ (d. 1104): Italian bishop. Feast day: February 25.

# Germanus

Meaning: Latin "Germanic"

+ Germanus of Auxerre (d. 448): Bishop of Auxerre, France. Feast day: July 31.

+ Germanus of Paris (d. 576): Bishop of Paris, France. Feast day: May 28.

+ Germanus of Capua (d.c. 545):

Bishop of Capua, Italy. Feast day: October 30.

+ (d.c. 677): Benedictine bishop. Feast day: February 21.

+ (d. 732): Patriarch of Constantinople (modern Istanbul, Turkey). Feast day: May 12.

+ (d. 1104): Bishop. Feast day: February 25.

## Germoc

Meaning: unknown

+ (d. sixth century): Irish chieftain. Feast day: June 24.

+ (d. 978): Nobleman who became a hermit in Switzerland. Feast day: April 19.

## Gerry, Gerald

See Gerard

## Gibbie

See Gabriel

## Gibrian

Meaning: Latin "aristocrat"

+ (d.c. 515): Irish priest-hermit. Feast day: May 8.

## Gideon

Meaning: Hebrew "mighty warrior"

+ (biblical): Judge in Israel (Judges 6:11).

## Gilbert

Meaning: Old German "bright pledge"

+ (d. 1245): Scottish bishop. Feast day: April 1.

+ Gilbert of Sempringham (d. 1189): Founder of the Gilbertine Order. Feast day: February 4.

*(Gibbon, Gibbs, Gibson, Gil)*

## Gildard

Meaning: unknown

+ (d.c. 514): Bishop of Rouen, France. Feast day: June 8.

## Gildas

Meaning: Latin "heritage"

+ (d.c. 570): Scottish bishop and author. Feast day: January 29.

## Giles

Meaning: Greek "young goat" or "bearded"

+ (d. eighth century): Benedictine abbot, patron of cripples, beggars, and blacksmiths. Feast day: September 1.

*(Gilles, Gyles)*

## Giovani

See John

## Girald

Meaning: probably a form of Gerald

+ (d. 1031): Benedictine abbot who was murdered by an irate monk. Feast day: December 29.

## Goar

Meaning: Latin "fighter"

+ (d.c. 575): Priest of Aquitaine, France, honored by Charlemagne. Feast day: July 6.

*(Goer)*

## Goban

Meaning: unknown

+ (d. 670): Benedictine martyr murdered by bandits. Feast day: June 20.

## Godehard

Meaning: Old German "God's flocks"

+ (d. 1038): Bishop and patron of St. Gothard Pass in the Alps. Feast day: May 4.

*(Gothard)*

## Godfrey

Meaning: Old German "god of peace"

+ (d. 1115): French bishop. Feast day: November 8.

+ (d. 1572): Two martyrs of the same name hanged by Calvinists. Feast day: July 9.

*(Geoff, Geoffrey, Geoffy, Geofrey, Jefery, Jeff, Jefferey, Jefferson, Jeffery, Jeffree, Jeffrie, Jeffry)*

## Godric

Meaning: Anglo-Saxon "ruling through God"

+ (d. 1170): English hermit, mystic and poet. Feast day: May 21.

## Godwin

Meaning: Old English "divine"

+ (d.c. 690): Benedictine abbot and a noted scholar. Feast day: October 28.

## Goeric

Meaning: possibly from the Latin "fighter"

+ (d. 647): French bishop. Feast day: September 19.

## Gollen

Meaning: Unknown

+ (d. seventh century): Welsh saint. Feast day: May 21.

*(Colan, Collen)*

## Goncalco

Meaning: unknown

+ Goncalco Garcia (d. 1597): Martyr of Japan. Feast day: February 6.

## Gonzaga

Meaning: unknown, perhaps from St. Aloysius Gonzaga

+ Gonzaga Gonza (d. 1886): Martyr of Uganda. Feast day: June 3.

## Gordian

Meaning: possibly from Anglo-Saxon "round hill"

+ (d. 362): Martyr. Feast day: May 10.

*(Gordan, Gordie, Gordon, Gordy)*

## Gorman

Meaning: Irish "little blue-eyed one"

+ (d. 965): Danish bishop. Feast day: August 28.

*(Gormon)*

## Gosbert

Meaning: unknown

+ (d.c. 859): German bishop. Feast day: February 13.

## Goswin

Meaning: unknown

+ (d. 1165): Benedictine abbot. Feast day: October 9.

## Govan

Meaning: unknown

+ (d. sixth century): Welsh hermit. Feast day: June 20.

## Gregory

Meaning: Greek "watchful"

+ Gregory Thaumaturgus (d. 270): Bishop whose title, Thaumaturgus, means "Wonder-Worker." Feast day: November 17.

+ Gregory the Illuminator (d. 332): The Apostle of Armenia. Feast day: September 30.

+ Gregory Nazianzus the Elder (d. 374): Bishop and confessor, Doctor of the Church, father of St. Gregory Nazianzus the Younger. Feast day: January 1.

+ Gregory Nazianzus the Younger (d. 390): Patriarch and Doctor of the Church, called "the Divine." Feast day: January 2.

+ Gregory of Elvira (d.c. 394): Spanish bishop. Feast day: April 24.

+ Gregory of Nyssa (d. 395): Bishop and brother of St. Basil. Feast day: March 9.

+ Gregory of Terracina (d.c. 570): Disciple of St. Benedict. Feast day: December 12.

+ Gregory of Tours (d.c. 594): Bishop and historian. Feast day: November 17.

+ Gregory I, Pope (served from 590-604): Benedictine monk and Doctor of the Church, called "the Great." Feast day: September 3.

+ Gregory of Utrecht (d. 776): Benedictine abbot who forgave two men who murdered his half brothers. Feast day: August 25.

+ Gregory of Einsiedeln (d. 996): Benedictine abbot who was an Anglo-Saxon pilgrim. Feast day: November 8.

+ (d. 999): Benedictine abbot in Germany. Feast day: November 4.

+ Gregory VII, Pope (served from 1073-1085): King Henry IV is said to have stood for three days in the snows outside Canossa to receive the Pope's forgiveness. Feast day: May 25.

+ Gregory Barbardico (d. 1697): Cardinal who worked for reconciliation between the Eastern and Western Churches. Feast day: June 17.

+ Gregory Grassi, Blessed (d. 1900): Franciscan martyr of China. Feast day: July 8.

*(Greg, Gregg, Gregor, Grigor)*

## Grimbald

Meaning: Old German or French "bold son"

+ (d. 901): Benedictine abbot. Feast day: July 8.

*(Grimwald)*

## Grimoaldo

Meaning: unknown

+ Grimoaldo Santamaria (d. 1902): Passionist priest.

## Guibert

Meaning: Old German "from a bright hope"

+ (d. 962): Military man who became a hermit. Feast day: May 23.

## Guido

Meaning: Italian "guide"

+ Guido Maria Conforti, Blessed (d. 1931): Modern missionary.

## Guiseppe

See Joseph

## Gulstan

Meaning: unknown

+ (d.c. 1010): Benedictine monk. Feast day: November 29.

## Gundebert

Meaning: unknown

+ (d.c. 676): Bishop. Feast day: February 21.

+ (d. eighth century): Martyr of Ireland. Feast day: April 20.

## Gundisalvus

Meaning: unknown

+ Gundisalvus Fusai, Blessed (d. 1622): Native-born Japanese martyr. Feast day: September 10.

+ Gundisalvus Garcia (d. 1597): Franciscan martyr of Japan. Feast day: February 6.

## Gurias

Meaning: unknown

+ (d. 305): Martyr in Edessa (city in present-day Turkey). Feast day: November 15.

## Gus

See Augustine

## Guthlac

Meaning: unknown

+ (d. 714): Benedictine hermit, mystic and prophet. Feast day: April 11.

## Guy

Meaning: Old German "warrior"

+ (d. 940): Benedictine abbot. Feast day: June 18.

+ (d. 1046): Benedictine abbot . Feast day: March 31.

+ (d.c. 1012): Pilgrim. Feast day: September 12.

## Gyavire

Meaning: unknown

+ (d. 1886): Martyr of Uganda. Feast day: June 13.

# H

## Hadelin

Meaning: unknown

+ (d.c. 690): Benedictine abbot in France. Feast day: February 3.

## Haduin

Meaning: possibly Old German "dear friend in battle"

+ (d.c. 662): Bishop of Le Mans, France. Feast day: August 20.

*(Hadwin, Hadwyn, Wynn)*

## Hal

See Harold, Henry

## Hallvard

Meaning: Scandinavian "from the castle of the king"

+ (d.c. 1043): Royal noble of Norway. Feast day: May 14.

## Hank

See Henry

## Hannibal

Meaning: Phoenician "grace"

+ Hannibal Maria di Fancia, Blessed (d. 1927): Founder of the Rogationist Fathers and Daughters of the Holy Zeal.

## Haran

Meaning: Hebrew "enlightened"

+ (biblical): brother of Abraham (Genesis 11:26)

*(Harran)*

## Hardoin

Meaning: possibly Old English "brave friend"

+ (d. seventh century): French Bishop. Feast day: November 29.

*(Hardan, Hardin, Hardwin)*

## Harold

Meaning: Old English "army power"

+ (d. 1168): Martyred child of Gloucester, England. Feast day: March 25.

*(Harrold, Harald, Hal, Harry)*

## Harry

See Harold, Henry

## Harvey

See Hervé

## Hedda

Meaning: Old German "strife"

+ (d. 705): Benedictine bishop, an Anglo-Saxon of Whitby, England. Feast day: July 7.

+ (d.c. 870): Martyred Benedictine abbot of Peterborough, England. Feast day: April 9.

## Heimrad

Meaning: unknown

+ (d. 1019): Benedictine hermit and pilgrim. Feast day: June 28.

## Heldrad

Meaning: unknown

+ (d. 842): Benedictine abbot who helped rescue Alpine travelers. Feast day: March 13.

## Helier

Meaning: unknown

+ (d. sixth century): Martyr on the island of Jersey, Britain. Feast day: July 16.

## Henry

Meaning: Old English "home ruler"

+ Henry II (d. 1024): Holy Roman Emperor, called "the Good," the patron saint of the Benedictine Oblates. Feast day: July 13.

+ Henry of Cocket (d. 1127): Danish hermit. Feast day: January 16.

+ Henry of Uppsala (d.c. 1156): Bishop and patron of Finland. Feast day: January 19.

+ Henry Suso, Blessed (d. 1366): German Dominican mystic. Feast day: January 23.

+ Henry Walpole (d. 1595): Jesuit and one of the Forty Martyrs of England and Wales. Feast day: April 7.

+ Henry Abbot, Blessed (d. 1597): Martyr of England. Feast day: July 4.

+ Henry Morse (d. 1645): English Jesuit priest, one of the Forty Martyrs of England and Wales. Feast day: February 1.

*(Enrico, Enrique, Hal, Hank, Harry, Henrik, Henri, Henricus, Henryk, Herry)*

## Herbert

Meaning: Old German "bright shining army"

+ (date unknown): French bishop. Feast day: October 30.

+ (d. 687): English hermit. Feast day: March 20.

+ Herbert Hoscam (d. 1180): Archbishop and patron saint of Conze, Italy. Feast day: August 20.

*(Herb, Herbie)*

## Herculanus (Hercules)

Meaning: Greek "gift"

+ (d. second century): Martyred Roman soldier. Feast day: September 25.

+ (d.c. 549): Bishop of Perugia, Italy. Feast day: November 7 and March 1.

## Heribert

Meaning: perhaps the same as Herbert

+ (d. 1022): Archbishop of Cologne, Germany, and chancellor of Emperor Otto III. Feast day: March 16.

## Herman

Meaning: Old German "army man"

+ Herman Joseph (d. 1241): German mystic. Feast day: April 7.

*(Hermann, Hermon)*

## Hermes

Meaning: Greek "messenger of the gods"

+ (d. 120): Roman martyr. Feast day: August 28.

## Hernan

Meaning: unknown

+ (d. sixth century): British hermit who lived in France. Feast day: September 15.

## Hernando

See Ferdinand

## Heron

Meaning: unknown

+ (d.c. 136): Martyred bishop, the successor of St. Ignatius at Antioch, Turkey. Feast day: October 17.

+ (d. 250): Egyptian martyr. Feast day: December 14.

## Herulph

Meaning: unknown

+ (d. 785): Benedictine bishop of Langres, France. Feast day: August 13.

## Hervé

+ Meaning: French "warrior"

+ (d.c. 575): Welsh bard. Feast day: June 17.

*(Harvey, Herveus)*

## Hilarion

Meaning: Latin "cheerful"

+ (d.c. 371): Abbot and disciple of St. Anthony the Great. Feast day: October 21.

## Hilary

Meaning: Latin "cheerful"

+ (d.c. 284): Martyr. Feast day: March 16.

+ Hilary of Poitiers (d. 368): Bishop and Doctor of the Church. Feast day: January 13.

+ (d.c. 449): Bishop of Arles, France. Feast day: May 5.

+ Hilary, Pope (served from 461-468): Fought the Nestorian heresy. Feast day: February 28.

+ (d. 558): Hermit who won the respect of King Theodoric of the Ostrogoths. Feast day: May 15.

*(Hilaire)*

## Hildebert

Meaning: possibly Old German "battle-bright"

+ (d. 752): Benedictine abbot and martyr. Feast day: April 4.

## Himelin

Meaning: unknown

+ (d.c. 750): Irish or Scottish priest. Feast day: March 10.

## Hippolytus

Meaning: Greek refers to "horses"

+ (d.c. 235): Martyr of Rome. Feast day: August 13.

## Hiram

Meaning: Hebrew "noble"

+ (biblical): King of Tyre who traded with David and Solomon (2 Chronicles 2:3).

*(Hi, Hirom)*

## Hon, Honus

See John

## Honorat

Meaning: probably from the Latin "man of honor"

+ Honorat a Biala (Kozminski), Blessed (d. 1916): Polish Franciscan.

## Honorius

Meaning: Latin "man of honor"

+ Honorius of Canterbury (d. 653): Archbishop of Canterbury, England. Feast day: September 30.

+ (d. 1250): Cattle merchant slain by his own servants in France. Feast day: January 9.

## Hubert

Meaning: Old German "bright, shining mind"

+ (d.c. 714): Benedictine monk. Feast day: May 30.

+ (d. 727): Bishop of Maastricht, Netherlands. Feast day: November 3.

*(Hubbard, Hubie)*

## Hugh

Meaning: Old German "mind," "soul," "thought"

+ Hugh of Rouen (d. 730): Benedictine bishop of Rouen, Paris, and Bayeux, France. Feast day: April 9.

+ Hugh of Anzy-le-Duc (d. 930): Benedictine prior. Feast day: April 20.

+ Hugh the Great (d. 1109): Benedictine abbot and one of the most influential men of his era. Feast day: April 29.

+ Hugh of Grenoble (d. 1132): Benedictine bishop of Grenoble, France. Feast day: April 1.

+ (d. 1172): Cistercian abbot. Feast day: November 17.

+ Hugh of Lincoln (d.c. 1200): Missionary to England. Feast day: November 17.

+ Hugh de Lippi-Uggucioni (d. 1282): One of the seven founders of the Servite Order. Feast day: February 17.

+ Hugh Faringdon, Blessed (d. 1539): Benedictine abbot, once a friend of King Henry VIII. Feast day: November 15.

+ Hugh More, Blessed (d. 1588): Martyr of England. Feast day: August 28.

+ Hugh Green, Blessed (d. 1642): Martyr of England. Feast day: August 19.

*(Hew, Howe, Howse, Huey, Hughes, Hughey, Hughie, Hughy, Hugo, Huw)*

# Humbert

Meaning: Old German "famous giant"

+ (d. 680): Benedictine abbot in Flanders, Belgium. Feast day: March 25.

# Humphrey

Meaning: Old German "peaceful Hun"

+ (d. 871): Benedictine bishop. Feast day: March 18.

+ Humphrey Middlemore, Blessed (d. 1535): Carthusian martyr of England. Feast day: June 19.

+ Humphrey Lawrence (d. 1591): Martyr of England. Feast day: July 7.

*(Humfrey, Humfrye, Humphery, Humphry)*

# Hyacinth

Meaning: the "hyacinth" flower

+ (d. 1257): Dominican missionary called "the Apostle of Poland." Feast day: formerly August 17.

+ Hyacinth Orfanel, Blessed (d. 1622): Martyr of Japan. Feast day: September 10.

+ Hyacinth Castaneda (d. 1773): Martyr of Vietnam. Feast day: November 7.

+ Hyacinth Marie Cormier (d. 1916): Master General of the Dominican Order.

# Hywyn

Meaning: possibly Gaelic "young warrior"

+ (d.c. 516): Founder of a Welsh monastery. Feast day: January 6.

*(Ewen, Owen)*

# I

# Iain, Ian

See John

# Ibar

Meaning: unknown

+ (d. fifth century): Missionary to Ireland, bishop. Feast day: April 23.

*(Iberius, Ivor)*

# Ichabod

Meaning: Hebrew "where is glory?"

+ (biblical): Grandson of Eli (1 Samuel 4:21)

# Ignatius

Meaning: Latin "ardent"

+ Ignatius of Antioch (d.c. 107): Bishop of Antioch and early martyr. Feast day: October 17.

+ Ignatius of Constantinople (d.c. 877): Patriarch of Constantinople (modern Istanbul, Turkey). Feast day: October 23.

+ Ignatius Loyola (d. 1556): Founder of the Jesuits. Patron of all spiritual exercises. Feast day: July 31.

+ Ignatius de Azevedo and Companions (d. 1570): Forty Jesuit martyrs. Spanish and Portuguese by descent. Feast day: July 15.

+ Ignatius Jorjes, Blessed (d. 1622): Martyr in Japan. Feast day: September 10.

+ Ignatius de Laconi (d. 1781): Franciscan mystic and confessor. Feast day: May 11.

+ Ignatius Delgado (d. 1838): Dominican martyr in Vietnam. Feast day: July 12.

*(Ignatious, Iggie, Inigo)*

# Ike

See Isaac

# Ildephonse

Meaning: form of Alfred

+ (d. 667) Archbishop of Toledo, honored in Spain as a Doctor of the Church. Feast day: January 23.

+ Ildephonse Schuster (d. 1954): Cardinal who opposed Fascism.

# Illtyd

Meaning: unknown

+ (d.c. 535): Welsh saint, traditionally thought to be a cousin of King Arthur of the Round Table. Feast day: November 6.

# Imelin

See Emilian

# Indract

Meaning: unknown

+ (d.c. 710): Irish chieftain and martyr. Feast day: February 5.

# Ine

Meaning: possibly from the Irish "pure"

+ (d. 727): King of Wessex. Feast day: September 8.

# Ingelbert

See Engelbert

# Inigo

See Ignatius, Eneco

# Innocent

Meaning: "without blame"

+ Innocent of Tortona (d.c. 350): Bishop and confessor. Feast day: April 17.

+ Innocent I, Pope (served from 401-417): Promoted celibacy for the clergy. Feast day: July 28.

+ Innocent V, Pope, Blessed (served from January to June, 1276): First Dominican to be elected pope, colleague of St. Thomas Aquinas. Feast day: June 22.

+ Innocent XI, Pope, Blessed (served from 1676-1689): Condemned quietism. Feast day: August 12.

# Irchard

Meaning: unknown

+ (d. seventh century): Called "the Apostle to the Picts" in Briton. Feast day: August 24.

# Irenaeus

Meaning: unknown

+ Irenaeus of Lyons (d.c. 200): Bishop of Lyons and one of the church's first theologians. Feast day: June 28.

+ (d.c. 258): Leader of a group of martyrs who were executed during the persecutions of Emperor Valerian. Feast day: December 15.

+ Irenaeus of Sirmium (d.c. 304): Bishop and martyr near present-day Belgrade. Feast day: March 25.

# Isaac

Meaning: Hebrew "laughter"

+ (biblical): Son of Abraham. (Genesis 17:19).

+ (d.c. 410): Abbot. Feast day: May 30.

+ Isaac the Great (d. 440): Bishop and

founder of the Armenian Church. Feast day: September 9.

+ (d.c. 550): Syrian hermit known for miracles and prophecies. Feast day: April 11.

+ Isaac of Córdoba (d. 852): Martyr of Spain. Feast day: June 3.

+ Isaac Jogues (d. 1646): Jesuit martyr in North America. Feast day: October 19.

*(Ike, Isac, Isak, Ishaq, Itzak, Izaak, Izzy, Yitzak, Yitzhak, Zak)*

## Isaiah

Meaning: Hebrew "God is salvation"

+ (biblical): One of the great Hebrew prophets (Book of Isaiah).

*(Isaia, Isiah, Izaiah)*

## Isaias

Meaning: possibly from the Hebrew "Lord"

+ (d. 309): Martyr. Feast day: January 14.

## Isidore

Meaning: Greek "gift of Isis"

+ Isidore of Chios (d.c. 251): Martyred Egyptian. Feast day: May 15.

+ Isidore of Alexandria (d. 404): Priest from Egypt. Feast day: January 15.

+ Isidore of Pelusium (d.c. 450): Abbot of Pelusium, Egypt. Feast day: February 4.

+ Isidore of Seville (d. 636): Bishop and Doctor of the Church. Feast day: April 4.

+ Isidore the Farmer (d. 1130): Patron of farmers and the city of Madrid. Feast day: May 10.

+ Isidore Bakanja, Blessed (d. 1909): Native of the former Belgian Congo.

+ Isidore of St. Joseph de Loor, Blessed (d. 1916): Passionist lay brother.

## Ismael

Meaning: Hebrew "God hears"

+ (biblical): Son of Abraham by Hagar (Genesis 16:11).

+ (d. sixth century): Welsh bishop. Feast day: June 16.

*(Ishmael, Ismael, Ishmaiah, Ishmeil, Ismail)*

## Israel

Meaning: Hebrew "wrestler with God"

+ (biblical): Another name of Jacob, the son of Isaac (Genesis 32:28).

*(Izrael, Yisrael)*

## Ivan

Meaning: form of John

+ (d. ninth century): Hermit of Bohemia. Feast day: June 24.

*(Iven)*

## Ivo

Meaning: Teutonic "yew wood"

+ (date unknown): Persian-born bishop and hermit in Huntingdonshire, England. Feast day: April 24.

+ Ivo of Chartres (d.c. 1115): Augustinian bishop and royal counselor. Feast day: May 23.

+ Ivo Hélory (d. 1303): Patron of lawyers. Feast day: May 19.

## Ivor

See Ibar

## Iwene

Meaning: unknown

+ (d. 1964): Trappist monk of Nigeria, also known as Cyprian Michael Tansi.

# J

## Jack

See John

## Jacques

See James

## Jacob

Meaning: Hebrew "supplanter"

+ (biblical): Son of Isaac. (Genesis 25:25).

+ Jacob of Nisibis (d.c. 338): Bishop, participated in the Council of Nicaea. Feast day: July 15.

+ Jacob Desiré Laval, Blessed (d. 1864): First saint of the Congregation of the Holy Spirit and Immaculate Heart of Mary.

+ Jacob Cusmano, Blessed (d. 1888): Physician and priest.

+ Jacob Kern, Blessed (d. 1924): World War II veteran and priest.

+ Jacob Gapp, Blessed (d. 1943): Marianist martyr and enemy of the Nazis in Austria.

*(Jacobb, Jacobs, Jakab, Jake, Jakiv, Jakov, Yakov)*

## Jacut

Meaning: unknown

+ (d. fifth century): Disciple of St. Budoc. Feast day: February 8.

## Jambert

Meaning: unknown

+ (d. 792): Benedictine archbishop of Canterbury. Feast day: August 12.

## James

Meaning: Latin form of Jacob

+ (biblical): Apostle, called "the Less" or "the "Younger." First bishop of Jerusalem. (Letter of James.) Feast day: May 3.

+ (biblical): Apostle, called "the Greater." Brother of John, son of Zebedee (Matthew 4:21-22). First apostle to be martyred. Patron of Spain, honored at the great shrine of Compostela. Feast day: July 25.

+ James Intercisus (d. 421): Persian martyr, so named because he was sliced into twenty-eight parts during his suffering ("intercisus" means "cut into pieces"). Feast day: November 27.

+ James the Deacon (d. seventh century): Italian monk and deacon. Feast day: August 17

+ James of Sasseau (d.c. 865): Benedictine hermit. Feast day: November 19.

+ James della Marca (d. 1475): Franciscan friar and missionary. Feast day: November 28.

+ James Walworth, Blessed (d. 1537): English monk hanged by King Henry VIII of England. Feast day: May 11.

+ James Andrade, Blessed (d. 1570): Jesuit who was thrown into the sea near the Canary Islands. Feast day: July 15.

+ James Lacop (d. 1572): One of the many martyrs of Gorkum. Feast day: July 9.

+ James Thompson, Blessed (d. 1582): English martyr. Feast day: November 28.

+ James Bell, Blessed (d. 1584): Martyr in England. Feast day: April 20.

+ James Fenn, Blessed (d. 1584): Martyr in England. Feast day: February 12.

+ James Claxton, Blessed (d. 1588): Martyr in England. Feast day: August 28.

+ James Bird, Blessed (d. 1593): English martyr. Feast day: March 25.

+ James Salés, Blessed (d. 1593): Jesuit martyr. Feast day: February 7.

+ James Kisai (d. 1597): Native Japanese martyr. Feast day: February 6.

+ James Duckett, Blessed (d. 1602): Martyr of England. Feast day: April 19.

+ James Guengoro, Blessed (d. 1620): Japanese martyr. Feast day: August 18.

+ James Denshi, Blessed (d. 1622): Japanese martyr. Feast day: August 19.

+ James Carvalho, Blessed (d. 1624): Jesuit martyr in Japan. Feast day: March 14.

+ James Fayashida, Blessed (d. 1628): Native Japanese martyr. Feast day: September 8.

+ James Nam (d. 1838): Native Vietnamese martyr. Feast day: August 12.

+ James Buzabalio (d. 1886): Martyr in Uganda. Feast day: June 3.

+ James Hilarius Barbal, Blessed (d. 1937): Victim in the Spanish Civil War.

*(Jacques, Jamie, Jaime, Jim, Jimmy, Jimmie)*

## Jamie

See Benjamin, James

## Jan

Meaning: form of John

+ Jan Sarkander (d. 1620): Martyr. Feast day: March 17.

## Januarius

Meaning: the month of "January"

+ (d. 304): Bishop and martyr, popular because his blood reportedly liquefies each year on his feast day. Feast day: September 19.

+ Januarius Maria Sarnelli (d. 1744): Prolific religious writer.

*(Gennaro)*

## Jarlath

Meaning: Latin "man of control"

+ (d.c. 480): Irish bishop and disciple of St. Patrick. Feast day: February 1.

+ (d.c. 550): Irish abbot and bishop. Feast day: June 6.

*(Jari)*

## Jason

Meaning: form of Joshua

+ (biblical): Disciple and patron of St. Paul (Acts 17:5-9). Feast day: July 12.

*(Jacen, Jaeson, Jaison, Jasan, Jasen, Jasun, Jaysen, Jayson)*

## Jean

Meaning: Scottish "God is gracious" or French form of John

+ Jean-Bernard Rousseau (d. 1867): Worked among slaves, also known as Blessed Scubilion.

## Jedediah

Meaning: Hebrew "loved by God"

+ (biblical): Name given to King Solomon (2 Sam. 12:25).

*(Jeb, Jed, Jedidiah)*

## Jeffrey

See Godfrey

## Jenkins

See John

## Jeremiah

Meaning: Hebrew "God will raise up"

+ (biblical): One of the great Hebrew prophets (Book of Jeremiah).

+ Jeremiah a Valachia Kostistk, Blessed (d. 1625): First Romanian saint.

*(Jerry, Jeremy)*

## Jermyn

Meaning: possibly "German"

+ Jermyn Gardiner, Blessed (d. 1544): Martyr in England. Feast day: March 7.

*(Jerman)*

## Jerry

See Gerald, Gerard, Jeremiah, Jerome

## Jesse

Meaning: Hebrew "gift"

+ (biblical): Father of King David (1 Samuel 16:1).

*(Jesee, Jess, Jessee, Jessie)*

## Jerome

Meaning: Greek "sacred name"

+ (d.c. 420): Doctor of the Church, translated the Bible into Latin, called the Vulgate. Feast day: September 30.

+ Jerome Emiliani (d. 1537): Patron saint of orphanages and abandoned children. Feast day: February 8.

+ Jerome of Werden (d. 1572): Franciscan martyr. Feast day: July 9.

+ Jerome de Angelis, Blessed (d. 1623): Jesuit martyr of Japan. Feast day: December 4.

+ Jerome de Torres (d. 1632): Native Japanese martyr. Feast day: September 3.

+ Jerome Lu, Blessed (d. 1858): Native of China martyred in Vietnam. Feast day: January 28.

+ Jerome Hermosilla (d. 1861): Bishop and martyr in Vietnam. Feast day: November 1.

*(Jérome, Jerôme, Jerrome, Jerry)*

## Jim

See James

## Joachim

Meaning: possibly Hebrew "pious"

+ (biblical): Traditional name of the father of the Blessed Virgin Mary. Feast day: July 26.

+ Joachim Sakachibara (d. 1597): Native Japanese martyr, physician. Feast day: February 6.

+ Joachim Firayama-Diz, Blessed (d. 1622): Martyr of Japan, ship captain. Feast day: August 19.

+ Joachim Royo, Blessed (d. 1748): Dominican martyr of China. Feast day: October 28.

+ Joachim Ho, Blessed (d. 1839): Native Chinese martyr. Feast day: November 24.

*(Joaquin, Jocquin, Juquin)*

## Joanninus

Meaning: form of John

+ Joanninus de San Juan, Blessed (d. 1570): Martyred with Blessed Ignatius de Azevedo. Feast day: July 15.

## Joavan

Meaning: unknown

+ (d.c. 570): Bishop. Feast day: March 2.

## Job

Meaning: unknown

+ (biblical): Man who was tested by God (Book of Job).

*(Jobe)*

## Joel

Meaning: Hebrew "Yaweh is God"

+ (biblical): One of the Hebrew prophets (Book of Joel).

+ (d. 1185): Abbot. Feast day: January 25.

*(Jôel, Joél, Jole)*

## John

Meaning: Hebrew "God has been gracious"

+ (biblical): John the Baptist, the cousin of Jesus and his precursor (John 1:19-28). Feast day: June 24 and August 29.

+ (biblical): Apostle, called the "Beloved Disciple" and John the Evangelist. (Gospel of John, Letters of John, Book of Revelation). Feast day: December 27.

+ John of Egypt (d.c. 394): Early desert hermit. Feast day: March 27.

+ John Chrysostom (d.c. 407): Doctor of the Church, noted bishop of Constantinople (Istanbul in present-day Turkey). Feast day: November 13 (in the Eastern Church) and September 13 (in the Western Church).

+ John Angeloptes (d. 433): Bishop of Ravenna, Italy. Feast day: November 27.

+ John Cassian (d. 433): Eastern monk and theological writer. Feast day: July 23.

+ John Zedazneli (d. sixth century): Abbot who helped to evangelize Georgia (in modern Russia). Feast day: November 4.

+ John I, Pope (served from 523-526): Tuscan priest became pope but died in prison under Emperor Theodoric. Feast day: May 18.

+ John the Almoner (d.c. 616): Patriarch of Alexandria, Egypt. Feast day: January 23.

+ John Climacus (d.c. 649): Named after his book, *The Ladder of Divine Ascent,* a guide for ascetics. Feast day: March 30.

+ John of Beverley (d. 721): Benedictine bishop of Hexham and York, England. Feast day: May 7.

+ John Damascene (d.c. 749): Doctor of the Church. Feast day: December 4.

+ John de Atarés (d. 750): Spanish hermit. Feast day: May 29.

+ John the Saxon, Blessed (d. 895): Monk and martyr. Feast day: February 22.

+ John Gualbert (d. 1073): Benedictine abbot, known for forgiving his brother's murderer. Feast day: July 12.

+ John of Matha (d. 1213): Founder of the Order of the Most Holy Trinity. Feast day: February 8.

+ John Duns Scotus, Blessed (d.

1308): Early defender of the doctrine of the Immaculate Conception.

+ John of Bridlington (d. 1379): Augustinian prior and patron of women who face difficult childbirth. Feast day: October 11.

+ John Nepomucene (d.c. 1393): Martyr and patron saint of Bohemia. Feast day: May 16.

+ John of Capistrano (d. 1456): Franciscan priest, led army against the Turkish invasion of Eastern Europe. Feast day: October 23.

+ John Cantius (d. 1473): Patron saint of Poland and Lithuania. Feast day: December 23.

+ John Fisher (d. 1535): Martyred English cardinal of England, close friend of St. Thomas More and Desiderius Erasmus. Feast day: June 22.

+ John Haile, Blessed (d. 1535): Martyr of England. Feast day: May 5.

+ John Houghton (d. 1535): One of the Forty Martyrs of England and Wales. Feast day: May 4.

+ John Forest, Blessed (d. 1538): Martyr of England, the confessor of the first wife of King Henry VIII, Queen Catherine of Aragon. Feast day: May 22.

+ John Stone (d. 1538): One of the Forty Martyrs of England and Wales. Feast day: May 12.

+ John Beche, Blessed (d. 1539): Martyr of England, friend of St. John Fisher and St. Thomas More. Feast day: December 1.

+ John Ireland, Blessed (d. 1544): English martyr, chaplain to St. Thomas More. Feast day: March 7.

+ John of God (d. 1550): Founder of the Brothers Hospitallers (Brothers of St. John of God), patron of the sick and hospitals. Feast day: March 8.

+ John of Ávila (d. 1569): Spiritual advisor of Sts. Teresa, Francis Borgia, John of the Cross, Peter of Alcantara, and others. Feast day: May 10.

+ John Storey, Blessed (d.c. 1571): Martyr of England. Feast day: June 1.

+ John Payne (d. 1582): English martyr, also called John Paine. Feast day: May 4.

+ John Bodey, Blessed (d. 1583): English martyr and schoolmaster. Feast day: November 2.

+ John Finch, Blessed (d. 1584): Martyr of England, Lancashire farmer. Feast day: April 20.

+ John Amias, Blessed (d. 1589): English martyr, also called John Anne. Feast day: March 16.

+ John of the Cross (d. 1591): Doctor of the Church, founder, with Teresa of Avila, of the Discalced Carmelites, and mystical poet. Feast day: December 14.

+ John Boste (d. 1594): One of the Forty Martyrs of England and Wales. Feast day: July 24.

+ John Cornelius, Blessed (d. 1594): Martyred Jesuit of England. Feast day: July 4.

+ John Ingram, Blessed (d. 1594): Martyr of Scotland. Feast day: July 26.

+ John Speed, Blessed (d. 1594): An English martyr, also called John Spence. Feast day: February 4.

+ John Soan de Goto (d. 1597): Japanese-born martyr. Feast day: February 6.

+ John Kisaka (d. 1597): Japanese martyr who was a silk weaver. Feast day: February 6.

+ John Rigby (d.c. 1600): Martyr of

England. Feast day: June 21.

+ John Leonardi (d. 1609): Founder of the Clerks Regular of the Mother of God. Feast day: October 9.

+ John Roberts (d. 1610): Benedictine member of the Forty Martyrs of England and Wales. Feast day: December 9.

+ John Almond (d. 1612): One of the Forty Martyrs of England and Wales. Feast day: December 5.

+ John Ogilvie (d.c. 1615): Jesuit martyr of Scotland. Feast day: March 10.

+ John Baptist Machado (d. 1617): Jesuit martyr of Japan. Feast day: May 22.

+ John Ivanango and John Montajana, Blessed (d. 1619): Martyrs of Japan. Feast day: November 27.

+ John Shoun, Blessed (d. 1619): Native-born martyr of Japan. Feast day: November 18.

+ John Berchmans (d. 1621): Jesuit confessor and patron of altar boys and girls. Feast day: August 13.

+ John Inamura, Blessed (d. 1622): Japanese martyr. Feast day: September 8.

+ John Kingoku, Blessed (d. 1622): Japanese martyr. Feast day: September 10.

+ John of Korea, Blessed (d. 1622): Martyr of Japan, son of Blessed Anthony and Blessed Mary of Korea. Feast day: September 10.

+ John Baptist Zola, Blessed (d. 1626): Martyred Jesuit of Japan. Feast day: June 20.

+ John Kinsako, Blessed (d. 1626): Martyr of Japan. Feast day: June 20.

+ John Naisen, Blessed (d. 1626): Wealthy native-born martyr of Japan. Feast day: July 12.

+ John Tanaka, Blessed (d. 1626): Martyr of Japan. Feast day: July 12.

+ John Maki, Blessed (d. 1627): Martyr of Japan. Feast day: September 7.

+ John Tomaki, Blessed (d. 1628): Japanese martyr. Feast day: September 8.

+ John Kokumbuko (d. 1630): Martyr of Japan. Feast day: September 28.

+ John-Francis Regis (d. 1640): Jesuit evangelist and preacher. Feast day: December 31.

+ John de Massias (d. 1645): Dominican monk in Peru. Feast day: September 18.

+ John de Brébeuf and Companions (d. 1649): Jesuits martyred in North America. Feast day: October 19.

+ John Nangata, Blessed (d. 1662): Martyr of Japan. Feast day: August 19.

+ John Yano, Blessed (d. 1662): Martyr of Japan. Feast day: August 19.

+ John Foyamon, Blessed (d. 1662): Martyr of Japan. Feast day: August 19.

+ John Kemble (d. 1679): One of the Forty Martyrs of England and Wales. Feast day: August 22.

+ John Lloyd (d. 1679): One of the Forty Martyrs of England and Wales. Feast day: July 22.

+ John Wall (d. 1679): One of the Forty Martyrs of England and Wales. Feast day: August 22.

+ John Eudes (d. 1680): Founder, with St. Margaret Mary Alacoque, of devotion to the Sacred Heart. Feast day: August 19.

+ John de Britto (d. 1693): Jesuit martyr in India. Feast day: February 4.

+ John Plesington (d. 1697): One of

the Forty Martyrs of England and Wales. Feast day: July 19.

+ John Baptist de la Salle (d. 1719): Teacher and founder of the Institute of the Brothers of the Christian Schools. Feast day: April 7.

+ John-Joseph of the Cross (d. 1734): Franciscan monk, mystic and prophet. Feast day: March 5.

+ John Gaspard Cratz, Blessed (d. 1737): Jesuit martyr in China. Feast day: January 12.

+ John Alcober, Blessed (d. 1748): Dominican martyr of China. Feast day: December 30.

+ John Baptist de Rossi (d. 1764): Missionary and catechist among farmers, herdsmen, teamsters, prisoners, and the sick. Feast day: May 23.

+ John Dat (d. 1798): Native martyr of Vietnam. Feast day: October 28.

+ John Lantrua of Triora, Blessed (d. 1816): Franciscan martyr of China. Feast day: February 13.

+ John Charles Cornay (d. 1837): Martyr of Vietnam. Feast day: September 20.

+ John Baptist Thanh (d. 1840): Native Vietnamese martyr. Feast day: April 28.

+ John Baptist Con (d. 1840): Martyr of Vietnam. Feast day: November 8.

+ John-Gabriel Perboyre, Blessed (d. 1840): Martyr of China. Feast day: September 11.

+ John-Louis Bonnard (d. 1852): Martyr of Vietnam. Feast day: May 1.

+ John Baptist Mazzuconi, Blessed (d. 1855): Martyr of the Australian regions.

+ John Baptist Vianney (d. 1859): Priest known as "The Curé of Ars," patron of parish priests. Feast day: August 4.

+ John Nepomucene Neumann (d. 1860): First American bishop to be canonized. Feast day: January 5.

+ John Baptist Lo, Blessed (d. 1861): Martyr of China. Feast day: July 29.

+ John Hoan (d. 1861): Vietnamese priest and martyr. Feast day: May 26.

+ John Maria Muzeyi (d. 1886): Martyr of Uganda. Feast day: June 3.

+ John Mary Mzec (d. 1887): Martyr of Uganda. Feast day: June 3.

+ John Bosco (d. 1888): Founder of the Salesians and mentor of St. Dominic Savio. Feast day: January 31.

+ John Baptist Scalabrini, Blessed (d. 1905): Italian bishop, founder of the Congregation of the Missionaries of St. Charles Borromeo (the Scalabrini Fathers).

+ John Maria Boccardo, Blessed (d. 1913): Parish priest.

+ John Piamarta, Blessed (d. 1913): Founder of the Congregation of the Holy Family and the Humble Servants of the Lord.

+ John Calabria, Blessed (d. 1954): Founder of a program for orphaned boys.

*(Giovani, Hann, Hon, Honn, Honus, Ian, Iain, Jack, Jan, Jean, Jehan, Jen, Jenkins, Johnson, Jon, Jones, Johnathan, Jonathan, Johnnie, Johnny, Sean)*

## Jorge
See George

## Jonah, Jonas
Meaning: Latin "dove"

+ (biblical): Legendary prophet who was swallowed by a fish (Book of Jonah).

+ (d. third century): Companion of St.

Denis of Paris. Feast day: September 22.

+ (d. fourth century): Egyptian monk and gardener. Feast day: February 11.

*(Jonah, Jona, Yona, Yonah)*

# Jonathan

Meaning: Hebrew "God has given"

+ (biblical): King Saul's oldest son and King David's best friend (1 Samuel 14:1).

# Josaphat

Meaning: unknown

+ (d. 1623) Archbishop of Polotsk and martyr. First saint of the Eastern Church to be formally canonized. Feast day: November 12.

# Josemaria

Meaning: combination of names "Joseph" and "Maria"

+ Josemaria Escrivá de Balaguer, Blessed (d. 1975): Founder of Opus Dei.

# Joseph

Meaning: Hebrew "God adds"

+ (biblical): Spouse of the Blessed Virgin Mary and foster father of Jesus (Matthew 1:18-25). Patron of workers and Italy and Poland. Feast day: March 19.

+ Joseph of Arimathea (biblical): Secret disciple of Jesus who gave his tomb to Jesus (Luke 23:50-54). Feast day: March 17.

+ Joseph Barsabbas (biblical): The competitor of St. Matthias for Judas Iscariot's place as one of the twelve Apostles (Acts 1:21-26). Feast day: July 20.

+ Joseph the Hymnographer (d.c. 886): Prolific Greek hymn writer. Feast day: April 3 in the Eastern Church and June 14 in the Western Church.

+ Joseph de Anchieta, Blessed (d. 1597): Missionary to Brazil.

+ Joseph of Leonissa (d. 1612): Franciscan who served as a missionary to Christian galley slaves. Feast day: February 4

+ Joseph of St. Hyacinth, Blessed (d. 1622): Dominican martyr of Japan. Feast day: September 10.

+ Joseph Calasanctius (d. 1648): Founder of the Clerks Regular of the Religious Schools, called the Scolopi or Piarists. Feast day: August 25.

+ Joseph of Cupertino (d. 1663): Franciscan mystic and the patron of pilots and air passengers. Feast day: September 18.

+ Joseph Oriol (d. 1702): Confessor, miracle worker, and prophet. Feast day: March 23.

+ Joseph Pignatelli (d. 1811): The "restorer of the Jesuits." Feast day: November 11.

+ Joseph Tshang-ta-Pong, Blessed (d.c. 1815): Martyr of China. Feast day: March 12.

+ Joseph Yuen, Blessed (d. 1815): Native-born martyr of Vietnam. Feast day: June

+ Joseph Marchand (d. 1835): Martyr of Vietnam. Feast day: November 30.

+ Joseph Canh (d. 1838): Native physician of Vietnam, martyr. Feast day: September 5.

+ Joseph Fernandez, Blessed (d. 1838): Dominican martyr of Vietnam. Feast day: July 24.

+ Joseph Nien Vien (d. 1838): Martyr

of Vietnam. Feast day: August 21.

+ Joseph Peter Uyen (d. 1838): Native-born martyr of Vietnam. Feast day: July 3.

+ Joseph Hien (d. 1840): Dominican martyr of Vietnam. Feast day: June 27.

+ Joseph Nghi (d. 1840): Native-born martyr of Vietnam. Feast day: November 8.

+ Joseph Benedict Cottolengo (d. 1842): Founder of the Little House of Divine Providence, also called the Brothers of St. Vincent and the Daughters of St. Vincent. Feast day: April 30.

+ Joseph Luu (d.c. 1854): Native Vietnamese martyr. Feast day: May 2.

+ Joseph Cafasso (d. 1860): Famous confessor and ascetic. Feast day: June 22.

+ Joseph Thi (d. 1860): Native-born martyr of Vietnam. Feast day: October 24.

+ Joseph Khang (d. 1861): Martyr of Vietnam. Feast day: November 6.

+ Joseph Tshang, Blessed (d.c. 1861): Native-born martyr of China. Feast day: July 29.

+ Joseph Mukasa (d. 1886): Martyr of Uganda. Feast day: June 3.

+ Joseph Gérard, Blessed (d. 1914): Oblate missionary to Africa.

+ Joseph Moscati (d. 1927): Italian physician. Feast day: November 16.

*(Guiseppe, Joe, Joey, Joeseph, José, Josef, Joseff, Josephe, Josephus, Jozef, Yosef, Yoseff, Yosif, Yusif)*

## Joshua
Meaning: Hebrew "God is my salvation"

+ (biblical): Successor to Moses, led Hebrews into the Promised Land (Book of Joshua).

*(Jeshua, Jeshuah, Josh, Joshe)*

## Juan
Meaning: Spanish form of John

+ Juan Diego, Blessed (date unknown): Mexican native who saw Our Lady of Guadalupe.

## Jude
Meaning: Hebrew "praise"

+ (biblical): One of the twelve Apostles and author of the Letter of Jude, also called Thaddeus (Mark 3:18). Patron saint of lost causes. Feast day: October 28.

*(Thaddeus)*

## Julian
Meaning: Latin "bearded"

+ (date unknown): Martyr and confessor. Feast day: March 23.

+ (date unknown): Martyr. Feast day: August 25.

+ Julian the Hospitaler (date unknown): Patron of boatmen, innkeepers, and travelers. Feast day: February 12.

+ Julian of Le Mans (d. third century): First bishop of Le Mans, France. Feast day: January 27.

+ (d.c. 250): Martyr of Alexandria. Feast day: October 30 and February 27.

+ Julian of Anazarbus (d.c. 302): Martyr praised by St. John Chrysostom. Feast day: March 16.

+ Julian of Auvergne (d.c. 304): Martyred officer of the Roman army. Feast day: August 28.

+ Julian of Caesarea (d. 309): Martyr. Feast day: February 17.

+ Julian of Toledo (d.c. 690): Archbishop of Toledo. Feast day: March 8.

*(Jule, Jules, Juliano, Julias, Julien, Jullian, Julius)*

## Julius

Meaning: Latin "bearded" or "softhaired"

+ (d. 190): Roman senator and martyr. Feast day: August 19.

+ Julius of Dorostorum (d.c. 302): Martyr in what is now Romania. Feast day: May 25.

+ Julius I, Pope (served from 337-352). Built several churches in Rome, fought the Arian heresy. Feast day: April 12.

## Junipero

Meaning: maybe from "juniper" tree

+ Junipero Serra, Blessed (d. 1784): California missionary.

## Juquin

See Joachim

## Jurmin

Meaning: possibly "German"

+ (d. seventh century): Prince of East Anglia, England. Feast day: February 23.

## Justin

Meaning: Latin "just"

+ Justin Martyr (d.c. 165): Martyr, philosopher, and defender of Christianity. Feast day: June 1.

+ (d. 259): Martyred priest. Feast day: September 17.

+ Justin de Jacobis (d. 1860): Vincentian bishop and missionary to Ethiopia. Feast day: July 31.

*(Justan, Justen, Justinn, Justinus, Juston, Juston, Justyn)*

## Justus

Meaning: Latin "just"

+ (date unknown): Roman military veteran and martyr. Feast day: July 14.

+ Justus of Beauvais (d.c. 287): Martyred nine-year-old. Feast day: October 18.

+ Justus of Lyons (d. 390): Bishop and hermit. Feast day: September 2 and October 14.

+ Justus of Urgel (d.c. 527): Bishop and writer. Feast day: May 28.

+ Justus of Canterbury (d. 627): Benedictine archbishop of Canterbury, England. Feast day: November 10.

*(Justas, Justice, Justis)*

# K

## Kaleb

See Caleb

## Kanten

Meaning: unknown

+ (d. eighth century): Welsh monk. Feast day: November 15.

*(Cannen)*

## Karl

Meaning: German "tiller"

+ Karl Leisner (d. 1945): Martyred by the Nazis.

*(Carl, Carel, Carle, Carlis, Karal, Karel, Karle, Karlis)*

## Kashmere, Kasimir

See Casimir

## Kaspar

See Caspar

## Kay

See Kea

## Kea

Meaning: African "very small one"

+ (d. sixth century): British saint. Feast day: November 5.

*(Kay, Kenan, Quay)*

## Keilach

See Cellach

## Kenan

Meaning: Hebrew "to possess"

+ (biblical): Son of Enoch (Genesis 5: 9).

+ (d.c. 500): Irish bishop, disciple of St. Martin of Tours. Feast day: November 24.

*(Keenan, Keanan, Keenen, Keenon, Kienan, Kienon)*

## Kenelm

Meaning: Old English "brave warrior"

+ (d. 821): Martyred king of Mercia, England. Feast day: July 17.

## Kenneth

Meaning: "fair one" or "fire-sprung"

+ (d. sixth century): Welsh prince. Feast day: August 1.

*(Ken, Kennith, Kenny)*

## Kentigern

Meaning: unknown

+ Kentigern Mungo (d. 603): Missionary to Northwestern England and Southwestern Scotland. Feast day: January 13.

## Kessag

Meaning: unknown

+ (d.c. 560): Irish prince. Feast day: March 10.

## Kevin

Meaning: Irish "handsome at birth"

+ (d.c. 618): Abbot, one of the patrons of Dublin. Feast day: June 3.

*(Kevan, Keverne, Keva, Kev, Kevinn, Kevon)*

## Khristophe, Kristopher, Kris

See Christopher

## Kieran

Meaning: Irish "dark"

+ (d.c. 530): First bishop of Ossory and founder of monastery at Sier-Ciaran, Ireland. Feast day: March 5.

+ (d.c. 556): One of the "Twelve Apostles of Ireland," surnamed "the Younger". Feast day: September 9.

*(Keiran, Keiren, Keiron, Kieren, Kieron, Kyran)*

## Kilian

Meaning: Irish "strife"

+ (d. seventh century): Irish abbot who

wrote a biography of St. Brigid. Feast day: July 29.

+ (d.c. 689): Irish martyr. Feast day: July 8.

*(Killian)*

## Kizito

Meaning: unknown, of African origin

+ Kizito, Blessed (d. 1886): Youngest martyr of Uganda. Feast day: June 3.

## Klement

See Clement

## Knute

See Canut

## Konrad

See Conrad

## Korban, Korbin

See Corbinian

## Kosma, Kosmos

See Cosmos

## Kristian, Kristjan

See Christian

# L

## Lactan

Meaning: unknown

+ (d. 672): Irish abbot. Feast day: March 19.

## Ladislas

Meaning: perhaps derived from "servant"

+ (d. 1095): King of Hungary. Feast day: June 27.

*(Lance, Lancelet, Lancelot, Laucelot, Launcelet)*

## Laetus

Meaning: unknown

+ (d. 553): French priest. Feast day: November 5.

## Lambert

Meaning: Old German "land bright"

+ (d.c. 680): Benedictine monk. Feast day: October 9.

+ Lambert of Lyon (d. 688): Benedictine archbishop. Feast day: April 14.

+ Lambert of Maastricht (d.c. 709): Bishop and martyr. Feast day: September 17.

+ Lambert of Saragossa (d.c. 900): Martyr of Spain. Feast day: April 16.

+ Lambert Peloquin (d. 1154): French Benedictine bishop. Feast day: May 26.

*(Lambard)*

## Lancelot

See Ladislas

## Landericus

Meaning: unknown

+ (d. seventh century): French Benedictine bishop. Feast day: April 17.

+ Landericus of Paris (d.c. 660): Bishop of Paris, France, the founder of St. Christopher's Hospital, which became Hotel-Dieu. Feast day: June 10.

*(Landry)*

# Landoald
Meaning: unknown

+ (d.c. 668): Missionary to Belgium and northeastern France. Feast day: March 19.

# Larry
See Lawrence

# Laserian
Meaning: unknown

+ (d. 639): Bishop and papal legate. Feast day: April 18.

# Laurentinus
Meaning: Latin "foster"

+ (d. third century): African martyr. Feast day: February 3.

# Laurus
Meaning: Latin "bay" or "laurel"

+ (d. seventh century): Welsh abbot. Feast day: September 30.

*(Lery, Lerry)*

# Lauto
Meaning: unknown

+ (d.c. 568): French Bishop. Feast day: September 22.

# Lawrence
Meaning: Latin "from the city of Laurentinium" or "crowned"

+ (d. 258): Martyred deacon of Rome, mentioned in the first Eucharistic Prayer. Feast day: August 10.

+ Lawrence of Novara (d.c. 397): Martyred priest. Feast day: April 30.

+ Lawrence of Siponto (d.c. 546): Italian bishop. Feast day: February 7.

+ Lawrence of Spoleto (d. 576): Bishop of Spoleto, Italy, also called "the Illuminator" because of his ability to cure physical and spiritual blindness. Feast day: February 3.

+ Lawrence of Canterbury (d. 619): Archbishop of Canterbury, England. Feast day: February 2.

+ Lawrence O'Toole (d. 1180): Augustinian archbishop of Dublin, Ireland. Feast day: November 14.

+ Lawrence Nerucci, Blessed (d. 1420): Servite martyr in Bohemia. Feast day: August 11.

+ Lawrence Giustiniani (d. 1455): Bishop of Venice, mystic and contemplative writer. Feast day: September 5.

+ Lawrence Richardson, Blessed (d. 1582): Martyr of England. Feast day: May 30.

+ Lawrence Humphrey, Blessed (d. 1591): Martyr of England. Feast day: July 7.

+ Lawrence of Brindisi (d. 1619): Capuchin monk and Doctor of the Church. Feast day: July 21.

+ Lawrence Rokuyemon, Blessed (d. 1622): Native-born martyr of Japan. Feast day: August 19.

+ Lawrence Jamada, Blessed (d. 1628): Martyr of Japan. Feast day: September 8.

+ Lawrence Riuz (d.c. 1630): Filipino native, martyr in Japan. Feast day: September 28.

+ Lawrence Shizu, Blessed (d. 1630): Native-born martyr of Japan. Feast day: September 28.

+ Lawrence Imbert (d. 1846): Bishop and martyr of Korea. Feast day: September 20.

+ Lawrence Huong (d. 1856): Native-born martyr of Vietnam. Feast day: April 27.

+ Lawrence Pe-Man, Blessed (d. 1856): Martyr of China. Feast day: November 24.

+ Lawrence Salvi, Blessed (d. 1856): Missionary and healer.

+ Lawrence Wang, Blessed (d. 1858): Native-born Chinese martyr. Feast day: January 28.

*(Labhras, Larry, Lars, Laurence, Laurance, Lauritz, Lawrance, Loeren, Lonrenz, Loren, Lorenzo, Lorrenzo)*

## Lazarus

Meaning: Hebrew "God may help"

+ (biblical): Disciple and friend of Jesus, brother of Martha and Mary, raised from the dead (John 11:38-44). Feast day: July 29.

+ Lazarus Zographos (d.c. 867): Monk and painter. Feast day: February 23.

## Leander

Meaning: Greek "lion man"

+ (d. 600): Archbishop of Seville, Spain. Feast day: February 27.

## Lenny

See Leonard

## Leo

Meaning: Latin "lion"

+ (date unknown): Martyr at Lycia (modern Turkey). Feast day: August 18.

+ Leo I, Pope (served from 440-461): Doctor of the Church, one of only two popes (with Gregory I) to earn the title "the Great." Feast day: November 10.

+ Leo of Sens (d. 541): Bishop of Sens, France. Feast day: April 22.

+ Leo of Catania (d. 787): Bishop of Catania, Sicily. Feast day: February 20.

+ Leo III, Pope (served from 795-816): Crowned Charlemagne and inaugurated the Holy Roman Empire. Feast day: June 12.

+ Leo IV, Pope (served from 847-855): Built the wall around St. Peter's and the Vatican Hill, fought the Saracen invasion. Feast day: July 17.

+ Leo Luke (d.c. 900): Italian abbot. Feast day: March 1.

+ Leo of Rouen (d. 900): Bishop of Rouen, France. Feast day: March 1.

+ (d. 1597): Korean-born martyr. Feast day: February 5.

+ Leo Tanaka (d. 1617): Native-born martyr of Japan. Feast day: June 1.

+ Leo Nakanishi, Blessed (d. 1619): Native-born martyr of Japan. Feast day: November 27.

+ Leo Satsuma, Blessed (d. 1622): Martyr of Japan. Feast day: September 10.

+ Leo Suchiemon, Blessed (d. 1622): Martyr of Japan. Feast day: August 19.

+ Leo Kombiogi, Blessed (d. 1628): Martyr of Japan. Feast day: September 8.

*(Lee, Lionel)*

## Leobald

Meaning: Old German "people bold"

+ (d. 593): Hermit and disciple of St. Gregory of Tours, France. Feast day: January 18.

+ (d. 650): French Benedictine abbot. Feast day: August 8.

+ Leopold (d. 1136): Austrian nobleman. Feast day: November 15.

# Leonard

Meaning: Old German "lion brave"

+ Leonard of Noblac (d.c. 559): Hermit-abbot. Feast day: November 6.

+ Leonard Wegel (d. 1572): One of the martyrs of Gorkum, Holland. Feast day: July 9.

+ Leonard Kimura (d. 1619): Japanese noble and martyr. Feast day: November 18.

+ Leonard of Port Maurice (d. 1751): Franciscan who founded the devotion of the Stations of the Cross. Feast day: November 26.

+ Leonard Muraildo (d. 1890): Founder of the Congregation of St. Joseph. Feast day: March 30.

*(Len, Lenard, Lennard, Lennie, Lenno, Lenny, Leno, Leonardo)*

# Leonides

Meaning: probably "brave"

+ Leonides of Alexandria (d. 202): Martyred father of Origen. Feast day: April 22.

+ (d. 304): Martyr of Egypt. Feast day: January 28.

# Leontius

Meaning: probably "brave"

+ (d.c. 300): Martyr. Feast day: August 1.

+ (d.c. 320): Martyr in Nicopolis (modern Bulgaria or Armenia). Feast day: July 10.

+ Leontius of Caesarea (d. 337): Bishop of Caesarea and a participant in the Council of Nicaea. Feast day: January 13.

+ Leontius the Elder (d.c. 541): Bishop of Bordeaux, France. Feast day: August 21.

+ Leontius the Younger (d. 565): Bishop of Bordeaux, France. Feast day: July 11.

+ Leontius (d. 1077): Bishop and missionary in Russia. Feast day: May 23.

# Leothade

Meaning: unknown

+ (d. 718): French Benedictine bishop. Feast day: October 23.

# Lester

See Sylvester

# Leucius

Meaning: unknown

+ Leucius of Brindisi (d.c. 180): Italian Bishop. Feast day: January 11.

# Leudomer

Meaning: unknown

+ (d.c. 585): Bishop of Chartres, France. Feast day: October 2.

# Lezin

Meaning: unknown

+ (d. early seventh century): French bishop. Feast day: February 13.

# Liberius

Meaning: Latin "free"

+ (d.c. 200): Italian bishop. Feast day: December 30.

# Libert

Meaning: probably from Latin "free"

+ (d. 783): Benedictine martyr. Feast day: July 14.

+ (d. 1076): French bishop. Feast day: June 23.

## Licerius
Meaning: unknown
+ (d.c. 548): French bishop. Feast day: August 27.

## Ligorius
Meaning: unknown
+ (date unknown): Martyr. Feast day: September 13.

## Linus
Meaning: Greek "flax"
+ Linus, Pope (served from about 67-76): Immediate successor of St. Peter. Feast day: formerly September 23.

*(Linas)*

## Loaran
Meaning: possibly Basque "son of the famous warrior"
+ (d. fifth century): Irish disciple of St. Patrick. Feast day: August 30.

*(Larian, Larien, Laurin, Lawren, Loren, Lorin, Loring, Lorne, Lorren, Lorrin, Loryn)*

## Loman
Meaning: possibly from the Hebrew "peace"
+ (d.c. 450): Nephew of St. Patrick. Feast day: February 17.

## Lomer
Meaning: unknown
+ (d. 593): French hermit. Feast day: January 5.

## Loren
See Loaran, Lawrence

## Lorenzo
See Lawrence

## Lotharius
Meaning: unknown
+ (d.c. 756): French Benedictine bishop and monk. Feast day: June 14.

## Louis
Meaning: French form of German "famous in battle"
+ Louis IX (d. 1270): King of France. Feast day: August 25.

+ Louis of Toulouse (d. 1297): Franciscan bishop, related to St. Elizabeth of Hungary. Feast day: August 19.

+ Louis Bertran (d. 1581): Dominican priest, relative of St. Vincent Ferrer, aided St. Teresa of Ávila. Called the Apostle to Columbia, South America. Feast day: October 9.

+ Louis Ibachi (d. 1597): 12-year-old martyr of Japan. Feast day: February 5.

+ Louis Flores, Blessed (d. 1622): Dominican martyr of Japan. Feast day: August 19.

+ Louis Kawara, Blessed (d. 1622): Native-born martyr of Japan. Feast day: September 10.

+ Louis Shakichi, Blessed (d. 1622): Native-born martyr of Japan. Feast day: October 2.

+ Louis Baba, Blessed (d. 1624): Martyr of Japan. Feast day: August 25.

+ Louis Sasanda, Blessed (d. 1624): Native-born martyr of Japan. Feast day: August 25.

+ Louis Sotelo, Blessed (d. 1624): Franciscan martyr of Japan. Feast day: August 25.

+ Louis Naisen, Blessed (d. 1626): Child martyr of Japan. Feast day: July 12.

+ Louis Someyon, Blessed (d. 1627): Martyr of Japan. Feast day: August 17.

+ Louis Nifaki, Blessed (d. 1628): Martyr of Japan. Feast day: September 8.

+ Louis Bertran, Blessed (d. 1629): Dominican martyr of Japan. Feast day: July 29.

+ Louis de Montfort (d. 1716): Marian devotee, founder of the Sisters of Divine Wisdom. Feast day: April 28.

+ Louis Zephyrinus Moreau, Blessed (d. 1901): Canadian bishop.

*(Lou, Louie, Luigi, Luis)*

## Lua

Meaning: possibly from Old German "battle"

+ (d. 609): Irish abbot. Feast day: August 4.

## Lucerius

Meaning: Latin "circle of light"

+ (d. 739): Benedictine abbot. Feast day: December 10.

## Lucian

Meaning: Latin "light"

+ (date unknown): African martyr at Tripoli, Libya. Feast day: December 24.

+ (d.c. 250): Martyr in what is now present-day Turkey. Feast day: October 26.

+ (d.c. 290): French martyr. Feast day: January 8.

+ Lucian of Antioch (d. 312): Theologian, scholar, and martyr. Feast day: January 7.

## Lucius

Meaning: Latin "light"

+ Lucius of Cyrene (biblical): One of the "prophets and doctors" of the early church (Acts 13:1). Feast day: May 6.

+ (date unknown): Roman martyr. Feast day: December 1.

+ (d.c. 200): Ruler of Britain. Feast day: December 3.

+ (d. 350): Bishop and martyr of Adrianople (in modern Turkey). Feast day: February 11.

*(Lucas, Lucian, Luciano, Lucien)*

## Ludan

Meaning: unknown

+ (d.c. 1202): Scottish pilgrim. Feast day: February 12.

## Ludwin

Meaning: unknown

+ (d. 713): German Benedictine bishop. Feast day: September 29.

## Luigi

Meaning: Italian form of Louis

+ Luigi Scrosoppi, Blessed (d. 1884): Priest who worked with the deaf.

+ Luigi Orione, Blessed (d. 1940): Founder of the Sons of Divine Providence, the Little Missionary Sisters of Charity, the Blind Sacramentive Sisters, and the Hermits of St. Albert. Feast day: March 12.

## Luke

Meaning: Greek "from Lucania"

+ (biblical): Companion of St. Paul and evangelist (Gospel of Luke, Acts of the Apostles). Patron of painters and physicians. Feast day: October 18.

+ Luke the Younger (d.c. 946): Hermit and wonder-worker. Feast day: February 7.

+ Luke Kirby (d. 1582): One of the Forty Martyrs of England and Wales. Feast day: May 30.

+ Luke Kiemon, Blessed (d. 1627): Native-born martyr of Japan. Feast day: August 17.

+ Luke Loan (d. 1840): Native-born martyr of Vietnam. Feast day: June 5.

+ Luke Banabakiutu (d. 1886): Martyr of Uganda. Feast day: June 3.

*(Luc, Lucas, Luck, Luk, Luke)*

## Lull
Meaning: unknown

+ (d. 787): Benedictine bishop and a relative of St. Boniface. Feast day: October 16.

# M

## Macarius
Meaning: unknown

+ (date unknown): Martyr of Alexandria, Egypt. Feast day: December 8.

+ (d.c. 250): Martyr, reportedly a potter by trade. Feast day: February 28.

+ Macarius of Jerusalem (d.c. 335): Bishop of Jerusalem, aided St. Helena in identifying the True Cross. Feast day: March 10.

+ (d.c. 350): Bishop of Petra (in present-day Jordan). Feast day: June 20.

+ Macarius the Great (d.c. 390): Egyptian hermit. Feast day: January 15.

+ Macarius the Younger (d.c. 394): Hermit and disciple of St. Macarius the Great. Feast day: January 2.

+ Macarius the Wonder-Worker (d.c. 830): Abbot. Feast day: April 1.

+ Macarius of Ghent (d. 1012): Bishop of Antioch in Pisidia (in present-day Turkey). Feast day: April 10.

*(Marc)*

## Macartan
Meaning: unknown

+ (d.c. 505): First bishop of Clogher, Ireland. Feast day: March 24.

## Maccallin
Meaning: probably Irish "son of Callin"

+ (d.c. 497): Irish bishop of Lusk. Feast day: September 6.

+ (d. 978): Benedictine abbot. Feast day: January 21.

## Macedonius
Meaning: probably "from Macedonia"

+ (d.c. 304): Martyr at Nicomedia (in present-day Turkey). Feast day: March 13.

+ (d. 362): Martyr in Phrygia (in present-day Turkey). Feast day: September 12.

+ (d.c. 430): Hermit of Syria, ate only grain. Feast day: January 24.

## Machai
Meaning: unknown

+ (d. fifth century): Disciple of St. Patrick. Feast day: April 11.

## Machar

Meaning: unknown

+ (d. sixth century): Bishop, companion of St. Columba. Feast day: November 12.

## Madern

Meaning: unknown

+ (d.c. 545): Hermit of Cornish descent. Feast day: May 17.

## Maelmuire

Meaning: unknown

+ Maelmuire O' Gorman (d.c. 1167): Abbot of Knock, Ireland, and poet. Feast day: July 3.

## Maidoc

Meaning: perhaps from the Welsh "lucky"

+ (d. fifth century): Irish abbot. Feast day: March 23.

+ (d. sixth century): Abbot and bishop. Feast day: February 28.

## Majolus

Meaning: unknown

+ (d.c. 994): Benedictine abbot, friend of emperors and popes. Feast day: May 11.

## Malachi

Meaning: Hebrew "my messenger"

+ (biblical): One of the last of the Hebrew prophets (Book of Malachi).

*(Malachy)*

## Malachy

Meaning: Hebrew "my messenger"

+ Malachy O' More (d. 1148): Bishop famous for writing prophecies of the popes. Feast day: November 3.

## Malard

Meaning: unknown

+ Malard (d.c. 650): Bishop of Chartres. Feast day: January 15.

## Malchus

Meaning: Hebrew "angel"

+ (d.c. 390): Syrian hermit. Feast day: October 21.

+ (d. twelfth century): Irish Benedictine. Feast day: April 10.

## Mâlo

Meaning: unknown

+ (d.c. 640): Welsh bishop and missionary to France. Feast day: November 15.

## Mamas

Meaning: unknown

+ (d.c. 275): Martyred shepherd . Feast day: August 17.

## Mancius

Meaning: unknown

+ (d. fifth or sixth century): Roman martyred by Portuguese slave masters. Feast day: March 15.

+ Mancius Araki, Blessed (d. 1626): Native-born martyr of Japan. Feast day: July 8.

+ Mancius of the Holy Cross, Blessed (d. 1629): Native-born martyr of Japan. Feast day: July 29.

+ Mancius Shisisoiemon, Blessed (d. 1630): Native-born martyr of Japan. Feast day: September 25.

+ Mancius of St. Thomas, Blessed (d.

1630): Native-born martyr of Japan. Feast day: September 12.

## Manettus

Meaning: unknown

+ (d. 1268): One of the founders of the Servite Order. Feast day: February 17.

## Manuel

Meaning: Spanish form of Emanuel

+ (d. 362): Persian martyr. Feast day: June 17.

*(Manny, Manney)*

## Marcellinus

Meaning: from Latin "Mars" or "the god of war"

+ (d.c. 303): Martyr in Egypt. Feast day: August 27.

+ (d. 304): Martyr in Rome, Italy, mentioned in the first Eucharistic Prayer. Feast day: June 2.

+ (d.c. 374): African missionary. Feast day: April 20.

+ (d. 413): Martyr, close friend of St. Augustine. Feast day: April 6.

+ Marcellinus of Ancona (d.c. 566): Bishop of Ancona, Italy. Feast day: January 9.

+ (d.c. 762): Anglo-Saxon, called the Apostle to Holland. Feast day: July 14.

## Marcellus

Meaning: from Latin "Mars" or "the god of war"

+ (d.c. 178): Martyred priest of Lyons, France. Feast day: September 4.

+ Marcellus the Centurion (d. 298): Roman officer martyred at Tingis (in modern Morocco). Feast day: October 30.

+ Marcellus I, Pope (served from 308-309): Roman, died in exile. Feast day: January 16.

+ (d. 389): Bishop of Apamea (in modern Syria.) Feast day: August 14.

+ (d.c. 430): Bishop of Paris. Feast day: November 1.

+ (d. 474): French bishop. Feast day: April 9.

+ Marcellus Akimetes (d.c. 485): Abbot at Constantinople (Istanbul in modern Turkey). Feast day: December 29.

+ Marcellus (d.c. 869): Irish or Scottish Benedictine. Feast day: September 27.

## Marculf

Meaning: unknown

+ (d. 558): Patron of skin diseases. Feast day: May 1.

## Marek

Meaning: unknown

+ Marek Krizin (d. 1619): Martyr in Hungary. Feast day: September 7.

## Marinus

Meaning: unknown

+ (d. fourth century): Bishop and hermit. Feast day: September 4.

+ (d. 731): Benedictine martyr. Feast day: November 24.

## Marius

Meaning: Hebrew "bitter," Roman family name

+ (d.c. 270): Persian martyr. Feast day: January 19.

*(Mariano, Marino, Mario)*

# Mark

Meaning: from Latin "Mars" or "the god of war"

+ (biblical): Companion of Sts. Peter and Paul, evangelist (Gospel of Mark). Feast day: April 25.

+ Mark of Galilee (d. 92): Galilean by birth, missionary to Italy. Feast day: April 28.

+ (d.c. 156): First bishop of Jerusalem not of Jewish descent. Feast day: October 22.

+ Mark and Marcellian (d.c. 287): Roman martyrs, twin brothers and deacons. Feast day: June 18.

+ (d.c. 303): Martyr of Antioch in Pisidia (in present-day Turkey). Feast day: September 28.

+ (d. 304): Egyptian martyr. Feast day: October 4.

+ Mark of Lucera (d.c. 328): Italian bishop. Feast day: June 14.

+ Mark, Pope (served January to August 336): Built two basilicas on land donated by the Emperor Constantine. Feast day: October 7.

+ (d.c. 362): Bishop, martyred on Mount Lebanon. Feast day: March 29.

+ Mark Criado, Blessed (d. 1569): Spanish Trinitarian martyred by the Moors. Feast day: September 25.

+ Mark Caldeira, Blessed (d. 1570): Portuguese martyr. Feast day: July 15.

+ Mark Barkworth, Blessed (d. 1601): Martyr of England. Feast day: February 27.

+ Mark Shineiemon, Blessed (d. 1622): Martyr of Japan. Feast day: August 19.

*(Marc, Marciano, Marcio, Marco, Marcos, Marcus, Marek, Marke, Markeese, Markei, Markey, Markice, Markques, Markus, Marqui, Marquis, Marx)*

# Marnock

Meaning: unknown

+ (d.c. 625): Irish bishop. Feast day: March 1 and October 25.

# Maro

Meaning: unknown

+ (d.c. 99): Martyr. Feast day: April 15.

+ (d.c. 435): Syrian hermit. Feast day: February 14.

# Martial

Meaning: from Latin "Mars" or "the god of war"

+ (date unknown): Martyred with St. Lawrence. Feast day: September 28.

+ (d.c. 300): Martyr. Feast day: August 22.

+ Martial of Limoges (d.c. 300): First bishop of Limoges, France. Feast day: June 30.

*(Marschal, Marshal, Marshall, Marshel, Marshell)*

# Martin

Meaning: from Latin "Mars" or "the god of war"

+ Martin of Vienne (d.c.132): French bishop. Feast day: July 1.

+ Martin of Tongres (d.c. 350): Bishop of Tongres, in France. Feast day: June 21.

+ Martin of Tours (d. 397): Former soldier, famous for giving his cloak away. Feast day: November 11.

+ Martin of Saujon (d.c. 400): Abbot and founder of Saujon Monastery. Feast day: December 7.

+ Martin of Braga (d.c. 580): Bishop and evangelist. Feast day: March 20.

+ Martin I, Pope (served from 649-655): Venerated as the last of the popes to be martyred. Feast day: April 13.

+ Martin of Arades (d. 726): Benedictine monk. Feast day: November 26.

+ Martin Cid (d. 1152): Cistercian abbot. Feast day: October 8.

+ Martin Manuel (d. 1156): Portuguese martyr. Feast day: January 31.

+ Martin of León (d. 1203): Augustinian monk. Feast day: January 12.

+ Martin de Hinojosa (d. 1213): Spanish bishop. Feast day: September 3.

+ Martin de Aguirre (d. 1597): Missionary and martyr of Japan. Feast day: February 6.

+ Martin Gomez, Blessed (d. 1627): Martyr of Japan. Feast day: August 17.

+ Martin de Porres (d. 1639): Dominican mystic and friend of St. Rose of Lima. Patron of interracial justice. Feast day: November 3.

+ Martin Tinh and Martin Tho (d. 1840): Martyrs of Vietnam. Feast day: November 8.

+ Martin, Blessed (d. 1862): Native-born martyr of China. Feast day: February 18.

*(Martain, Marten, Martinez, Marton, Marty, Martyn)*

## Martius

Meaning: from Latin "Mars" or "the god of war"

+ (d.c. 530): Hermit. Feast day: April 13.

## Matthew

Meaning: Hebrew "gift of God"

+ (biblical): One of the Twelve Apostles, also called Levi, tax collector and evangelist (Gospel of Matthew). Feast day: September 21.

+ Matthew of Beauvais (d.c. 1098): Crusader and martyr. Feast day: March 27.

+ Matthew de Eskandely, Blessed (d.c. 1309): Martyr in China. Feast day: October 8.

+ Matthew Alvarez, Blessed (d. 1628): Native-born Japanese martyr. Feast day: September 8.

+ Matthew Alonso Leziniana (d. 1745): Spanish Dominican martyred in Vietnam. Feast day: January 22.

+ Matthew Gam, Blessed (d. 1847): Vietnamese martyr. Feast day: May 11.

+ Matthew Phuong (d. 1861): Native-born martyr in Vietnam. Feast day: May 26.

*(Mateo, Mathew, Mathieux, Matt)*

## Matthias

Meaning: Greek form of Matthew

+ (biblical): Chosen to replace Judas Iscariot as one of the Twelve Apostles (Acts 1:21-26). Feast day: May 14.

+ (d.c. 120): Bishop of Jerusalem. Feast day: January 30.

+ Matthias of Meako (d. 1597): Native-born martyr of Japan. Feast day: February 6.

+ Matthias Kosaka and Matthias Nakano, Blesseds (d. 1619): Native-born martyrs of Japan. Feast day: November 27.

+ Matthias of Arima, Blessed (d. 1622): Native-born martyr of Japan. Feast day: May 22.

+ Matthias Araki, Blessed (d. 1626): Native-born martyr of Japan. Feast day: July 12.

+ Matthias Murumba (d. 1886): Muslim judge who became a Protestant and then converted to Catholicism. Martyred in Uganda. Feast day: June 3.

+ Mathias Mulumba (d. 1886): Martyr of Uganda, chief of several villages. Feast day: June 3.

## Maurice
Meaning: Latin "dark-skinned"

+ Maurice of Carnoët (d.c. 1191): Cistercian abbot and reformer. Feast day: October 13.

*(Maury, Morice, Moris, Morrice, Morris, Morriss, Morry, Moss)*

## Maurilius
Meaning: Latin "sympathizer"

+ (d.c. 453): Bishop of Angers, France. Feast day: September 13.

+ (d. 1067): Benedictine archbishop. Feast day: August 9.

## Maurus
Meaning: perhaps from Latin "dark-skinned"

+ (date unknown): Martyr of Rome. Feast day: November 22.

+ (d.c. 117): Martyr. Feast day: July 27.

+ (d. 383): Second bishop of Verdun, France. Feast day: November 8.

+ (d.c. 555): French monk and famous prophet. Feast day: January 27.

+ (d. 946): Benedictine bishop . Feast day: January 20.

+ Maurus Scott, Blessed (d. 1612): Benedictine martyr of England. Feast day: May 30.

## Maxentius
Meaning: from the Latin "excellence"

+ (d. 515): Abbot and miracle worker. Feast day: June 26.

## Maximian
Meaning: Latin "excellence"

+ (d. 404): Bishop of North Africa. Feast day: October 3.

+ Maximian of Constantinople (d. 434): Patriarch of Constantinople. Feast day: April 21.

+ Maximian of Ravenna (d.c.556): Bishop of Ravenna, Italy. Feast day: February 22.

+ Maximian of Syracuse (d. 594): Benedictine bishop. Feast day: June 9.

## Maximilian
Meaning: Latin "excellence"

+ Maximilian of Lorch (d. 284): Martyred bishop. Feast day: October 12.

+ (d. 295): Martyr. Feast day: March 12.

+ Maximilian Kolbe (d. 1941): Franciscan missionary martyred at Auschwitz by the Nazis. Feast day: August 14.

*(Max, Maximillian, Maxx)*

## Maximinus
Meaning: Latin "excellence"

+ Maximinus of Aix (d. first century): First bishop of Aix, in Provence, France. Feast day: June 8.

+ Maximinus of Trier (d.c. 347): Bishop of Trier, Germany. Feast day: May 29.

+ (d.c. 520): French abbot. Feast day: December 15.

## Maximus

Meaning: Latin "best"

+ (d.c. 250): Martyr in Ephesus in Asia Minor (present-day Turkey). Feast day: April 30.

+ (d. 282): Patriarch of Alexandria, Egypt. Feast day: December 27.

+ Maximus the Confessor (d. 662): Abbot, mystic, and Doctor of the Church. Feast day: August 13.

## Mbaga

Meaning: unknown, probably of Ugandan origin

+ Mbaga Tuzinde (d. 1886): Martyr of Uganda, adopted son of the chief executioner. Feast day: June 3.

## Meara

See Mura

## Medard

Meaning: Latin "student"

+ (d.c. 558): French bishop. Feast day: June 8.

## Medericus

Meaning: unknown

+ (d.c. 700): Benedictine abbot. Feast day: August 29.

*(Merry)*

## Meinrad

Meaning: unknown

+ (d. 861): Benedictine hermit and martyr in Switzerland. Feast day: January 21.

## Meira

See Mura

## Mel

Meaning: unknown

+ (d.c. 490): Nephew of St. Patrick. Feast day: February 6.

## Melas

Meaning: unknown

+ (d.c. 385): Bishop. Feast day: January 16.

## Melchior

Meaning: unknown

+ (biblical): Traditional name of one of the Three Wise Men (Matthew 2).

## Meldon

Meaning: Old English "hill"

+ (d. sixth century): Irish hermit. Feast day: February 7.

## Mellitus

Meaning: Perhaps from Greek "honey"

+ (d. 624): Archbishop of Canterbury. Feast day: April 24.

## Mellon

Meaning: unknown

+ (d. 314): First bishop of Rouen, France, native of Cardiff, Wales. Feast day: October 22.

## Menas

Meaning: unknown

+ (d. 552): Patriarch of Constantinople (Istanbul in modern Turkey). Feast Day: August 25.

## Mennas

Meaning: unknown

+ (d.c. 295): Egyptian martyr. Feast day: November 11.

+ (d.c. 312): Martyr in Alexandria, Egypt. Feast day: December 10.

+ (d. sixth century): Italian hermit. Feast day: November 11.

# Meriadoc

Meaning: unknown

+ (d.c. 886): Bishop of Vannes, France. Feast day: June 7.

+ (d. 1302): Bishop of Vannes, in Brittany. Feast day: June 7.

# Merinus

+ (d.c. 620): Bishop honored in both Scotland and Ireland. Feast day: September 15.

# Micah

Meaning: Hebrew "who is like the Lord?"

+ (biblical): One of the Hebrew prophets (Book of Micah).

# Michael

Meaning: Hebrew "who is like the Lord?"

+ (biblical): Archangel who fought against Satan (Revelation 12: 7-9). Feast day: September 29.

+ Michael Ulumbijski (d. sixth century): Evangelist to Russia. Feast day: May 7.

+ Michael of Synnada (d.c. 820): Bishop of Constantinople (Istanbul in present-day Turkey). Feast day: May 23.

+ Michael Kozaki (d. 1597): Native-born martyr of Japan. Feast day: February 6.

+ Michael Takeshita, Blessed (d. 1619): Native-born martyr of Japan. Feast day: November 27.

+ Michael Diaz, Blessed (d. 1622): Martyr of Japan. Feast day: August 19.

+ Michael Shumpo, Blessed (d. 1622): Martyr of Japan. Feast day: September 10.

+ Michael Yamiki, Blessed (d. 1622): Five-year-old martyr of Japan. Feast day: September 10.

+ Michael Carvalho, Blessed (d. 1624): Martyr of Japan. Feast day: August 25.

+ Michael Tomaki, Blessed (d. 1626): Thirteen-year-old martyr of Japan. Feast day: September 8.

+ Michael Tozo, Blessed (d. 1626): Native-born martyr of Japan. Feast day: June 20.

+ Michael Kiraiemon, Blessed (d. 1627): Martyr of Japan. Feast day: August 17.

+ Michael Fimonaya, Blessed (d. 1628): Native-born martyr of Japan. Feast day: September 16.

+ Michael Jamada, Blessed (d. 1628): Native-born martyr of Japan. Feast day: September 8.

+ Michael Nakashima, Blessed (d. 1628): Native-born martyr of Japan. Feast day: December 25.

+ Michael Kinoshi, Blessed (d. 1630): Martyr of Japan. Feast day: September 28.

+ Michael My (d. 1838): Native-born martyr of Vietnam. Feast day: August 12.

+ Michael Ghebre, Blessed (d. 1855): Vincentian martyr of Ethiopia, also called Mika'el Gabra. Feast day: September 1.

+ Michael Ho-Dinh-Hy (d. 1857): Native-born martyr of Vietnam. Feast day: May 22.

+ Michael Garicoits (d. 1863): Founder of the Priests of the Sacred Heart, the Betharran Fathers. Feast day: May 14.

+ Michael Cordero (d. 1910): First native born Ecuadorian to be ordained. Feast day: February 9.

*(Mic, Micael, Micah, Michal, Micheal, Mick, Micky, Miguel, Mik, Mike, Mikel, Mitch, Michel)*

## Midan

Meaning: unknown

+ (d.c. 610): Venerated in Anglesey, Wales. Feast day: September 30.

## Miles

Meaning: Old German "generous"

+ Miles Gerard, Blessed (d. 1590): Martyr of England. Feast day: April 30.

*(Myles)*

## Milles

Meaning: probably Old German "merciful"

+ (d. 380): Martyr in Persia (modern Iran). Feast day: April 22.

## Mira

See Mura

## Mirin

Meaning: Polish "peace"

+ (d. seventh century): Irish missionary abbot. Feast day: September 15.

*(Miron, Miran, Myron)*

## Mitch

See Michael

## Modan

Meaning: unknown

+ (d. sixth century): Abbot, son of Irish chieftain. Feast day: February 4.

## Monan

Meaning: unknown

+ (d. 874): Scottish martyr. Feast day: March 1.

## Monas

Meaning: unknown

+ (d. 249): Bishop of Milan. Feast day: October 12.

## Morris

See Maurice

## Moses

Meaning: Hebrew "deliverer" or "drawn from the water"

+ (biblical): Great Hebrew leader of the Exodus, recipient of the ten commandments (Book of Exodus).

+ (d.c. 250): Martyr of Africa. Feast day: December 18.

+ (d. 251): Martyred priest of Rome. Feast day: November 25.

+ (d.c. 372): Arab hermit and bishop. Feast day: February 7.

+ Moses the Black (d.c. 405): Ethiopian hermit and martyr. Feast day: August 28.

*(Moe, Moïse, Moisei, Moises, Moishe, Moises, Mose, Moshe, Moyses, Mozes)*

## Mugagga

Meaning: unknown, of Ugandan origin

+ (d. 1886): Martyr of Uganda. Feast day: June 3.

## Mukasa

Meaning: unknown, of Ugandan origin

+ Mukasa Kiriwawanvu (d. 1886): Martyr of Uganda. Feast day: June 3.

## Mura

Meaning: Japanese "village"

+ Mura McFeredach (d.c. 645): Irish abbot, disciple of St. Columba. Feast day: March 12.

*(Meara, Meira, Mira, Murah)*

## Myron

Meaning: Greek "sweet-smelling oil"

+ (d.c. 250): Bishop of Crete. Feast day: August 17.

+ (d. 350): Priest martyred in present-day Turkey. Feast day: August 8.

*(Miron, Myran)*

# N

## Nabor

Meaning: unknown

+ (d.c. 304): Martyr in Milan. Feast day: July 12.

## Narnus

Meaning: unknown

+ (d. first century): First bishop of Bergamo, Italy. Feast day: August 27.

## Narses

Meaning: unknown

+ (d.c. 340): Martyred bishop of Persia. Feast day: January 3.

## Natalis

Meaning: Latin "birth"

+ Natalis Pinot, Blessed (d. 1794): French martyr. Feast day: February 21.

## Nathalan

Meaning: probably from Latin "birth"

+ (d.c. 678): Scottish hermit and bishop. Feast day: January 19.

## Nathan

Meaning: Hebrew "God has given"

+ (biblical): One of the Hebrew prophets (2 Samuel 5:14).

## Nathanael, Nathaniel

Meaning: Hebrew "Gift of God"

+ (biblical): One of the Twelve Apostles, also called Bartholomew (John 21:2).

*(Nat, Natan, Nataniel, Nate, Nathan, Nathanial, Nathann, Nathon, Natt, Naython, Nethanial, Nethanyal)*

## Nathy

Meaning: unknown

+ (d.c. 610): Irish bishop. Feast day: August 9.

## Nectan

Meaning: unknown

+ (d. sixth century): Hermit and martyr from Wales or Ireland. Feast day: June 17.

## Ned

See Edmund, Edward

## Nennius

Meaning: unknown

+ (d. sixth century): Called one of the

"Twelve Apostles of Ireland." Feast day: January 17.

## Nennus

Meaning: unknown

+ (d. seventh century): Irish abbot. Feast day: June 14.

## Neot

Meaning: unknown

+ (d.c. 880): English hermit, relative of King Alfred the Great. Feast day: July 31.

## Nereus

Meaning: unknown

+ (d.c. 100): Member of the elite Roman Praetorian Guard, martyr. Feast day: May 12.

+ (d. 343): Persian bishop and martyr. Feast day: November 20.

+ Nerses the Great (d. 373): Armenian bishop and martyr. Feast day: November 19.

+ Nerses Glaiëtsi (d. 1173): Armenian bishop. Feast day: August 13.

+ Nerses Lambronazi (d. 1198): Armenian bishop. Feast day: July 17.

## Nestor

Meaning: unknown

+ (d. 251): Bishop of Magydos, Pamphylia (in present-day Turkey), martyr. Feast day: February 26.

+ (d.c. 304): Martyr executed at Thessalonika under Emperor Diocletian. Feast day: October 8.

+ (d. 362): Youthful martyr in Gaza. Feast day: September 8.

## Neville, Nevin

See Abban

## Nicander

Meaning: unknown

+ (date unknown): Martyr, possibly in Bulgaria. Feast day: June 17.

## Nicanor

Meaning: unknown

+ (biblical): One of the first deacons chosen by the Apostles (Acts 6:5). Feast day: January 10.

## Nicasius

Meaning: unknown

+ Nicasius Jonson (d.c. 1572): Dutch martyr. Feast day: July 9.

## Nicholas

Meaning: Greek "victory people"

+ Nicholas (d.c. 350): Bishop of Myra, traditionally known as the saintly model for Santa Claus, patron of sailors and Russia, Greece, Apulia, Sicily, and Lorraine, France. Feast day: December 6.

+ Nicholas Studites (d. 863): Turkish abbot. Feast day: February 4.

+ Nicholas I, Pope (served from 858 to 867): Promoted the institution of marriage. Feast day: November 13.

+ Nicholas the Mystic (d. 925): Patriarch of Constantinople. Feast day: May 15.

+ Nicholas Chrysoberges (d. 996): Patriarch of Constantinople (Istanbul in present-day Turkey). Feast day: December 16.

+ Nicholas of Tolentino (d. 1305): Augustinian preacher, venerated for his miracles. Feast day: September 10.

+ Nicholas Tavigli (d. 1391): Franciscan martyred in Jerusalem. Feast day: December 5.

+ Nicholas von Flüe (d. 1487): Swiss

hermit, patron of Switzerland. Feast day: March 21.

+ Nicholas Dinnis, Blessed (d. 1570): Jesuit martyred near the Canary Islands. Feast day: July 15.

+ Nicholas Pieck (d. 1572): One of the Franciscan martyrs of Gorkum. Feast day: July 9.

+ Nicholas Poppel (d. 1572): One of the Franciscan martyrs of Gorkum. Feast day: July 9.

+ Nicholas Factor (d. 1582): Franciscan preacher. Feast day: December 23.

+ Nicholas Owen (d. 1606): Jesuit member of the Forty Martyrs of England and Wales. Feast day: March 2.

+ Nicholas Thé (d. 1839): Vietnamese martyr. Feast day: June 13.

*(Colin, Nichols, Nick, Nikolas, Nic, Niccolas, Nicki, Nik, Niki, Niklas, Nikolaus)*

## Nicodemus

Meaning: Greek "victory of the people"

+ (biblical): Pharisee who came to Jesus by night for instruction and assisted at Jesus' burial (John 3:1-21). Feast day: August 3.

+ Nicodemus of the Holy Mountain (d.c. 1809): Greek monk and writer. Feast day: July 14.

## Nicomedes

Meaning: unknown

+ (d.c. 90): Martyr, buried in the catacombs. Feast day: September 15.

## Nicon

Meaning: perhaps from Latin "victory"

+ (d.c. 250): Martyred Roman soldier. Feast day: March 23.

+ (d. 998): Missionary. Feast day: November 26.

## Niels

Meaning: unknown

+ Niels Stensen, Blessed (d. 1686): Bishop, anatomist and geologist.

## Nilus

Meaning: unknown

+ Nilus the Elder (d.c. 430): Bishop, friend of St. John Chrysostom. Feast day: November 12.

+ Nilus the Younger (d. 1004): Abbot. Feast day: September 26.

*(Niles)*

## Nimatullah

Meaning: unknown

+ Nimatullah Youssef Kassab Al-Hardini, Blessed (d. 1859): Saint of the Maronite Rite of the Church.

## Ninian

Meaning: unknown

+ (d.c. 432): Scottish missionary and bishop. Feast day: August 26.

## Nissen

Meaning: unknown

+ (d. fifth century): Irish abbot. Feast day: July 25.

## Nithard

Meaning: unknown

+ (d. 845): Benedictine monk and martyr. Feast day: February 4.

## Noah, Noe

Meaning: Hebrew "rest"

+ Noah (biblical): Survived the great flood by building an ark. (Genesis 5:29).

+ Noe Mawaggali (d. 1886): Ugandan martyr. Feast day: June 3.

## Norbert

Meaning: German "famous in the North"

+ (d.c. 1134): Bishop. Feast day: June 6.

## Nothelm

Meaning: unknown

+ (d.c. 740): Archbishop of Canterbury. Feast day: October 17.

# O

## Obadiah

Meaning: Hebrew "servant of God"

+ (biblical): One of the Hebrew prophets (Book of Obadiah).

*(Obadieh)*

## Obitius

Meaning: unknown

+ (d.c. 1204): Benedictine monk and penitent. Feast day: February 4.

## Octavian, Octavius

Meaning: Latin "eighth" or "born"

+ Octavius (d. 297): Martyr and patron of Turin, Italy. Feast day: November 20.

+ Octavian (d. 484): Martyred by the Vandals. Feast day: March 22.

*(Octavien, Octavio, Octavious)*

## Odilo

Meaning: Latin "the refined son"

+ Odilo of Cluny (d. 1049): Abbot. Feast day: May 11.

*(Odell, Odie)*

## Odo

Meaning: German "possessions" or Latin "refined"

+ Odo of Beauvais (d. 880): Abbot and bishop. Feast day: January 28.

+ Odo of Cluny (d. 942): Second abbot of Cluny. Feast day: May 11.

+ Odo the Good (d. 959): Archbishop of Canterbury. Feast day: July 4.

+ Odo of Urgell (d. 1122): Spanish bishop.. Feast day: July 7.

*(Otho, Otto)*

## Odrian

Meaning: unknown

+ (d.c. fifth century): One of the first bishops of Waterford, Ireland. Feast day: May 8.

## Ogmund

Meaning: unknown

+ (d. 1121): Bishop of Holar, Iceland. Feast day: March 8.

## Olaf

Meaning: Norse "ancestor"

+ Olaf of Norway (d. 1030): King of Norway and martyr, patron of Norway. Feast day: July 29.

+ Olaf of Sweden (d. 1024): Martyred Swedish king. Feast day: July 30.

*(Ola, Olave, Olav, Olavus, Ole, Oleh, Olef, Olle, Olov, Oluf)*

# Oliver

Meaning: possibly Old German "elf-host" or Old Norse "affectionate"

+ Oliver Plunket (d. 1681): Archbishop of Armagh, Ireland, martyr in England. Feast day: July 11.

*(Olley, Ollie, Olliver)*

# Omer

Meaning: Hebrew "eloquent"

+ (d.c. 670): Benedictine bishop and miracle worker. Feast day: September 9.

*(Omar, Omarr)*

# Onesimus

Meaning: unknown

+ (biblical): Former slave, martyr (Letter to Philemon). Feast day: February 16.

+ (d.c. 361): Bishop of Soissons, France. Feast day: May 13.

# Ormond

Meaning: Irish "red"

+ (d. late sixth century): French abbot. Feast day: January 23.

*(Armand)*

# Oren

Meaning: Hebrew "fir tree"

+ (biblical): Descendent of Judah (1 Chronicles 2:25)

*(Orrie, Orrin, Orinn)*

# Osmund

Meaning: Old English "divine protector"

+ (d. 1099): Bishop of Salisbury, helped compile the Domesday Book. Feast day: December 4.

*(Osmond)*

# Oswald

Meaning: Old English "god power"

+ (d. 642): King of Northumbria . Feast day: August 5.

+ (d. 992): Benedictine archbishop of York. Feast day: February 28.

*(Oswall, Oswell, Oswold)*

# Oswin

Meaning: Old English "god-friend"

+ (d. 651): Martyred king of Deira, England. Feast day: August 20.

# Othmar

Meaning: unknown

+ (d. 759): Benedictine abbot. Feast day: November 16.

# Otto

Meaning: Old German "possessions"

+ Otto of Bamberg (d.c. 1139): Bishop. Feast day: July 2.

*(Oto)*

# Ouen

Meaning: probably from Greek "distinguished"

+ (d. 684): French bishop, son of St. Authaire. Feast day: August 24.

*(Aldwin, Owen)*

# Owen

Meaning: Welsh "well-born"

+ (d.c. 680): English Benedictine monk. Feast day: March 4.

# P

## Pabiali

Meaning: unknown

+ (d. fifth or sixth century): Son of King Brychan, brother of St. Cledwyn. Patron of Wales. Feast day: November 1.

## Pabo

Meaning: unknown

+ (d.c. 510): Son of a Scottish boarder chieftain, founder of monastery of Llanbabon, Aglesey in Wales. Feast day: November 9.

## Pacian

Meaning: Latin "man of peace"

+ (d. 390): Bishop of Barcelona. Feast day: March 9.

## Pacificus

Meaning: probably from Latin "peace"

+ Pacificus of Cerano, Blessed (d. 1482): Franciscan friar and renowned preacher. Feast day: June 8.

## Paldo

Meaning: unknown

+ (d. eighth century): Benedictine abbot. Feast day: January 11.

## Palladius

Meaning: unknown

+ (d.c. 432): First bishop of Ireland, immediate predecessor to St. Patrick. Feast day: July 7.

+ (d. 661): Bishop of Auxerre, France. Feast day: April 10.

## Pancras

Meaning: unknown

+ (d.c. 304): Martyr under the Diocletian persecutions in Rome. Patron of children receiving First Communion. Feast day: May 12.

## Paris

Meaning: unknown

+ (d. 346): Bishop of Teano, Italy. Feast day: August 5.

*(Parras, Parris)*

## Parisius

Meaning: unknown

+ (d. 1267): Camaldolese spiritual director. Feast day: June 11.

## Paschal

Meaning: French "Easter child"

+ Paschal I, Pope (served from 817-824). Superior of the monastery of St. Stephen, which cared for pilgrims in Rome. Feast day: May 14.

+ Paschal Baylon (d. 1592): Franciscan lay brother and mystic. Feast day: May 17.

*(Pascale, Paschale, Pascual, Pascuale)*

## Patiens

Meaning: possibly from Latin "patience"

+ (d.c. 150): Bishop and patron of Metz (in present-day France). Feast day: November 12.

+ (d.c. 491): Archbishop of Lyons, (in (present-day France). Feast day: September 11.

## Patrick

Meaning: Latin "noble man"

+ (date unknown): Bishop of Malaga, Spain. Feast day: March 16.

+ Patrick of Prusa (date unknown): Martyr. Feast day: April 28.

+ Patrick the Elder (d.c. 450): Abbot, relative of St. Patrick. Feast day: August 24.

+ (d. 461): Missionary and Bishop, patron of Ireland. Feast day: March 17.

+ (d.c. 469): Fourth bishop of Bayeux, France. Feast day: May 24.

+ Patrick Salmon, Blessed (d. 1594): Martyr of England. Feast day: July 4.

*(Paddy, Padraig, Pat, Patrik, Patrique, Patryck, Patryk)*

# Patto

Meaning: possibly Old English "from the warrior's town"

+ (d.c. 788): Bishop of Werden, Saxony, Germany. Feast day: March 30.

*(Patten, Patton)*

# Paul

Meaning: Latin "small"

+ (biblical): Apostle of the Gentiles, martyr, and first great missionary (Acts of the Apostles, Letters of Paul). Feast day: June 29.

+ Paul and Companions (date unknown): Seven martyrs during the Roman persecutions. Feast day: March 20.

+ Paul and Tatta (date unknown): Martyred husband and wife. Feast day: September 25.

+ Paul of Narbonne (d.c. 290): Missionary to Gaul (modern France). Feast day: March 22.

+ Paul the Simple (d.c. 339): Hermit

and disciple of St. Anthony of Egypt. Feast day: March 7.

+ Paul the Hermit (d.c. 342): Also known as Paul the First. Feast day: January 15.

+ Paul of Constantinople (d. 350): Bishop of Constantinople (Istanbul in present-day Turkey). Feast day: June 7.

+ Paul of Trois-Châteaux (d.c. 405): Hermit and bishop. Feast day: February 1.

+ Paul Aurelian (d.c. 573): Welsh bishop. Feast day: March 12.

+ Paul of Verdun (d.c. 649): Hermit and bishop. Feast day: February 8.

+ Paul of Cyprus (d.c. 760): Martyr for the cause of venerating icons. Feast day: March 17.

+ Paul I, Pope (served from 757-767). Brother of Pope Stephen, resisted the encroachments of Byzantine forces in the West. Feast day: June 28.

+ Paul of St. Zoilus (d. 851): Spanish martyr. Feast day: July 20.

+ Paul of Latros (d. 956): Byzantine hermit. Feast day: December 15.

+ Paul and Ninety Companions (d. 1240): Dominican martyrs. Feast day: February 10.

+ Paul Miki and Companions (d. 1597): Martyrs of Japan. Feast day: February 6.

+ Paul Navarro, Blessed (d. 1622): Martyr of Japan. Feast day: November 1.

+ Paul Sanchiki, Blessed (d. 1622): Martyr of Japan. Feast day: August 19.

+ Paul Tanaka, Blessed (d. 1622): Japanese martyr. Feast day: September 10.

+ Paul Shinsuki, Blessed (d. 1626): Native-born Japanese martyr. Feast day: June 20.

+ Paul Aybara (d. 1628): Japanese martyr. Feast day: September 8.

+ Paul Fimonaya, Blessed (d. 1628): Japanese martyr. Feast day: September 16.

+ Paul Tomaki, Blessed (d. 1628): Young Japanese martyr. Feast day: September 8.

+ Paul of the Cross (d. 1775): Founder of the Congregation of the Discalced Clerks of the Most Holy Cross and Passion of Our Lord Jesus Christ, the Passionists. Feast day: October 19.

+ Paul Lieou, Blessed (d. 1818): Chinese martyr. Feast day: February 13.

+ Paul Tong Buong (d. 1833): Native-born Vietnamese martyr. Feast day: October 23.

+ Paul My (d. 1838): Vietnamese martyr. Feast day: December 18.

+ Paul Khoan (d. 1840): Native born Vietnamese martyr. Feast day: April 28.

+ Paul Ngan (d. 1840): Native-born Vietnamese martyr. Feast day: November 8.

+ Paul Tinh (d. 1857): Native-born Vietnamese martyr. Feast day: April 6.

+ Paul Hanh (d. 1859): Vietnamese martyr. Feast day: May 28.

+ Paul Loc (d. 1859): Native-born Vietnamese martyr. Feast day: February 13.

+ Paul Tcheng, Blessed (d. 1861): Martyr of China. Feast day: July 29.

*(Pablo, Paolo, Pasha, Pauley, Pauli, Paulis, Pavel)*

## Paulinus

Meaning: Latin "very little"

+ Paulinus of Trier (d. 358): Bishop of Trier, enemy of the Arian heresy. Feast day: August 31.

+ Paulinus of Nola (d.c. 431): Bishop of Nola, writer. Feast day: June 22.

+ Paulinus of York (d.c. 644): Missionary and bishop of York, England. Feast day: October 10.

+ Paulinus of Aquileia (d.c. 802): Noted preacher. Feast day: January 28.

+ Paulinus of Capua (d. 843): Bishop of Capua, Italy. Feast day: October 10.

## Pelagius

Meaning: uncertain, perhaps "sea sorrow"

+ Pelagius of Laodicea (d.c. 381): Bishop of Laodicea. Feast day: March 25

+ (d.c. 925): Martyr in Córdoba, Spain. Feast day: June 26.

## Pepin

Meaning: unknown

+ Pepin of Landen, Blessed (d. 640): Ancestor of Charlemagne. Feast day: February 21.

## Peregrinus

Meaning: unknown

+ Peregrinus Laziosi (d. 1345): Preacher, patron of fight against cancer. Feast day: May 1.

*(Peregrine)*

## Peris

Meaning: unknown

+ (date unknown): Patron of Llanberis, Wales. Feast day: December 11.

# Peter

Meaning: Greek "rock"

+ (biblical) Simon the Fisherman, head of the Twelve Apostles (Matthew 16:13-20, also Acts of the Apostles, Letters of Peter). Served as the first pope, martyred in Rome. Feast day: June 29.

+ (d. mid-third century): Martyr under Emperor Trajanus Decius. Feast day: May 15.

+ Peter of Nicomedia (d. 303): Martyr. Feast day: March 12.

+ Peter of Alexandria (d.c. 311): Bishop of Alexandria, Egypt. Feast day: November 26.

+ Peter Absalon (d. 311): Martyred under Emperor Galerius. Feast day: January 3.

+ Peter of Sebaste (d.c. 391): Bishop. Feast day: January 9.

+ Peter (d. mid-fifth century): African martyr. Feast day: March 14.

+ Peter Chrysologus (d. 450): Doctor of the Church, famous preacher. Feast day: July 30.

+ Peter the Deacon (d.c. 605): Papal secretary to Pope St. Gregory I. Feast day: March 12.

+ Peter of Canterbury (d.c. 607): Benedictine abbot. Feast day: January 6.

+ Peter of Mount Athos (d. eighth century): First hermit to reside upon famed Mount Athos in northern Greece. Feast day: June 12.

+ Peter Urseolus (d. 987): Benedictine hermit. Feast day: January 10.

+ Peter Martínez (d.c. 1000): Archbishop, one of the composers of the hymn, Salve Regina. Feast day: September 10.

+ Peter Damian (d. 1072): Cardinal and Doctor of the Church. Feast day: February 21.

+ Peter Igneus (d.c. 1089): Cardinal and Benedictine. Feast day: February 8.

+ Peter of Anagni (d. 1105): Benedictine bishop, papal legate. Feast day: August 3.

+ Peter of Poitiers, Blessed (d. 1115): Bishop. Feast day: April 4.

+ Peter of Pappacarbone (d. 1123): Benedictine bishop. Feast day: March 4.

+ Peter the Venerable, Blessed (d.c. 1156): Abbot of Cluny. Feast day: May 11.

+ Peter of Tarantaise (d. 1175): Cistercian archbishop. Feast day: May 8.

+ Peter Parenzi (d. 1199): Papal legate and martyr. Feast day: May 22.

+ Peter of Castelnau, Blessed (d. 1208): Martyred Cistercian papal legate. Feast day: January 15.

+ Peter Gonzalez (d. 1246): Dominican protector of captives and sailors. Feast day: April 14.

+ Peter Nolasco (d.c. 1256): Founder of the Order of Mercedarians with St. Raymond of Peñafort. Feast day: January 28.

+ Peter de la Cadireta, Blessed (d. 1277): Dominican martyr. Feast day: December 20.

+ Peter Tecelano, Blessed (d. 1287): Franciscan mystic, comb-maker. Feast day: December 10.

+ Peter Pascual (d. 1300): Bishop and preacher. Feast day: December 6.

+ Peter Armengol (d. 1304): Mercedarian martyr. Feast day: April 27.

+ Peter of Luxembourg, Blessed (d.

1387): Cardinal and bishop. Feast day: July 4.

+ Peter de Dueñas, Blessed (d. 1397): Martyr. Feast day: May 19.

+ Peter Alcántara (d. 1562): Founder of the Spanish Discalced Franciscans, patron of Brazil. Feast day: October 19.

+ Peter of Asche (d. 1572): Franciscan lay brother and member of the Gorkum Martyrs. Feast day: July 9.

+ Peter Berna, Blessed (d. 1583): Jesuit martyr in India. Feast day: July 15.

+ Peter Canisius (d. 1597): Jesuit theologian and Doctor of the Church. Feast day: December 21.

+ Peter Baptist (d. 1597): Franciscan martyr in Japan. Feast day: February 6.

+ Peter Shukeshiko (d. 1597): Native-born Japanese martyr. Feast day: February 6.

+ Peter of the Assumption, Blessed (d. 1614): Martyr of Japan. Feast day: May 22.

+ Peter of Ávila, Blessed (d. 1622): Franciscan martyr in Japan. Feast day: September 10.

+ Peter Onizuko, Blessed (d. 1622): Native-born Japanese martyr. Feast day: November 1.

+ Peter-Paul of St. Claire (d. 1622): Native-born Japanese martyr. Feast day: September 12.

+ Peter Zuñiga, Blessed (d. 1622): Martyr in Japan. Feast day: August 19.

+ Peter Sampo, Blessed (d. 1622): Native-born Japanese martyr. Feast day: September 10.

+ Peter Sanga, Blessed (d. 1622): Three-year-old Korean boy martyred in Japan. Feast day: September 10.

+ Peter Vasquez, Blessed (d. 1624): Martyr in Japan. Feast day: August 25.

+ Peter Araki Kobioje, Blessed (d. 1626): Native-born Japanese martyr. Feast day: July 12.

+ Peter Rinshei, Blessed (d. 1626): Native-born Japanese martyr. Feast day: June 20.

+ Peter of the Holy Mother of God, Blessed (d. 1629): Native-born Japanese martyr. Feast day: July 29.

+ Peter Kufioji, Blessed (d. 1630): Native-born martyr in Japan. Feast day: September 28.

+ Peter Fourier (d. 1640): Founder of the Congregation of Notre Dame. Feast day: December 9.

+ Peter Wright, Blessed (d. 1651): Jesuit martyr in England. Feast day: May 19.

+ Peter Claver (d. 1654): The "Apostle of the Negroes," worked with the slaves in the new world. Feast day: September 9.

+ Peter Sanz, Blessed (d. 1747): Martyred bishop in China. Feast day: May 26.

+ Peter Roque, Blessed (d. 1796): Martyred in the French Revolution. Feast day: March 1.

+ Peter Ou, Blessed (d. 1814): Native-born Chinese martyr. Feast day: November 7.

+ Peter Tuy (d. 1833): Vietnamese martyr. Feast day: October 11.

+ Peter Lieou, Blessed (d. 1834): Native-born martyr of China. Feast day: March 17.

+ Peter Truat (d. 1838): Vietnamese martyr. Feast day: December 18.

+ Peter Tu (d. 1838): Native-born Vietnamese martyr. Feast day: September 5.

+ Peter Tuan (d. 1838): Vietnamese martyr. Feast day: July 15.

+ Peter Domoulin-Bori (d. 1838): Martyr in Vietnam. Feast day: November 24.

+ Peter Duong (d. 1838): Native-born Vietnamese martyr. Feast day: December 10.

+ Peter Thi (d. 1839): Native-born Vietnamese martyr. Feast day: December 20.

+ Peter Chanel (d. 1840): First martyr of Oceania. Feast day: April 28.

+ Peter Hieu (d. 1840): Native-born Vietnamese martyr. Feast day: April 28.

+ Peter Khanh (d.c. 1842): Native Vietnamese martyr. Feast day: July 12.

+ Peter Van (d. 1857): Native-born Vietnamese martyr. Feast day: May 25.

+ Peter Quy (d. 1859): Native-born Vietnamese martyr. Feast day: July 31.

+ Peter-Francis Néron (d. 1860): Martyr in Vietnam. Feast day: November 3.

+ Peter Almafo, Blessed (d. 1861): Spanish Dominican and martyr in Japan. Feast day: November 1.

+ Peter Julian Eymard (d. 1868): Founder of the Congregation of the Priests of the Blessed Sacrament. Feast day: August 3.

+ Peter Donders, Blessed (d. 1887): Priest, cared for lepers in Batavia.

+ Peter To Rot, Blessed (d. 1945): Native of Papua, New Guinea and martyr.

*(Peat, Pete, Petar, Peterr, Petr, Petre, Petros, Pierto, Pierce, Piers)*

## Petronius
Meaning: Latin family name

+ (d.c. 445): Bishop of Bologna. Feast day: October 4.

## Phileas
Meaning: unknown

+ (d.c. 307): Martyr born in Thumis, Egypt. Feast day: February 4 and November 26.

## Philemon
Meaning: Greek "kiss"

+ (biblical) Christian owner of runaway slave (Letter to Philemon).

## Philibert
Meaning: Old German "bright"

+ (d.c. 685): Benedictine abbot and bishop. Feast day: August 20.

*(Filbert)*

## Philip
Meaning: Greek "lover of horses"

+ (biblical): One of the Twelve Apostles (John 1:43-46). Feast day: May 3.

+ (biblical): One of the seven deacons chosen by the Apostles (Acts 6:5-6). Feast day: June 6.

+ Philip of Heraclea (d. 304): Bishop of Heraclea and martyr. Feast day: October 22.

+ Philip of Zell (d.c. 770): Anglo-Saxon priest, pilgrim and hermit. Feast day: May 3.

+ Philip Benizi (d. 1285): Servite cardinal and preacher. Feast day: August 23.

+ Philip Howard (d. 1595): One of the Forty Martyrs of England and Wales. Feast day: October 19.

+ Philip Neri (d. 1595): Missionary, founder of the Congregation of the Oratory. Feast day: May 26.

+ Philip of Jesus (d. 1597): Franciscan martyr in Japan. Feast day: February 5.

+ Philip Powel, Blessed (d. 1646): Benedictine English martyr. Feast day: June 30.

+ Philip Evans, Blessed (d. 1679): One of the Forty Martyrs of England and Wales. Feast day: July 22.

+ Philip Minh (d. 1853): Native-born Vietnamese martyr. Feast day: July 3.

*(Phil, Pip)*

## Piato
Meaning: unknown

+ (d. 286): Martyr, in Gaul (modern France). Feast day: October 1.

## Pier
Meaning: Italian form of Peter

+ Pier Giorgio Frassati, Blessed (d. 1925): College student and social justice activist.

## Pierre
Meaning: French form of Peter

+ Pierre Toussaint, Venerable (d. 1853): Freed Haitian slave from New York, hairdresser.

## Pior
Meaning: unknown

+ (d. 395): Hermit and disciple of St. Anthony in Egypt. Feast day: January 17.

## Pip
See Philip

## Piran
Meaning: probably a form of Peter

+ (d.c. 480): Hermit and patron of miners. Feast day: March 5.

*(Perran, Pieran)*

## Pius
Meaning: Latin "pious"

+ Pius V, Pope (served from 1566-1572): Church reformer, known for his charitable works and piety. Feast day: April 30.

+ Pius X, Pope (served from 1903 to 1914): Condemned modernism, encouraged frequent reception of Holy Communion. Last pope to be canonized. Feast day: August 21.

## Placid
Meaning: Latin "calm"

+ (d. sixth century): Monk. Feast day: October 5.

## Plato
Meaning: name of the Greek philosopher

+ (d.c. 306): Martyr at Ancyra (modern Ankara, Turkey). Feast day: July 22.

+ (d. 813): Greek monk and abbot. Feast day: April 4.

*(Plaeto, Platon)*

## Polycarp
Meaning: unknown

+ Polycarp of Smyrna (d.c. 155): Bishop of Smyrna, early Church leader, martyr. Feast day: February 23.

+ (d. 202): Martyr in Alexandria, Egypt. Feast day: June 28.

+ (d.c. 300): Martyr. Feast day: February 23.

+ Polycarp of Alexandria (d. 303): Martyr in Egypt. Feast day: April 2.

## Polydore
Meaning: unknown

+ Polydore Plasden (d. 1591): One of the Forty Martyrs of England. Feast day: December 10.

## Pontian
Meaning: possibly from Latin "lover of water"

+ Pontian, Pope (served from 230-235): First pope to abdicate the papacy. Feast day: August 13.

+ Pontian Ngondwe (d. 1886): Ugandan martyr. Feast day: June 3.

## Poppo
Meaning: Latin "poppy flower"

+ (d. 1048): Benedictine abbot. Feast day: January 25.

*(Poppey, Poppi, Poppie, Poppy)*

## Primael
Meaning: unknown

+ (d. mid-fifth century): Hermit from Brittany. Feast day: May 16.

*(Primal)*

## Prior
Meaning: Latin "head of the monastery"

+ (d. late fourth century): Egyptian hermit. Feast day: June 17.

*(Pryor)*

## Proclus
Meaning: unknown

+ (d. 447): Patriarch of Constantinople, disciple of St. John Chrysostom.

Feast day: October 24 in the West and November 20 in the East.

## Prosper
Meaning: Latin "always"

+ Prosper of Aquitaine (d.c. 436): Theologian. Feast day: July 7.

+ Prosper of Orléans (d.c. 453): Bishop of Orléans, France. Feast day: July 29.

## Protus
Meaning: unknown

+ (d.c. 257): Roman martyr. Feast day: September 11.

## Ptolemy
Meaning: Greek name of several rulers of Egypt

+ (d. first century): Martyred bishop, disciple of St. Peter. Feast day: August 24.

+ (d.c. 165): Roman martyr. Feast day: October 19.

## Quay
See Kea

## Quentin
Meaning: Latin "fifth"

+ (d. 287): Missionary to Gaul (modern France) and martyr. Feast day: October 31.

*(Quint, Quinton, Quitin, Quiton)*

## Quintian

Meaning: Latin "fifth"

+ (date unknown): French bishop. Feast day: June 14.

+ (d.c. 430): African martyr. Feast day: May 23.

+ (d.c. 527): Native-born African bishop. Feast day: November 13.

## Quintius

Meaning: Latin "fifth"

+ (d. 570): Martyr, refused the advances of a Frankish Queen. Feast day: October 4.

## Quintus

Meaning: Latin "fifth"

+ (d.c. 255): Martyr under Emperor Trajanus Decius. Feast day: December 18.

## Quirinus

Meaning: Latin "fifth"

+ (d.c. 117): Roman tribune and martyr. Feast day: March 30.

+ (d.c. 269): Roman martyr. Feast day: March 25.

+ (d. 308): Bishop and martyr. Feast day: June 4.

# R

## Rabanus

Meaning: unknown

+ Rabanus Maurus, Blessed (d. 856): German abbot and theologian, probably the author of hymn Veni Creator Spiritus. Feast day: February 4.

## Racho

Meaning: unknown

+ (d.c. 660): First bishop of Autun, France. Feast day: January 25.

## Rafael

Meaning: Hebrew "God has healed"

+ Rafael Melchior Chylinski, Blessed (d. 1741): Polish priest.

## Ralph

Meaning: Old English "wolf counsel"

+ (d. 866): Benedictine bishop. Feast day: June 21.

+ Ralph Crockett, Blessed (d. 1588): English martyr. Feast day: October 1.

+ Ralph Milner, Blessed (d. 1591): English martyr. Feast day: July 7.

+ Ralph Sherwin (d. 1581): One of the Forty Martyrs of England and Wales. Feast day: December 1.

+ Ralph Ashley, Blessed (d. 1606): Jesuit martyr of England. Feast day: April 7.

+ Ralph Corby, Blessed (d. 1644): Jesuit martyr of England. Feast day: September 7.

*(Radolphus, Radulf, Rafe, Ralf, Raul, Raulf, Raulin, Rawlings)*

## Rambert

Meaning: Old German "mighty brilliant"

+ (d.c. 680): French martyr. Feast day: June 13.

## Rambold

Meaning: unknown

+ (d. 1001): Benedictine abbot. Feast day: June 17.

## Raphael

Meaning: Hebrew "God has healed"

+ (biblical): Archangel mentioned by name in the Bible. (Tobit 3:17).

+ Raphael Arnáuz Baron, Blessed (d. 1938): Spiritual writer.

*(Rafe, Rafi)*

## Raymond

Meaning: Old English "counsel-protection"

+ Raymond of Barbastro (d. 1126): Augustinian bishop. Feast day: June 21.

+ Raymond of Fitero (d. 1163): Cistercian abbot and founder of the Order of Calatrava. Feast day: March 15.

+ Raymond Nonnatus (d. 1240): Cardinal, called Nonnatus from the Latin non natus or "not born," because he was delivered by caesarian section. Patron saint of midwives. Feast day: August 31.

+ Raymond of Peñafort (d. 1275): Dominican friar and associate of Thomas Aquinas. Codified canon law. Feast day: January 7.

+ Raymond Lull, Blessed (d.c. 1316): Mystic and philosopher. Feast day: July 3.

+ Raymond of Capua, Blessed (d. 1399): Second "founder" of the Dominicans and close friend of St. Catherine of Siena. Feast day: October 5.

*(Raimondo, Raimund, Rayment, Raymonde, Raymund, Raymunde, Roman)*

## Raynald

Meaning: Old German "mighty"

+ Raynald de Bar, Blessed (d. 1151): Cistercian abbot. Feast day: December 16.

+ Raynald of Nocera (d. 1225): Benedictine bishop. Feast day: February 9.

+ Raynald of Ravenna, Blessed (d. 1321): Archbishop of Ravenna. Feast day: August 18.

## Reginald

See Ronald

## Reinold

Meaning: Old German "mighty"

+ (d. 960): Patron of stonemasons. Feast day: January 7.

*(Rainald, Reynold)*

## Rembert

Meaning: unknown

+ (d. 888): Benedictine bishop and missionary to Scandinavia. Feast day: February 4.

## Remigius

Meaning: unknown

+ (d.c. 533): Called the "Apostle to the Franks." Feast day: October 1.

## René

Meaning: French "reborn"

+ René Goupil (d. 1642): Jesuit martyr in North America. Feast day: October 19.

*(Raenée, Rainato, Ranato, Renato, Rene, Renne, Rennie)*

## Reuben

Meaning: Hebrew "behold"

+ (biblical): Jacob's eldest son (Genesis 30:32).

*(Reuban, Reubin, Rheuben, Rube, Rubin)*

# Rhian

Meaning: Welsh "maiden," but used as a man's name in Middle Ages.

+ (date unknown): Welsh abbot. Feast day: March 8.

*(Rhyan, Rian, Riann, Ryan)*

# Ribert

Meaning: unknown

+ (d. seventh century): Benedictine abbot and possibly a bishop. Feast day: September 15.

+ Ribert (d.c. 790): Abbot. Feast day: December 19.

# Richard

Meaning: Old English "strong ruler"

+ (d. 720): Legendary saint, called "King of the English." Feast day: February 7.

+ Richard of Andria (d.c. 1196): Bishop of Andria, Italy. Feast day: June 9.

+ Richard of Chichester (d. 1253): Bishop. Feast day: April 3.

+ Richard Rolle de Hampole, Blessed (d. 1349): English mystic and hermit. Feast day: September 29.

+ Richard Reynolds (d. 1535): One of the Forty Martyrs of England and Wales. Feast day: May 4.

+ Richard Bere, Blessed (d. 1537): English martyr. Feast day: August 31.

+ Richard Whiting, Blessed (d. 1539): Benedictine abbot and martyr. Feast day: November 15.

+ Richard Featherstone, Blessed (d. 1540): English martyr, chaplain to Queen Catherine of Aragon. Feast day: July 30.

+ Richard Kirkman, Blessed (d. 1582): English martyr. Feast day: August 22.

+ Richard Thirkeld, Blessed (d. 1583): English martyr. Feast day: May 29.

+ Richard Gwyn (d. 1584): One of the Forty Martyrs of England and Wales. Feast day: October 17.

+ Richard Langley, Blessed (d. 1586): English martyr. Feast day: December 1.

+ Richard Leigh, Blessed (d. 1588): English martyr. Feast day: August 30.

+ Richard Martin (d. 1588): English martyr. Feast day: August 30.

+ Richard Newport, Blessed (d. 1612): English martyr. Feast day: May 30.

+ Richard of St. Ann, Blessed (d. 1622): Martyr of Japan. Feast day: September 10.

+ Richard Herst, Blessed (d. 1628): English farmer and martyr. Feast day: August 29.

+ Richard Langhorne, Blessed (d. 1679): English martyr. Feast day: July 14.

*(Dic, Dick, Dickie, Dik, Ric, Ricardo, Ricci, Rich, Richards, Rickie, Rick, Rickey, Ricki, Rickie, Rico, Ricquie, Rik, Rikk, Riks, Riq, Ritch, Ritchard, Rykk)*

# Rick

See Eric, Frederick, Richard

# Rigobert

Meaning: unknown

+ (d.c. 745): French Benedictine archbishop. Feast day: January 4.

# Rioch

Meaning: unknown

+ (d.c. 480): Irish bishop-abbot. Feast day: August 1.

# Rizzerio

Meaning: unknown

+ Rizzerio, Blessed (d. 1236): Early member of the Franciscans, companion of St. Francis of Assisi. Feast day: February 7.

# Robert

Meaning: Old English "famous"

+ Robert of Chaise-Dieu (d. 1067): Benedictine abbot. Feast day: April 17.

+ Robert of Molesmes (d.c. 1111): Benedictine abbot, founder of the abbey of Cîteaux, France, which became the motherhouse of the Cistercians. Feast day: April 29.

+ Robert of Bruges, Blessed (d. 1157): Cistercian abbot in France. Feast day: April 29.

+ Robert of Newminster (d. 1159): English Cistercian abbot. Feast day: January 26.

+ Robert Lawrence (d. 1535): One of the Forty Martyrs of England and Wales. Feast day: May 4.

+ Robert Salt, Blessed (d. 1537): Carthusian martyr. Feast day: June 6.

+ Robert Johnson, Blessed (d. 1582): English martyr. Feast day: May 28.

+ Robert Anderton, Blessed (d. 1586): English martyr. Feast day: April 25.

+ Robert Morton, Blessed (d. 1588): English martyr. Feast day: August 28.

+ Robert Sutton, Blessed (d. 1588): English martyr. Feast day: October 5.

+ Robert Widmerpool, Blessed (d. 1588): English martyr. Feast day: October 1.

+ Robert Wilcox, Blessed (d. 1588): English martyr. Feast day: October 1.

+ Robert Dalby, Blessed (d. 1589): English martyr. Feast day: March 16.

+ Robert Southwell (d. 1595): Martyr of England. Feast day: February 21.

+ Robert Watkinson, Blessed (d. 1602): English martyr. Feast day: April 20.

+ Robert Bellarmine (d. 1621): Cardinal and theologian. Feast day: September 17.

*(Bob, Bobby, Rob, Robb, Robbert, Robbie, Robby, Roberto, Roberts, Robertson, Robinson, Rupert)*

# Roch

Meaning: Germanic "repose"

+ (d.c. 1378): Devoted to the care of the sick, patron of plague victims. Called Rocco in Italy and Roque in Spain. Feast day: August 16.

*(Rochus, Rock, Rocky, Rollock, Roqu, Roque, Rokus, Rook)*

# Roderic

Meaning: Old German "fame-rule"

+ (d. 857): Martyr of Spain. Feast day: March 13.

*(Roddy, Roderick, Roderk, Rodric, Rodrick, Rodrigo, Rodriguez)*

# Roger

Meaning: Old English "fame-spear"

+ Roger of Todi, Blessed (d. 1237): Franciscan, friend of St. Francis of Assisi. Feast day: January 28.

+ Roger James, Blessed (d. 1539):

Monk at Glastonbury Benedictine monastery, martyr. Feast day: November 15.

+ Roger Dickinson, Blessed (d. 1591): English martyr. Feast day: July 7.

*(Rodger, Rogar, Rogre, Rogers)*

# Roland
Meaning: Old German "famous land"

+ Roland d'Medici, Blessed (d. 1386): Member of the famed Italian House of d'Medici. Feast day: September 15.

*(Rolando, Rolland, Rolle, Rollie, Rowland)*

# Romanus
Meaning: possibly from Latin "man of Rome"

+ Romanus of Subiaco (d. 258): Monk who influenced St. Benedict of Nursia. Feast day: May 22.

+ Romanus of Condat (d.c. 460): French abbot. Feast day: February 28.

+ Romanus the Melodist (d. mid-sixth century): Foremost Greek composer of hymns. Feast day: October 1.

+ Romanus of Rouen (d. 639): Bishop of Rouen, France. Feast day: October 23.

+ Romanus, Blessed (d. 1619): Native-born Japanese martyr. Feast day: November 27.

+ Romanus Aybara (d. 1628): Native-born Japanese martyr. Feast day: September 8.

*(Román, Romaine, Romeo, Romi, Romy)*

# Romaric
Meaning: unknown

+ (d. 653): Abbot and nobleman. Feast day: December 8.

# Romuald
Meaning: unknown

+ (d. 1027): Italian abbot. Feast day: June 19.

# Ronald
Meaning: Old English "counsel-power"

+ (d. 1158): Scottish warrior. Feast day: August 20.

*(Randald, Reginald, Renault, Renaldo, Renauld, Reynaldo, Rinaldo, Roneld)*

# Ronan
Meaning: Irish "little seal"

+ (date unknown): Irish bishop. Feast day: June 1.

*(Raanan, Rhiannon, Román, Rónán)*

# Rudesind
Meaning: unknown

+ (d. 977): Benedictine abbot and bishop. Feast day: March 1.

# Rudolf
Meaning: Old German "fame-wolf"

+ Rudolph of Gubbio (d.c. 1066): Benedictine abbot. Feast day: October 17.

+ Rudolf Acquaviva, Blessed (d. 1583): Jesuit martyr in India. Feast day: July 27.

*(Rodolph, Rolf, Rolph, Rudolphus, Rudy)*

# Rufus
Meaning: Latin "red-haired"

+ (biblical): Roman Christian called "chosen in the Lord" by St. Paul (Romans 16:13). Feast day: November 21.

+ (date unknown): Irish hermit, possibly a bishop. Feast day: April 2.

+ Rufus of Avignon (d.c. 200): First bishop of Avignon, France. Feast day: November 12.

+ Rufus and Companions (d. 304): Roman martyrs during the persecutions of Emperor Diocletian. Feast day: November 28.

*(Ruffus)*

# Rumold

Meaning: unknown

+ (d.c. 775): Flemish bishop. Feast day: June 24.

# Rumon

Meaning: unknown

+ (d. sixth century): English bishop. Feast day: June 1.

*(Ronan, Ruadon, Ruan)*

# Rumwald

Meaning: unknown

+ (d.c. 650): Legendary English saint who announced his profession of faith after his baptism at the age of three days and then died. Feast day: August 28.

# Rupert

Meaning: Germanic form of Robert

+ (d.c. 717): Bishop and missionary to Germany. Feast day: March 27.

+ Rupert Mayer, Blessed (d. 1945): Enemy of the Nazis.

# Ryan

See Rhian

# S

# Sabas

Meaning: Hebrew "rest"

+ (d. 272): Roman martyr. Feast day: April 24.

+ (d. 372): Martyr in the area of modern Romania. Feast day: April 12.

+ (d. 532): Disciple of St. Euthymius, appointed archimandrite over all the hermit monks of Jerusalem. Feast day: December 5.

*(Sabah, Sabbah, Sava)*

# Sabinian

Meaning: unknown

+ (d.c. 275): Martyr and missionary to Gaul (in modern France). Feast day: January 29.

+ (d.c. 720): Benedictine abbot. Feast day: November 22.

# Sabinus

Meaning: Latin "vine planter"

+ (d. 303): Martyr under Emperor Diocletian. Feast day: December 30.

+ (d. fifth century): Hermit. Feast day: October 9.

+ (d. 420): Bishop. Feast day: December 11.

+ (d. 566): Italian bishop. Feast day: February 9.

+ (d.c. 760): Bishop of Catania, Sicily. Feast day: October 15.

## Sacer

Meaning: unknown

+ (d. seventh century): Irish abbot. Feast day: March 3.

## Sadoc

Meaning: Hebrew "sacred"

+ Sadoc, Blessed (d. 1260): Dominican missionary and martyr in Poland. Feast day: June 2 and May 5.

## Sagar

Meaning: unknown

+ (d.c. 175): Martyred bishop of Turkey. Feast day: October 6.

## Salvator

Meaning: Latin "one who saves"

+ Salvator of Horta (d. 1567): Franciscan confessor. Feast day: March 18.

## Samson

Meaning: Hebrew "sun"

+ (biblical): Judge of Israel, noted for his strength. (Judges 13-16).

+ (d.c. 530): Physician to the poor in Constantinople (Istanbul in present-day Turkey). Feast day: June 27.

+ (d.c. 565): Welsh bishop and evangelizer. Feast day: July 28.

*(Sam, Sammie, Sammy, Sampson)*

## Samuel

Meaning: Hebrew "name of God"

+ (biblical): Prophet who anointed King Saul (Books of Samuel).

+ Samuel of Edessa (d. 496): Ecclesiastical writer. Feast day: August 9.

*(Sam, Sammy, Same, Sami, Samual)*

## Sanctan

Meaning: Latin "holy"

+ (d. sixth century): Irish bishop. Feast day: May 9.

## Sandy

See Alexander

## Saul

Meaning: Hebrew "borrowed"

+ (biblical): First King of Israel (1 Samuel 9:2).

*(Sawl, Sol)*

## Sava

Meaning: unknown

+ (d. 1235): Son of King Stephen I, abbot, also called Sabas. Patron of Serbia. Feast day: January 14.

## Sawl

Meaning: possibly form of Saul

+ (d. sixth century): Welsh chieftain. Feast day: January 15.

## Schotin

Meaning: unknown

+ (d. sixth century): Welsh hermit. Feast day: January 6.

## Scubilion

Meaning: unknown

+ (d. 1867): Worker among slaves. Born Jean-Bernard Rousseau.

## Sean

See John

## Sebald

Meaning: unknown

+ (d.c. 770): Hermit and missionary. Feast day: August 19.

## Sebastian

Meaning: Latin "man from Sebastia" or "august"

+ (d.c. 288): Roman martyr. Feast day: January 20.

+ Sebastian Newdigate, Blessed (d. 1535): Carthusian martyr of England. Feast day: June 19.

+ Sebastian Montánol, Blessed (d. 1616): Spanish Dominican missionary in Mexico. Feast day: December 10.

+ Sebastian Kimura, Blessed (d. 1622): Japanese martyr, grandson of the first Japanese convert. Feast day: September 10.

*(Sabastien)*

## Sebbi

Meaning: unknown

+ (d.c. 694): King of Essex, England. Feast day: August 29.

## Secondo

Meaning: Latin "second"

+ Secondo Pollo, Blessed (d. 1941): Italian priest, patron of chaplains.

## Sedna

Meaning: unknown

+ (d.c. 570): Irish bishop. Feast day: March 10.

## Seiriol

Meaning: unknown

+ (d. sixth century): Welsh monk and hermit. Feast day: February 1.

## Senach

Meaning: unknown

+ (d. sixth century): Irish bishop. Feast day: August 3.

## Senan

Meaning: unknown

+ (d.c. 550): Irish bishop. Feast day: March 8.

+ (d. seventh century): Welsh hermit. Feast day: April 29.

## Senoch

Meaning: unknown

+ (d. 576): Benedictine abbot, friend of St. Gregory of Tours. Feast day: October 24.

## Sergius

Meaning: Russian "servant"

+ Sergius I, Pope (served from 687-701): Encouraged music in the liturgy and introduced the Agnus Dei into the mass. Feast day: September 8.

+ (d.c. 1392): Russian saint and mystic. Feast day: September 25.

*(Serge, Sergey, Sergio, Sirgio, Sirgios)*

## Seth

Meaning: Hebrew "appointed"

+ (biblical): Son of Adam and Eve (Genesis 4:25).

*(Shet, Shethe)*

## Servan

Meaning: unknown

+ (d. sixth century): Bishop, possibly from Ireland. Feast day: July 1.

## Servus

Meaning: unknown

+ (d. 484): African martyr. Feast day: December 7.

## Severinus

Meaning: unknown

+ (d.c. 403): Bishop of Cologne. Feast day: October 23.

+ (d.c. 420): Bishop of Bordeaux. Feast day: October 23.

+ (d. 482): Monk and hermit Feast day: January 8.

+ (d.c. 507): Abbot and healer. Feast day: February 11.

+ Severinus Boethius (d.c. 524): Roman philosopher, theologian, statesman. Feast day: October 23.

+ (d.c. 540): French hermit. Feast day: November 27.

+ (d. 550): Italian bishop. Feast day: June 8.

## Severus

Meaning: unknown

+ (d.c. 300): Roman martyr. Feast day: August 20.

+ (d.c. 348): Bishop of Ravenna. Feast day: February 1.

+ (d. 409): Bishop of Naples. Feast day: April 29.

+ (d. 445): Missionary in Gaul (modern France). Feast day: August 8.

+ (d. 455): French bishop. Feast day: October 15.

+ (d.c. 500): Village priest. Feast day: August 1.

+ (d.c. 530): Italian priest. Feast day: February 15.

+ (d. 633): Spanish bishop and martyr. Feast day: November 6.

+ (d.c. 690): French bishop. Feast day: February 1.

## Sezni

Meaning: unknown

+ (d.c. 529): Bishop and missionary to Ireland. Feast day: August 4.

## Shapur

Meaning: unknown

+ (d. 339): Persian (modern Iranian) martyr. Feast day: November 30.

## Sidney

Meaning: unknown, possibly a corrupted form of "St. Denis"

+ Sidney Hodgson, Blessed (d. 1591): English martyr. Feast day: December 10.

*(Cid, Cyd, Cydney, Sid, Sindony, Syd, Sydnie)*

## Siffred

Meaning: unknown

+ (d. 540): Monk and bishop. Feast day: November 27.

## Sigebert

Meaning: unknown

+ (d. 635): King of East Anglia, Benedictine monk. Feast day: September 27.

+ (d. 656): King of early France, establish twelve monasteries. Feast day: February 1.

## Sigfrid

Meaning: Old German "glorious peace"

+ (d. 690): Benedictine scholar and abbot. Feast day: August 22.

+ (d.c. 1045): Benedictine priest and missionary to Sweden. Feast day: February 15.

## Sigibald

Meaning: unknown

+ (d.c. 740): Bishop. Feast day: October 26.

## Silas

Meaning: Greek "woods-dweller"

+ (biblical): Disciple and companion of St. Paul (Acts of the Apostles 15-17). Feast day: July 13.

*(Sy, Sylas)*

## Silaus

Meaning: Latin "one who lives in the woods"

+ (d. 1100): Irish bishop. Feast day: May 17.

## Sillan

Meaning: unknown

+ (d.c. 610): Irish abbot. Feast day: February 28.

## Silverius

Meaning: Latin "woods"

+ Silverius, Pope (served from 536-537): Son of Pope Hormisdas, deposed by the Byzantines. Feast day: June 20.

+ (d. mid-sixth century): Bishop of Verona. Feast day: September 12.

+ (d.c. 720): Benedictine bishop. Feast day: February 17.

## Simbert

Meaning: unknown

+ (d.c. 809): Benedictine bishop. Feast day: October 13.

## Simeon

Meaning: Greek "snub-nosed"

+ (biblical): Righteous elderly man who recognized the infant Jesus (Luke 2:25-36). Feast day: October 8.

+ (d. 341): Persian (modern Iranian) martyr. Feast day: April 21.

+ Simeon the Ancient (d.c. 390): Syrian hermit. Feast day: January 28.

+ Simeon Stylites (d. 459): Ascetic who lived on top of a pillar. Feast day: January 5.

+ Simeon Stylites the Younger (d. 597): Lived on top of a pillar, established a monastery. Feast day: September 3.

+ Simeon Salus (d. late sixth century): Egyptian hermit. Feast day: July 1.

+ Simeon Metaphrastes (d.c. 950): Hagiographer. Feast day: November 9.

+ Simeon of Padolirone (d. 1016): Benedictine hermit, monk, miracle worker. Feast day: July 26.

+ Simeon the New Theologian (d. 1022): Byzantine mystic and spiritual writer. Feast day: March 12.

+ Simeon of Syracuse (d. 1035): Hermit, second saint formally canonized by a pope. Feast day: June 1.

*(Simon)*

## Simon

Meaning: Greek "snub-nosed"

+ (biblical): One of the Twelve Apostles, called "the Zealot" (Luke 6:15). Feast day: October 28.

+ (biblical): Cousin, called a "brother," of Jesus (Mark 6:3) Bishop and martyr. Feast day: February 18.

+ Simon of Cyrene (biblical): Forced to carry cross for Jesus (Matthew 27:32).

+ Simon of Crespy (d.c. 1080): Benedictine monk, count. Feast day: September 18.

+ Simon Stock (d.c. 1265): Sixth master general of the Carmelites. Feast day: May 16.

+ Simon Acosta and Simon Lopez, Blesseds (d. 1570): Jesuit martyrs in the Canary Islands. Feast day: July 15.

+ Simon Yempo (d. 1623): Japanese martyr, originally a Buddhist monk. Feast day: December 4.

+ Simon de Rojas (d. 1624): Trinitarian priest and tutor to the Spanish royal family. Feast day: September 28.

+ Simon Kiota and Companions (d. 1625): Native-born Japanese martyr, a samurai and member of one of the oldest Christian families in Japan. Feast day: August 16.

+ Simon Hoa (d. 1840): Native-born Vietnamese martyr. Feast day: December 12.

*(Sim, Simms, Simonds, Simpson, Shimon, Simion, Symon)*

## Sincheall

Meaning: unknown

+ (d. late fifth century): Irish abbot. Feast day: March 26.

## Siviard

Meaning: unknown

+ (d.c. 729): Benedictine abbot. Feast day: March 1.

## Sixtus

Meaning: Latin "sixth"

+ Sixtus of Reims (d.c. 300): First bishop of Reims, France. Feast day: September 1.

## Socrates

Meaning: name of Greek philosopher

+ (d. 275): Martyr under Emperor Marcus Aurelius. Feast day: April 19.

*(Socratis)*

## Sol

See Saul, Solomon

## Sola

Meaning: Latin "alone"

+ (d. 794): Monk. Feast day: December 3.

*(Sol, Suolo)*

## Solomon

Meaning: Hebrew "peace"

+ (biblical): Son of David, King of Israel (2 Samuel 12:24).

+ (d.c. 269): First bishop of Genoa. Feast day: September 28.

+ Solomon I (d. fifth century): King and martyr. Feast day: June 25.

+ Solomon III (d. 874): King of Brittany. Feast day: June 25.

*(Salmon, Samon, Sol, Soloman, Sulaiman)*

## Sozon

Meaning: unknown

+ (d. early fourth century): Shepherd and martyr. Feast day: September 7.

## Spes

Meaning: Latin "hope"

+ (d.c. 513): Benedictine abbot. Feast day: March 28.

# Spiridion

Meaning: unknown

+ (d.c. 350): Bishop and martyr, originally a shepherd. Feast day: December 14.

# Stacey, Stacy

See Eustace

# Stanislaus

Meaning: Latin and Polish "glory-camp"

+ (d. 1079): Bishop of Cracow, martyr. Feast day: April 11.

+ Stanislas Kazimierczyk (d. 1489): Polish priest.

+ Stanislaus Kostka (d. 1568): Jesuit from Poland. Feast day: November 13.

*(Stan, Stanislaw, Stanly)*

# Stephen

Meaning: Greek "crown"

+ (biblical): One of the first deacons, first martyr of the Church (Acts 7). Feast day: December 26.

+ Stephen of Reggio (d. first century): Bishop and martyr. Feast day: July 5.

+ Stephen I, Pope (served from 254-257). Tradition says he was beheaded while saying mass in the catacombs. Feast day: August 2.

+ Stephen of Antioch (d. 481): Patriarch of Antioch, martyr. Feast day: April 25.

+ Stephen of Lyons (d. 512): Bishop of Lyons, France. Feast day: February 13.

+ (d. 764): Martyr, monk. Feast day: November 28.

+ Stephen of Cardena (d. 872): Abbot and martyr. Feast day: August 6.

+ Stephen of Cajazzo (d. 1023): Italian bishop. Feast day: October 29.

+ Stephen of Perugia (d. 1026): Italian abbot. Feast day: September 16.

+ Stephen, King of Hungary (d. 1038): Patron and first King of Hungry. Feast day: August 16 (in Hungary, August 20).

+ Stephen of Apt (d. 1046): Bishop of Apt, France. Feast day: November 6.

+ Stephen of Corvey (d.c. 1075): Missionary bishop to Sweden, martyr. Feast day: June 2.

+ Stephen of Pechersky (d. 1094): Russian monk and bishop. Feast day: April 27.

+ Stephen du Bourg (d. 1118): Carthusian monk. Feast day: January 4.

+ Stephen of Grandmont (d. 1124): Abbot. Feast day: February 8.

+ Stephen Harding (d. 1134): English abbot, co-founder of the Cistercian order. Feast day: April 17.

+ Stephen of Obazine (d. 1154): French Cistercian abbot. Feast day: March 8.

+ Stephen del Lupo (d. 1191): Abbot, companion of a wolf. Feast day: July 19.

+ Stephen of Châtillon (d. 1208): French Carthusian bishop. Feast day: September 7.

+ (d. 1209): Cistercian martyr. Feast day: April 11.

+ Stephen de Petervarad, Blessed (d. 1334): Franciscan friar and martyr of Hungary. Feast day: April 22.

+ Stephen (d. 1396): Russian bishop. Feast day: April 26.

+ Stephen de Zudaira, Blessed (d. 1570): Spanish Jesuit martyr. Feast day: July 15.

+ Stephen Vinh (d. 1839): Native-born Vietnamese martyr. Feast day: December 19.

+ Stephen Cuenot (d. 1861): French missionary bishop and martyr of Vietnam. Feast day: November 14.

*(Esteban, Estevan, Steen, Stefan, Stephan, Stephon, Steve, Stevens, Stevenson, Steven, Stevie, Stevon, Stevyn)*

## Straton

Meaning: unknown

+ (d.c. 301): Martyred with Sts. Cyprian, Philip and Eutychian. Feast day: September 9.

## Sulaiman

See Solomon

## Swithbert

Meaning: Old German "landowner"

+ (d. 713): Missionary bishop to Holland and Germany. Patron of those suffering from angina. Feast day: March 1.

+ Swithbert the Younger (d. 807): Benedictine monk and bishop. Feast day: April 30.

*(Swithbart)*

## Swithun

Meaning: Old German "land"

+ (d. 862): English bishop. Feast day: July 2.

+ Swithun Wells (d. 1591): One of the Forty Martyrs of England and Wales. Feast day: December 10.

*(Swithin)*

## Sylvanus

Meaning: Latin "woods"

+ (d.c. 311): Bishop of ancient Palestine, martyr. Feast day: May 4

+ (d. 312): Martyr during the reign of Maximinus . Feast day: February 6.

+ (d. fourth century): Monk of Egypt. Feast day: May 15.

+ (d.c. 450): Monk and Bishop of Troas in Phrygia. Feast day: December 2.

## Sylvester

Meaning: Latin "woody"

+ Sylvester I, Pope (served from 314 to 335): Fought heresies of Donatism and Arianism. Feast day: December 31.

+ (d.c. 420): Missionary in Ireland. Feast day: March 10.

+ (d.c. 525): Bishop of Châlons-sur-Saône. Feast day: November 20.

+ (d.c. 625): French abbot. Feast day: April 15.

+ Sylvester Gozzolini (d. 1267): Benedictine monk. Feast day: November 26.

*(Les, Lester, Silvester, Sylvain, Sylvestre)*

## Syrus

Meaning: unknown

+ (d. third or fourth century): First bishop of Pavia, Italy. Feast day: December 9.

+ Syrus of Genoa (d.c. 380): Bishop of Genoa, Italy. Feast day: June 29.

# T

## Talacrian

Meaning: unknown

+ (d. sixth century): Bishop of Scotland. Feast day: October 30.

*(Tarkin)*

## Talmach

Meaning: unknown

+ (d. seventh century): Irish monk. Feast day: March 14.

## Tanco

Meaning: unknown

+ (d. 808): Irish Benedictine abbot and bishop. Feast day: February 6.

*(Tancho, Tatta)*

## Tarasius

Meaning: unknown

+ (d. early fourth century): Roman martyr. Feast day: August 15.

+ (d. 806): Patriarch of Constantinople (Istanbul in present-day Turkey). Feast day: February 25.

## Tarkin

See Talacian

## Tassach

Meaning: unknown

+ (d.c. 495): Early disciple of St. Patrick, created croziers, patens and chalices. Gave Patrick the last rites. Feast day: April 14.

## Ted

See Edward, Edmund, Theodore

## Teilo

Meaning: unknown

+ (d. sixth century): Welsh bishop. Feast day: February 9.

## Tenenan

Meaning: unknown

+ (d. seventh century): Hermit and bishop. Feast day: July 16.

## Terence

Meaning: Roman family name

+ (d. first century): Bishop and martyr. Feast day: June 21.

+ (d. 250): Martyred under Emperor Trajanus Decius. Feast day: April 10.

+ Terence of Metz (d.c. 520): Bishop of Metz, France. Feast day: October 29.

*(Teran, Terin, Terrance, Terrant, Terrence, Terry)*

## Ternan

Meaning: unknown

+ (d. fifth century): Missionary and bishop in Scotland. Feast day: June 12.

## Tetricus

Meaning: unknown

+ (d. 572): Bishop of Langres, France. Feast day: March 20.

+ (d. 707): Benedictine abbot and bishop. Feast day: April 12.

## Thaddeus

Meaning: Aramaic "loving"

+ (biblical): Another name for St. Jude, one of the Twelve Apostles (Matthew 10:3). Feast day: October 28.

+ Thaddeus Lieu, Blessed (d. 1823):

Native-born Chinese martyr. Feast day: November 24.

*(Tad, Thad, Thadd, Thaddaeus)*

## Thalelaeus

Meaning: unknown

+ (d.c. 284): Physician and martyr. Feast day: May 20.

## Thamel

Meaning: unknown

+ (d.c. 125): Martyr under Emperor Hadrian. Feast day: September 4.

## Theobald

Meaning: Old German "people-bold"

+ Theobald of Vienne (d. 1001): Archbishop of Vienne, France. Feast day: May 21.

+ (d. 1066): Camaldolese hermit and monk, son of nobility. Feast day: June 30.

+ Theobald, Blessed (d. 1150): Patron of shoemakers and porters. Feast day: June 1.

+ Theobald of Marly (d. 1247): Cistercian abbot. Feast day: July 27.

## Theodard

Meaning: unknown

+ (d.c. 670): Bishop and martyr in present-day Belgium. Feast day: September 10.

+ (d. 893): French Benedictine bishop. Feast day: May 1.

## Theodore

Meaning: Greek "god's gift"

+ (d. 220): Roman soldier and martyr. Feast day: September 20.

+ (d. third century): Martyr during the persecutions of Emperor Gallienus. Feast day: March 26.

+ (d.c. 310): Martyr under Emperor Maximinus. Feast day: September 4.

+ Theodore of Cyrene (d.c. 310): Bishop of Cyrene in Libya, martyr. Feast day: July 4.

+ Theodore Trichinas (d.c. 330): Hermit, called Trichinas ("the hairy") because he wore a hair shirt. Feast day: April 20.

+ Theodore Tyro (d. early fourth century): Roman martyr. Feast day: November 9.

+ Theodore of Egypt (d. fourth century): Egyptian monk. Feast day: January 7.

+ Theodore Stratelates (d. early fourth century): Roman general and martyr. Feast day: February 7.

+ Theodore of Bologna (d.c. 550): Bishop of Bologna, Italy. Feast day: May 5.

+ (d.c. 575): French abbot. Feast day: October 29.

+ Theodore the Sacrist (d. sixth century): Sacristan in St. Peter's Basilica in Rome. Feast day: December 26.

+ Theodore of Sykeon (d. 613): Abbot and bishop. Feast day: April 22.

+ Theodore of Tarsus (d.c. 690): Archbishop of Canterbury, England. Feast day: September 19.

+ Theodore of Pavia (d. 778): Italian bishop. Feast day: May 20.

+ Theodore of Studites (d. 826): Abbot and monastic reformer. Feast day: November 11.

+ (d.c. 841): Monk and martyr. Feast day: December 27.

+ (d. 870): English abbot and martyr. Feast day: April 9.

*(Dietrich, Ted, Teddy, Theo, Tudor)*

# Theodoric

Meaning: Old German "ruler of the people"

+ Theodosius the Cenobiarch (d. 529): Abbot. Feast day: January 11.

+ (d.c. 533): French abbot. Feast day: July 1.

+ (d. 863): French bishop. Feast day: August 5.

+ (d. 880): Bishop and martyr. Feast day: February 2.

+ Theodoric of Orléans (d. 1022): Benedictine bishop. Feast day: January 27.

+ Theodosius Pechersky (d. 1074): Russian monk. Feast day: July 10.

+ Theodoric of Emden (d. 1572): Dutch Franciscan martyr. Feast day: October 9.

*(Dietrich, Diederic, Derek, Derrick)*

# Theofrid

Meaning: unknown

+ (d. 728): Abbot and martyr. Feast day: October 19.

# Theonas

Meaning: unknown

+ (d.c. 300): Bishop of Alexandria, Egypt. Feast day: August 23.

+ Theonas of Egypt (d.c. 395): Monk in Egypt. Feast day: April 4.

# Theophanes

Meaning: Greek "god"

+ (d.c. 818): Turkish abbot and martyr. Feast day: March 12.

+ Theophane Venard (d. 1861): Martyr of Vietnam. Feast day: December 4.

# Thethmar

Meaning: unknown

+ (d. 1152): Missionary in Germany. Feast day: May 17.

# Thiemo

Meaning: unknown

+ (d. 1102): Benedictine bishop and martyr. Feast day: September 28.

# Thomas

Meaning: Hebrew "twin"

+ (biblical): One of the Twelve Apostles, known as "the Twin." Doubted the Resurrection (John 20:24-29). Preached in Parthia and martyred in India. Feast day: July 3.

+ Thomas of Farfa (d.c. 720): Benedictine abbot. Feast day: December 10.

+ Thomas of Antioch (d. 782): Hermit. Feast day: November 18.

+ Thomas a Becket (d. 1170): Archbishop of Canterbury, martyred at the altar. Feast day: December 29.

+ Thomas Aquinas (d. 1274): Dominican Doctor of the Church, patron of universities, colleges and schools. Feast day: January 28.

+ Thomas of Hereford (d. 1282): Bishop of Hereford, also called Thomas Cantilupe. Feast day: October 2 and 3.

+ Thomas of Dover (d. 1295): Benedictine monk and martyr. Feast day: August 2.

+ Thomas of Tolentino, Blessed (d. 1322): Franciscan martyr. Feast day: April 9.

+ Thomas More (d. 1535): Lord chancellor of England, humanist, scholar, martyr. Feast day: June 22.

+ Thomas Green, Thomas Scryven, and Thomas Reding, Blesseds (d. 1537): English Carthusian martyrs. Feast day: June 15.

+ Thomas Johnson, Blessed (d. 1537): English Carthusian martyr. Feast day: September 20.

+ Thomas Abel, Blessed (d. 1540): English martyr. Feast day: July 30.

+ Thomas of Villanova (d. 1555): Augustinian bishop. Feast day: September 22.

+ Thomas Plumtree, Blessed (d. 1570): English martyr. Feast day: January 4.

+ Thomas Percy, Blessed (d. 1572): English martyr. Feast day: August 26.

+ Thomas Woodhouse, Blessed (d. 1573): English martyr. Feast day: June 19.

+ Thomas Sherwood, Blessed (d. 1578): English martyr. Feast day: February 7.

+ Thomas Cottam, Blessed (d. 1582): English martyr. Feast day: May 30.

+ Thomas Ford, Blessed (d. 1582): Martyr of England. Feast day: May 28.

+ Thomas Hemerford, Blessed (d. 1584): English martyr. Feast day: February 12.

+ Thomas Alfield, Blessed (d. 1585): English martyr. Feast day: July 6.

+ Thomas Felton, Blessed (d. 1588): English martyr. Feast day: August 28.

+ Thomas Holford, Blessed (d. 1588): English martyr. Feast day: August 28.

+ Thomas Bosgrave, Blessed (d. 1594): English martyr. Feast day: July 4.

+ Thomas Danki (d. 1597): Native-born Japanese martyr. Feast day: February 6.

+ Thomas Kozaki (d. 1597): Fifteen-year-old Japanese martyr. Feast day: February 6.

+ Thomas Warcop, Blessed (d. 1597): English martyr. Feast day: July 4.

+ Thomas Welbourne, Blessed (d. 1605): English martyr. Feast day: August 1.

+ Thomas Garnet (d. 1608): English Jesuit martyr. Feast day: June 23.

+ Thomas Somers, Blessed (d. 1610): English martyr. Feast day: December 10.

+ Thomas Maxfield, Blessed (d. 1616): English martyr. Feast day: July 1.

+ Thomas Tunstal, Blessed (d. 1616): English martyr. Feast day: July 13.

+ Thomas Kotenda, Blessed (d. 1619): Japanese martyr from a noble family. Feast day: November 27.

+ Thomas Guengoro, Blessed (d. 1620): Native-born Japanese martyr. Feast day: August 18.

+ Thomas Akafuji, Blessed (d. 1622): Native-born Japanese martyr. Feast day: September 19.

+ Thomas Koyanangi, Blessed (d. 1622): Japanese martyr. Feast day: August 19.

+ Thomas of the Holy Rosary, Blessed (d. 1622): Native-born Japanese martyr. Feast day: September 10.

+ Thomas Shikuiro, Blessed (d. 1622): Native-born Japanese martyr. Feast day: September 10.

+ Thomas Zumarraga, Blessed (d. 1622): Dominican martyr of Japan. Feast day: September 12.

+ Thomas Tsughi, Blessed (d. 1627):

Native-born Japanese martyr. Feast day: September 6.

+ Thomas Yinyemon, Blessed (d. 1627): Japanese martyr. Feast day: August 17.

+ Thomas of St. Hyacinth, Blessed (d. 1628): Native-born Japanese martyr. Feast day: September 8.

+ Thomas Tomaki, Blessed (d. 1628): Japanese martyr. Feast day: September 8.

+ Thomas Kufioji, Blessed (d. 1630): Japanese martyr. Feast day: September 28.

+ Thomas Holland, Blessed (d. 1642): English martyr. Feast day: December 12.

+ Thomas Reynolds, Blessed (d. 1642): English martyr. Feast day: January 21.

+ Thomas Pickering, Blessed (d. 1679): Benedictine martyr. Feast day: May 9.

+ Thomas Whitbread, Blessed (d. 1679): English Jesuit and martyr. Feast day: June 20.

+ Thomas Thwing, Blessed (d. 1680): English martyr. Feast day: October 23.

+ Thomas Dien (d. 1838): Native-born Vietnamese martyr. Feast day: September 21.

+ Thomas De (d. 1839): Vietnamese tailor, martyr. Feast day: December 19.

+ Thomas Du (d. 1839): Native-born Vietnamese martyr. Feast day: May 31.

+ Thomas Toan (d. 1840): Native-born Vietnamese martyr. Feast day: June 27.

*(Thom, Thompson, Tom, Tomas, Tomm, Tommy)*

## Thomian

Meaning unknown

+ (d.c. 660): Irish Archbishop. Feast day: January 10.

## Thorlac

Meaning: unknown, from Nordic sagas

+ Thorlac Thorhalli (d. 1193): Bishop and abbot, native of Iceland. Feast day: December 23.

## Tigernach

Meaning: Irish "lordly"

+ (d. 549): Irish abbot and bishop. Feast day: April 4.

*(Tierney, Tig, Tige, Tiger, Tyger)*

## Tikhon

Meaning: unknown

+ Tikhon of Zadonsk (d. 1783): Russian monk and bishop. Feast day: August 13.

## Tilbert

Meaning: unknown

+ (d. 789): Bishop of Hexham, England. Feast day: September 7.

## Tillo

Meaning: unknown

+ (d.c. 702): Benedictine monk. Feast day: January 7.

## Timon

Meaning: Greek "God-fearing"

+ (biblical): One of the first seven deacons chosen by the Apostles (Acts 6:5). Feast day: April 19.

## Timothy

Meaning: Greek "honoring God"

+ (biblical): Companion of St. Paul, first bishop of Ephesus (Acts of the Apostles, Letters to Timothy). Feast day: January 26.

+ (d.c. 250): Deacon in the African Church, martyr. Feast day: December 19.

+ (d.c. 298): Egyptian martyr with his wife Maura. Feast day: May 3.

+ (d.c. 306): Bishop of Gaza in present-day Israel, martyr. Feast day: August 19.

+ (d.c. 306): Roman martyr. Feast day: August 22.

+ (d. 362): Martyr and bishop. Feast day: June 10.

+ Timothy Giaccardo, Blessed (d. 1948): Priest, teacher and spiritual director.

*(Tim, Timmoty, Timmy, Timothi, Tymothee, Tymothy)*

## Titian

Meaning: unknown

+ (d.c. 536): Bishop of Brescia, Italy. Feast day: March 3.

## Titus

Meaning: Greek "giant"

+ (biblical): Disciple of St. Paul, bishop of Crete (Letter to Titus). Feast day: January 26.

+ (d. 410): Roman and martyr. Feast day: August 16.

+ Titus Brandsma, Blessed (d. 1942): Carmelite martyr who died at Dachau. Feast day: July 27.

*(Tito, Titos, Tytus)*

## Tony

See Anthony

## Tola

Meaning: unknown

+ (d.c. 733): Irish bishop. Feast day: March 30.

## Toribio

Meaning: unknown

+ Toribio Alfonso de Mogrovejo (d. 1606): Bishop, defender of the rights of natives of Peru. Feast day: March 23.

## Trason

Meaning: unknown

+ (d.c. 302): Roman martyr. Feast day: December 11.

## Tressan

Meaning: unknown

+ (d. 550): Irish missionary to Gaul (modern France). Feast day: February 7.

## Trien

Meaning: unknown

+ (d. fifth century): Disciple of St. Patrick. Feast day: March 22.

## Trojan

Meaning: Greek "from Troy"

+ (d. 533): Bishop. Feast day: November 30.

## Trudo

Meaning: unknown

+ (d.c. 695): Benedictine abbot. Feast day: November 23.

*(Tron, Trond)*

## Trumwin

Meaning: unknown

+ (d.c. 704): Scottish bishop. Feast day: February 10.

## Tudor
See Theodore

## Tudwal
Meaning: unknown

+ (d.c. 564): Welsh monk and bishop. Feast day: November 30.

## Tutilo
Meaning: unknown

+ (d.c. 915): Monk and artist. Feast day: March 28.

## Tychon
Meaning: Greek "wine grower"

+ (d.c. 450): Bishop of Cyprus and patron of wine growers. Feast day: June 16.

*(Tyce, Tysen, Tyson)*

## Tysilio
Meaning: unknown

+ (d. mid-seventh century): Welsh abbot. Feast day: November 8.

# U

## Ulfrid
Meaning: Old English "wolf-peace"

+ (d. 1028): Missionary to Germany and Sweden, martyr . Feast day: January 18.

*(Ulfred)*

## Ulric
Meaning: Old English "wolf-powerful"

+ (d.c. 973): Bishop of Augsburg, first saint officially canonized by a pope. Feast day: July 4.

*(Ulrich, Ulrick)*

## Ultan
Meaning: Welsh "holy"

+ (d. 657): Irish bishop. Feast day: September 4.

+ (d. 686): Benedictine abbot. Feast day: May 2.

+ (d. eighth century): Irish monk known for manuscript illumination. Feast day: August 8.

## Uni
Meaning: Latin "one"

+ (d. 936): Bishop and missionary to Sweden and Denmark. Feast day: September 17.

## Urban
Meaning: Latin "of the city"

+ Urban I, Pope (served from 222-230): Possibly martyred during the persecution of Alexander Severus. Feast day: formerly May 25.

+ (d.c. 356): Italian bishop. Feast day: December 7.

+ (d. 370): Martyred with St. Theodore on a ship off Africa. Feast day: September 5.

+ Urban of Langres (d.c. 390): Bishop, patron of vine dressers. Feast day: April 2.

+ (d.c. 940): Benedictine abbot. Feast day: April 6.

+ Urban II, Pope, Blessed (served from 1088-1099): Studied under St. Bruno, founder of the Carthusians.

Called for the first crusade. Feast
day: July 29.

+ Urban V, Pope, Blessed (served from
1362-1370): Benedictine abbot,
moved the papacy from Avignon,
France, to Rome, and back to
Avignon. Feast day: December 19.

*(Urbain)*

## Ursicinus

Meaning: unknown

+ (d.c. 67): Physician, martyred in
Ravenna, Italy. Feast day: June 19.

+ (d.c. 625): Irish missionary to
Luxeuil, France. Feast day: December 20.

## Ursmar

Meaning: unknown

+ (d. 713): Benedictine bishop and
abbot, missionary to Belgium. Feast
day: April 19.

# V

## Valens

Meaning: Latin "healthy"

+ (date unknown): Bishop and martyr.
Feast day: May 21.

+ (d. 309): Martyr in Caesarea (in ancient Palestine). Feast day: June 1.

+ (d. 531): Bishop of Verona, Italy.
Feast day: July 26.

*(Valin, Vaylin)*

## Valentine

Meaning: Latin "to be strong"

+ (d. 269): Roman priest, physician
and martyr. Patron of lovers. Feast
day: February 14.

+ (d.c. 304): Martyr, beheaded at
Viterbo, Italy. Feast day: November
3.

+ Valentine (d.c. 305): Bishop of Trier,
Germany, and martyr. Feast day:
July 16.

+ Valentine (d.c. 305): Martyr. Feast
day: December 16.

+ Valentine (d.c. 307): Bishop of
Genoa, Italy. Feast day: May 2.

+ (d. fourth century): Bishop of
Strassburg, France. Feast day: September 2.

+ Valentine (d.c. 470): Abbot and missionary bishop. Feast day: January
7.

+ Valentine Berrio-Ochoa (d. 1861):
Bishop and martyr in Vietnam. Feast
day: November 1.

*(Val)*

## Valerian

Meaning: Latin "strength"

+ (d. 178): Martyr. Feast day: September 15.

+ (d.c. 350): Bishop of Auxerre,
France. Feast day: May 13.

+ (d. 389): Italian bishop. Feast day:
November 27.

+ (d. 457): Bishop of Abbenza (modern Africa), and martyr. Feast day:
December 15.

+ (d.c. 460): Bishop and orator. Feast
day: July 23.

+ (d. fifth century): African bishop.
Feast day: November 28.

*(Val, Vallee, Valli, Vally)*

## Valerius

Meaning: Latin "strength"

+ (date unknown): First bishop of Conserans, France. Feast day: February 20.

+ (d.c. 287): Martyr in Gaul (modern France). Feast day: June 14.

+ (d. 315): Bishop of Saragossa, Spain. Feast day: January 28.

+ (d.c. 320): Bishop of Trier, Germany. Feast day: January 29.

+ (d.c. 453): Hermit and bishop. Feast day: January 16.

+ (d. 695): Abbot. Feast day: February 21.

## Vassilij, Vassily

See Basil

## Vedast

Meaning: unknown

+ (d. 539): Bishop and missionary among the Franks. Feast day: February 6.

*(Foster, Gaston, Vaast, Vaat)*

## Venturino

Meaning: unknown

+ Venturino of Bergamo (d. 1346): Dominican preacher and missionary. Feast day: March 28.

## Viator

Meaning: unknown

+ (d.c. 378): Bishop of Bergamo, Italy. Feast day: December 14.

+ (d. 389): Deacon of Lyons, France. Feast day: October 21.

## Vicelin

Meaning: unknown

+ (d.c. 1154): Missionary and bishop in Germany. Feast day: December 12.

## Victor

Meaning: Latin "conqueror"

+ Victor i, Pope (served from 189-199): From Africa, first to use Latin in the liturgy. Feast day: July 28.

+ (d.c. 250): Martyr during the reign of Emperor Trajanus. Feast day: March 10.

+ (d.c. 290): Martyr in Marseilles, Gaul (modern France). Feast day: July 21.

+ (d.c. 300): Martyr under Diocletian. Feast day: April 12.

+ (d.c. 303): Martyr executed at Nicomedia (in modern Turkey). Feast day: April 20.

+ Victor the Moor (d. 303): Martyr from Mauretania, Africa. Feast day: May 8.

+ Victor of Piacenza (d. 375): Italian bishop. Feast day: December 7.

+ Victor of Vita (d.c. 535): Bishop of Carthage. Feast day: August 23.

+ (d. 554): Bishop of Capua, Italy. Feast day: October 17.

+ (d.c. 950): Martyr. Feast day: August 26.

+ (d. 995): Hermit, French recluse. Feast day: February 26.

+ Victor III, Pope, Blessed (served from 1086-1087). Monk, fought the anti-pope, Clement III. Feast day: September 16.

*(Vic, Victer, Vik, Viktor)*

## Victricius

Meaning: unknown

+ (d.c. 405): Bishop of Trent, Italy, and martyr. Feast day: June 26.

+ (d.c. 407): Bishop and missionary, son of a Roman legionnaire. Feast day: August 7.

+ (d.c. 506): Italian bishop. Feast day: September 26.

+ (d. 685): French bishop and martyr. Feast day: March 11.

## Vigor

Meaning: Celtic "vigor"

+ (d.c. 537): Bishop and missionary. Feast day: November 1.

## Vincent

Meaning: Latin "to conquer"

+ (date unknown): Roman martyr. Feast day: July 24.

+ (date unknown): Spanish martyr. Feast day: September 1.

+ Vincent of Agen (d.c. 292): Martyr. Feast day: June 9.

+ Vincent of Bevagna (d. 303): Italian bishop. Feast day: June 6.

+ Vincent of Collioure (d.c. 304): Martyr. Feast day: April 19.

+ Vincent the Deacon (d. 304): Deacon and martyr, patron of vinedressers. Feast day: January 22.

+ Vincent of Digne (d. 380): Bishop of Digne, France, originally from Africa. Feast day: January 22.

+ Vincent of Lérins (d.c. 445): Monk and writer. Feast day: May 24.

+ Vincent of Troyes (d.c. 546): Bishop of Troyes, France. Feast day: February 4.

+ Vincent of León (d.c. 554): Spanish abbot and martyr. Feast day: September 11.

+ Vincent Madelgarus (d.c. 677): Benedictine abbot. Feast day: September 20.

+ (d.c. 950): Benedictine abbot. Feast day: May 9.

+ Vincent Kadlubek (d. 1223): Cistercian bishop from Poland. Feast day: March 8.

+ Vincent Ferrer (d.c. 1419): Spanish Dominican preacher. Feast day: April 5.

+ Vincent Kaun (d. 1626): Korean, martyred in Japan. Feast day: June 20.

+ Vincent de Paul (d. 1660): Founder of the Congregation of the Missions, the Lazarist (or Vincentian) Fathers, and, with St. Louise de Marillac, the Sisters of Charity. Patron of charitable groups. Feast day: September 27.

+ Vincent de Cunha, Blessed (d. 1737): Jesuit martyr of Vietnam. Feast day: January 12.

+ Vincent Liem (d. 1773): Native-born Vietnamese martyr. Feast day: November 7.

+ Vincent Strambi (d. 1824): Passionist bishop. Feast day: January 1.

+ Vincent Diem (d. 1838): Native-born Vietnamese martyr. Feast day: November 24.

+ Vincent Yen (d. 1838): Native-born Vietnamese martyr. Feast day: June 30.

+ Vincent Pallotti (d. 1850): Confessor and exorcist. Feast day: January 23.

+ Vincent Vilar David, Blessed (d. 1937): Victim of the Spanish Civil War.

+ Vincent Eugene Bossilkov (d. 1952): Martyr of Communism.

*(Vince, Vincente, Vinnie, Vinny)*

## Vilmos

Meaning: unknown

+ Vilmos Apor, Blessed (d. 1945): Martyred bishop of Hungary.

## Vitus

Meaning: Latin "alive"

+ (d.c. 303): Martyr in Lucania, Italy. Patron against epilepsy and storm, of dancers and actors. Feast day: June 15.

+ (d. 1095): Benedictine monk. Feast day: September 15.

## Vivian

Meaning: Latin "alive"

+ (d.c. 460): Bishop of Saintes, France. Feast day: August 28.

*(Viv, Vivia, Vivien)*

## Vladimir

Meaning: Slavic "ruler of all"

+ (d. 1015): Grandson of St. Olga, ruler of Russia, convert. Patron of Russian Catholics. Feast day: July 15.

*(Vlad, Vladi, Vladimar, Vladamar)*

## Voloc

Meaning: unknown

+ (d.c. 724): Irish missionary bishop. Feast day: January 29.

## Walbert

Meaning: unknown

+ (d.c. 678): French Duke. Feast day: May 11.

## Waldebert

Meaning: unknown

+ (d.c. 668): Benedictine abbot. Feast day: May 2.

## Walfrid

Meaning: Old German "peaceful"

+ (d.c. 765): Benedictine abbot. Feast day: February 15.

*(Walfred)*

## Walstan

Meaning: Anglo-Saxon "corner-stone"

+ (d.c. 1016): Gave away his inheritance and became a servant and farm laborer. Feast day: May 30.

## Walter

Meaning: Old German "ruling people"

+ (d. 1070): French abbot. Feast day: May 11.

+ Walter of Pontoise (d. 1099): French Benedictine abbot. Feast day: April 8.

+ (d.c. 1150): Benedictine abbot. Feast day: June 4.

+ (d.c. 1250): Benedictine hermit and abbot. Feast day: June 4.

+ Walter Pierson, Blessed (d. 1537): Carthusian martyr of England. Feast day: June 6.

*(Walt, Watkin, Watson)*

## Ward

See Edward

## Wenceslaus

Meaning: Old Slavic "wreath of glory"

+ (d. 929): King, patron of Bohemia, the "good king" of Christmas carol. Feast day: September 28.

## Wilfrid

Meaning: Old German "determined peace-maker"

+ Wilfrid of York (d. 709): Bishop of York, England. Feast day: October 12.

+ Wilfrid the Younger (d. 744): Benedictine abbot and bishop of York, England. Feast day: April 29.

## Willeic

Meaning: unknown

+ (d. 726): Benedictine monk in Germany. Feast day: March 2.

## William

Meaning: Old German "will helmet" or "protector"

+ William of Gellone (d. 812): Knight and Benedictine monk. Feast day: May 28.

+ William of Dijon (d. 1031): Benedictine abbot and reformer. Feast day: January 1.

+ William of Peñacorada (d.c. 1042): Benedictine monk. Feast day: March 20.

+ William of Roeskilde (d. 1067): Bishop and counselor to the Danish royal house. Feast day: September 2.

+ William Firmatus (d.c. 1103): Hermit, pilgrim and physician. Feast day: April 24.

+ William of Breteuil (d. 1130): Benedictine abbot. Feast day: July 14.

+ William of Vercelli (d. 1142): Abbot. Feast day: June 25.

+ William of York (d. 1154): Archbishop of York, England. Feast day: June 8.

+ William of Maleval (d. 1157): Hermit. Feast day: February 10

+ William of Pontoise (d. 1192): English hermit. Feast day: May 10.

+ William of Rochester (d. 1201): Scottish martyr. Feast day: May 23.

+ William of Eskilsoë (d. 1203): Missionary to Denmark. Feast day: April 6.

+ William of Bourges (d. 1210): Cistercian bishop. Feast day: January 10.

+ William Arnaud (d. 1242): Dominican and martyr. Feast day: May 29.

+ William Exmew, Blessed (d. 1535): Carthusian martyr. Feast day: June 19.

+ William Greenwood, Blessed (d. 1537): Carthusian martyr of England. Feast day: June 16.

+ William Horne, Blessed (d. 1540): Carthusian lay brother and martyr. Feast day: August 4.

+ William Filby, Blessed (d. 1582): Martyr in England. Feast day: May 30.

+ William Lacey, Blessed (d. 1582): Martyr in England. Feast day: August 22.

+ William Hart, Blessed (d. 1583): Martyr in England. Feast day: March 15.

+ William Marsden, Blessed (d. 1586): Martyr in England. Feast day: April 25.

+ William Dean, Blessed (d. 1588): English Protestant minister who converted to Catholicism, martyr. Feast day: August 28.

+ William Gunter, Blessed (d. 1588): Martyr in Wales. Feast day: August 28

+ William Hartley, Blessed (d. 1588): Former Anglican minister, martyr. Feast day: October 5.

+ William Way, Blessed (d. 1588): Martyr in England. Feast day: September 23.

+ William Patenson, Blessed (d. 1592): Martyr in England. Feast day: January 22.

+ William Harrington, Blessed (d. 1594): Martyr in England. Feast day: February 18.

+ William Freeman (d.c. 1595): Martyr in England. Feast day: August 13.

+ William Andleby, Blessed (d. 1597): Martyr in England. Feast day: July 4.

+ William Richardson, Blessed (d. 1603): Last martyr in the reign of Queen Elizabeth I of England. Feast day: February 7.

+ William Browne, Blessed (d. 1605): Martyr in England. Feast day: September 5.

+ William Ward, Blessed (d. 1641): Martyr in England. Feast day: July 26.

+ William Harcourt, Blessed (d. 1679): Jesuit martyr in England. Feast day: June 20.

+ William Ireland, Blessed (d. 1679): Jesuit martyr in England. Feast day: January 24.

+ William Howard, Blessed (d. 1680): Martyr in England. Feast day: December 29.

*(Bill, Billie, Billy, Wil, Wilkinson, Will, Willie, Willis, Wilson)*

## Willibald

Meaning: unknown

+ (d.c. 786): Bishop and missionary. Feast day: July 7.

## Willibrord

Meaning: unknown

+ (d. 739): Missionary and archbishop. Feast day: November 7.

## Winebald

Meaning: unknown

+ (d. 761): Benedictine abbot and missionary to Germany. Feast day: December 18.

## Winoc

Meaning: unknown

+ (d.c. 717): Monk, built hospital. Feast day: November 6.

## Wiro

Meaning: possibly Celtic "castle"

+ (d. mid-eighth century): Bishop and missionary to France. Feast day: May 8.

## Wistan

Meaning: unknown

+ (d.c. 850): Martyr in England. Feast day: June 1.

## Wolfgang

Meaning: German "wolf-strife"

+ (d. 994): German bishop and reformer. Feast day: October 31.

*(Wolf, Wolfe, Woolf, Woolfe)*

## Wulfram

Meaning: unknown

+ (d. early eighth century): Bishop and missionary. Feast day: March 20.

## Wulfric

Meaning: unknown

+ (d. 1154): English hermit and miracle worker. Feast day: February 20.

## Wulfstan

Meaning: unknown

+ (d. 1095): Bishop of Worcester, England, fought slave trade. Feast day: January 19.

*(Wolstan, Woolstan)*

## Wulmar

Meaning: unknown

+ (d. 689): Benedictine abbot. Feast day: July 20.

## Wulsin

Meaning: unknown

+ (d. 1002): Benedictine bishop and monk. Feast day: January 8.

## Wynn

See Haduin

## Xavier

Meaning: Arabic "bright"

+ Francis Xavier (d. 1552): Jesuit, one of world's greatest missionaries, patron of foreign missions. Feast day: December 3.

*(Xaven, Xavian, Xavion, Xavon, Zavier, Zavon)*

## Xystus

Meaning: unknown

+ Xystus I, Pope (served from 115-125): Roman, succeeded Pope St. Alexander I. Feast day: April 3.

+ Xystus II, Pope (served from 257-258): First pope to bear the same name as one of his predecessors, martyred during persecution of Valerian. Mentioned in the first Eucharistic Prayer. Feast day: August 7.

+ Xystus III, Pope (served from 432-440): Friend of St. Augustine. Fought Pelagian and Nestorian heresies. Feast day: March 28.

*(Sixtus)*

## Yakov

See Jacob

## Yitzak

See Isaac

## Yisrael

See Israel

## Ymar

Meaning: unknown

+ (d.c. 830): Benedictine martyr of England. Feast day: November 12.

## Yona, Yonah

See Jonah

## Yosef

See Joseph

## Yrchard

Meaning: unknown

+ (d. fifth century): Scottish bishop. Feast day: August 24.

## Yrieix

Meaning: unknown

+ (d. 591): French monk. Feast day: August 25.

## Ysarn

Meaning: unknown

+ (d. 1048): French Benedictine abbot. Feast day: September 24.

## Ywi

Meaning: unknown

+ (d.c. 690): English Benedictine monk and hermit. Feast day: October 8.

## Yusif

See Joseph

# Z

## Zacchaeus

Meaning: Aramaic "pure"

+ (d.c. 116): Bishop of Jerusalem. Feast day: August 23.

## Zachariah

Meaning: Hebrew "God has remembered"

+ (biblical): Father of St. John the Baptist Luke 1:5-25, 57-79). Feast day: November 15.

*(Zacariah, Zacarias, Zachary, Zachery, Zackery, Zak, Zechariah)*

## Zachary

Meaning: Hebrew "God has remembered"

+ (date unknown): Martyr in Nicomedia (in modern Turkey). Feast day: June 10.

+ (d.c. 106): French bishop and martyr. Feast day: May 26.

+ Zachary, Pope (served from 741-752): Rescued slaves from the Roman markets, supported St. Boniface's mission to the Germans. Feast day: March 15.

## Zak

See Isaac, Zachariah

## Zama

Meaning: unknown

+ (d.c. 268): First bishop of Bologna, Italy. Feast day: January 24.

## Zanitas

Meaning: unknown

+ (d. 326): Persian (modern Iranian) martyr. Feast day: March 27.

## Zavier

See Xavier

## Zavon

See Xavier

## Zebadiah

Meaning: Hebrew "gift of God"

+ (biblical): Son of Jacob (Genesis 30: 20).

## Zechariah

Meaning: Hebrew "remember the Lord"

+ (biblical): King of Israel (2 Kings 14:29).

## Zeik, Zeke

See Ezekiel

## Zenas

See Zeno

## Zeno

Meaning: unknown

+ (d.c. 300): Leader of a group of martyrs under the Emperor Diocletian. Feast day: July 9.

+ (d. 302): Martyr put to death at Nicomedia (modern Turkey). Feast day: September 2.

+ (d. 303): Soldier martyred in Nicomedia (modern Turkey). Feast day: December 22.

+ (d. 371): Bishop and theological writer. Feast day: April 12.

+ (d.c. 400): Bishop of Gaza, Israel. Feast day: December 26.

+ Zeno and Zenas (d.c. 304): Martyrs who suffered during the persecutions of Emperor Diocletian. Feast day: June 23.

## Zenobius

Meaning: Greek "force of Zeus"

+ (d. late third century): Martyred with his sister, St. Zenobia. Feast day: October 30.

+ (d. 310): Martyr, doctor and priest. Feast day: October 29.

+ (d.c. 390): Bishop of Florence, Italy. Feast day: May 25.

## Zosimus

Meaning: Greek "wealth"

+ (d. 110): Martyr during the reign of Emperor Trajan. Feast day: June 19.

+ (d. fifth century): Hermit. Feast day: April 4.

+ (d.c. 660): Bishop of Syracuse, Sicily. Feast day: March 30.

## Zoticus

Meaning: unknown

+ (d. 204): Bishop and martyr. Feast day: July 21.

+ (d.c. 350): Priest, patron of the poor. Feast day: December 31.

# Saints' Names

# GIRLS

# A

## Abigail

Meaning: Hebrew "father's joy"

+ (biblical): King David's wife (1 Samuel 25:3).

*(Abbie, Abbigail, Abbigayle, Abbygayle, Abby, Abigale)*

## Abra

Meaning: feminine form of Abraham

+ (d.c. 360): Consecrated virgin from France. Feast day: December 12.

## Actinea

Meaning: unknown

+ (d. fourth century): Martyr in Roman persecutions. Feast day: June 16.

## Ada

Meaning: Hebrew "ornament"

+ (biblical): Wife of Esau (Genesis 36:2).

+ (d. seventh century): Abbess and dedicated virgin. Feast day: December 4.

*(Adah, Adalee, Adenette, Adna, Adnette, Adonetta, Aida)*

## Adela

Meaning: Old German "nobility"

+ (d.c. 734): Abbess and Frankish princess. Feast day: December 24.

+ (d. 1071): Benedictine noblewoman. Feast day: September 8.

+ (d. 1137): English princess, daughter of William the Conqueror. Feast day: February 24.

*(Adeline)*

## Adelaide

Meaning: Old German "nobility"

+ (d. 999): Princess, regent, and foundress of convents and monasteries. Feast day: December 16.

+ Adelaide of Bellich (d. 1015): Abbess and miracle worker. Feast day: February 5.

+ (d. 1250): Flemish contemplative and miracle worker. Feast day: June 15.

*(Adelheid, Aleydis, Alice, Adela, Adele, Adeline, Addey, Addie, Alicia, Heidi)*

## Adelina

Meaning: Latin form of Adela

+ (d. 1125): Abbess and granddaughter of William the Conqueror. Feast day: October 20.

## Adeloga

Meaning: unknown

+ (d.c. 745): German Benedictine abbess. Feast day: February 2.

## Afra

Meaning: Hebrew "dust"

+ (d.c. 304): Martyr under Emperor Diocletian. Feast day: August 5.

*(Affery, Aphra)*

## Agape

Meaning: Greek "love"

+ (d.c. 273): Martyr and follower of St. Valentine. Feast day: February 15.

+ (d. 304): Martyr and virgin. Feast day: April 3.

## Agatha

Meaning: Greek "good"

+ (c. 250): Martyr and virgin, patron of earthquakes and volcanic eruptions, bell makers, nursemaids, goldsmiths, blast furnace workers, miners, weavers and breast disease. Feast day: February 5.

+ (d.c. 790): Nun and aide to St. Boniface. Feast day: December 12.

+ (d. 1024): Wife. Feast day: February 5.

+ Agatha Lin, Blessed (d. 1858): Native-born Chinese martyr. Feast day: February 18.

## Agia

Meaning: unknown

+ (d. sixth century): Widow. Feast day: September 1.

+ (d.c. 714): Benedictine nun. Feast day: April 18.

*(Aia, Aye)*

## Agilberta

Meaning: unknown

+ (d.c. 680): Abbess. Feast day: August 10.

## Agnes

Meaning: Greek "pure"

+ (d.c. 304): Virgin and martyr. Feast day: January 21.

+ Agnes of Poitiers (d. 586): Abbess. Feast day: May 13.

+ Agnes of Assisi (d. 1253): Sister of St. Clare of Assisi. Feast day: November 16.

+ Agnes of Bohemia (d.c. 1282): Princess, abbess, and miracle worker. Feast day: March 2.

+ Agnes of Montepulciano (d. 1317): Italian nun. Feast day: April 20.

+ Agnes Takea, Blessed (d. 1622): Martyr of Japan. Feast day: September 10.

+ Agnes of Jesus Galand de Langeac, Blessed (d. 1634): French nun.

+ (d. 1841): Vietnamese martyr. Feast day: July 12.

+ Agnes Tsao-Kouy, Blessed (d. 1856): Martyr of China. Feast day: November 24.

*(Ageneta, Aggie, Agness, Anice, Anis, Anise, Inez, Nessie, Nesta, Segna)*

## Agrippina

Meaning: Latin "pain of childbirth"

+ (d. third century): Martyr under Emperor Valerian or Diocletian. Feast day: June 23.

## Alberta

Meaning: feminine form of Albert

## Albina

Meaning: Latin "white"

+ (d. 250): Young martyr in present-day Israel. Feast day: December 16.

*(Albinia)*

## Alburga

Meaning: unknown

+ (d.c. 800): English abbess. Feast day: December 25.

## Aldegundis

Meaning: unknown

+ (d. 684): Virgin and abbess, raised by two saints. Feast day: January 30.

## Aldetrudis

Meaning: unknown

+ (d.c. 969): Niece of St. Aldegundis.
Feast day: February 25.

*(Trudi, Trudy)*

## Aleth

Meaning: Greek "truth"

+ Aleth, Blessed (d. 1105): Widow and
mother of St. Bernard of Clairvaux.
Feast day: April 4.

*(Alathea, Aleta, Aletha, Alethia,
Althea)*

## Alexandra

Meaning: feminine form of Alexander

+ (d.c. 303): Martyr under Emperor
Diocletian. Feast day: March 20.

*(Aleksandra, Alexandria, Alexa,
Alexia, Allex, Alexis, Aleksei,
Aleksey, Aleksi, Alexes, Alexi,
Alexus, Alexys, Allyx, Alyx)*

## Alfreda

Meaning: feminine form of Alfred

+ (d.c. 795): Virgin and hermitess.
Feast day: August 2.

*(Afreda, Alfritha, Aelfnryth)*

## Alice

See Adelaide

## Alkeld

Meaning: unknown

+ (d. tenth century): English saint.
Feast day: March 27.

## Almedha

Meaning: unknown

+ (d. sixth century): Welsh virgin and
martyr. Feast day: August 1.

*(Aled, Eiluned)*

## Alphonsa

Meaning: Italian "noble"

+ Alphonsa Muttathupandatu, Blessed
(d. 1946): Modern Indian saint.

## Amabilis

Meaning: Latin "beautiful"

+ (d.c. 634): Anglo-Saxon princess and
nun. Feast day: July 11.

## Amalberga

Meaning: Latin "industrious"

+ (d.c. 690): Mother of Sts. Emebert,
Gudula and Reineldis. Feast day:
July 10.

+ (d.c. 805): Miracle worker and virgin,
the one true love of Charlemagne.
Feast day: July 10.

*(Amelia)*

## Amanda

Meaning: feminine form of Amandus

## Amata

Meaning: Latin "loved"

+ (d.c. 1250): Niece of St. Clare of
Assisi. Feast day: February 20.

+ Amata, Blessed (d. 1270): Dominican nun in Rome. Feast day: June
10.

*(Amy, Amie)*

## Amelberga

Meaning: probably Latin "industrious"

+ (d.c. 690): Benedictine nun and
widow. Feast day: June 10.

+ (d.c. 772): Benedictine nun in Belgium. Feast day: July 10.

+ (d.c. 900): Dutch Benedictine abbess. Feast day: November 21.

# Amelia

See Amalberga, Emily

# Amy

See Amata

# Anastasia

Meaning: Greek "resurrection"

+ (d.c. 257): Martyr during the persecutions of Emperor Valerian. Feast day: October 28.

+ (d.c. 304): Martyr remembered in the second Mass celebrated on Christmas Day. Feast day: December 25.

+ Anastasia the Patrician (d. sixth century): Virgin hermitess. Feast day: March 10.

*(Anastasha, Anastashia, Anastassian, Anastyasya)*

# Anatolia

Meaning: feminine form of Anatol

+ (d.c. 250): Martyr on Lake Velino in Italy. Feast day: July 9.

# Andrea

Meaning: feminine form of Andrew

# Angela

Meaning: Latin "angel"

+ Angela of Foligno, Blessed (d. 1309): Third Order Franciscan and mystic. Feast day: January 4.

+ Angela Merici (d. 1540): Foundress of the Ursuline order and mystic. Feast day: January 27.

+ Angela Maria Truszkowska, Blessed (d. 1899): Foundress of the Felician Sisters.

+ Angela Salawa, Blessed (d. 1922): Polish Third Order Franciscan.

+ Angela Guerrero Gonzalez, Blessed (d. 1932): Foundress of the Company of the Cross.

*(Angela, Angelina, Angelia, Angelica, Angelika, Angelita, Angie)*

# Ann, Anna, Anne

Meaning: Hebrew "gracious"

+ Anne (biblical): Traditional name of the mother of the Blessed Virgin Mary. Patron of widows, pregnant women, plague victims, childless women, and nursemaids. Feast day: July 26.

+ Anna (biblical): Widow and prophetess who recognized the child Jesus (Luke 2:36-38). Feast day: September 1.

+ Anne (d. 820): Widow and monastic. Feast day: October 29.

+ Anne (d.c. 918): Hermitess. Feast day: July 23.

+ Anne Line (d. 1601): One of the Forty Martyrs of England and Wales. Feast day: February 27.

+ Anne of St. Bartholomew, Blessed (d. 1626): Carmelite mystic and secretary to St. Teresa of Ávila. Feast day: June 7.

+ Anna Monteagudo, Blessed (d. 1686): Dominican mystic of Peru.

+ Anne Jahouvey, Blessed (d. 1851): Missionary to French Guyana, Tahiti and Madagascar. Feast day: July 15.

*(Ana, Annabelle, Annette, Annie, Anita, Annika, Maura, Hannah, Nancy, Nina)*

# Annunciata

Meaning: Latin "the Annunciation"

+ Annunciata Cocchetti, Blessed (d. 1882): Foundress of the Sisters of St. Dorothy of Cemmo.

## Anstrudis

Meaning: unknown

+ (d. 688): French Benedictine abbess.
  Feast day: October 17.

*(Astrude)*

## Anthusa

Meaning: unknown

+ Anthusa the Younger (date unknown): Persian martyr. Feast day:
  August 27.

+ (d. eighth century): Abbess tortured
  by Byzantine Emperor Constantine
  V. Feast day: July 27.

## Antoinette

Meaning: feminine form of Anthony

+ Antoinette Roussel, Blessed (d.
  1794): Carmelite nun martyred during the French Revolution. Feast
  day: July 17.

## Antonia

Meaning: feminine form of Anthony

+ Antonia Mesina (d. 1935): Martyr for
  her chastity.

## Anysia

Meaning: unknown

+ (d. 304): Martyr of Greece. Feast
  day: December 30.

## Apollonia

Meaning: feminine form of Apollo

+ (d. 249): Martyr of Alexandria and the
  patron of dentists, often invoked
  against toothaches. Feast day: February 9.

## Apronia

Meaning: unknown

+ (d. fifth or sixth century): Nun. Feast
  day: July 15.

## Aquilina

Meaning: Latin "eagle"

+ (d. 293): Virgin martyr beheaded in
  Lebanon. Feast day: June 18.

## Arilda

Meaning: unknown

+ (date unknown): English virgin martyr. Feast day: October 30.

## Arthelais

Meaning: unknown

+ (d. sixth century): Virgin and patron
  of Benevento, Italy. Feast day: March
  3.

## Ascelina

Meaning: unknown

+ (d. 1195): Cistercian mystic and relative of St. Bernard. Feast day: August 23.

## Asella

Meaning: unknown

+ (d.c. 406): Virgin hermitess. Feast
  day: December 6.

## Asteria

Meaning: possibly from Latin "star"

+ (d.c. 307): Virgin martyr. Feast day:
  August 10.

## Athanasia

Meaning: female form of Athanasius

+ (d. 860): Greek widow and abbess.
  Feast day: August 14.

## Attracta

Meaning: unknown

+ (d. sixth century): Hermitess and colleague of St. Patrick. Feast day:
  August 11.

## Audrey

See Etheldreda

## Augusta

Meaning: feminine form of Augustus

+ (d. fifth century): Virgin martyr. Feast day: March 27.

## Aulaire, Aulazie

See Eulalia

## Aurea

Meaning: Latin "golden"

+ (d. 270): Italian martyr. Feast day: August 24.

+ (d. 666): Abbess of St. Martial in Paris. Feast day: October 4.

+ (d. eighth century): Abbess of Rouen. Feast day: October 6.

+ (d. 856): Widow and martyr of Spain. Feast day: July 19.

+ (d.c. 1069): Benedictine hermitess in the time of the Moors. Feast day: March 11.

*(Auriel, Auriol, Oriel)*

## Aurelia

Meaning: from Roman clan name "golden"

+ (date unknown): Virgin captured by the Saracens. Feast day: September 25.

+ (d. 1027): Austrian princess and hermitess. Feast day: October 15.

*(Auralia, Auarelea, Aureliana, Aurie, Aurielle, Aurilla)*

## Austreberta

Meaning: unknown

+ (d. 704): Benedictine abbess famed for her visions and miracles. Feast day: February 10.

*(Eustreberta)*

## Ava

Meaning: Hebrew "life"

+ (d.c. 850): Flemish Benedictine abbess. Feast day: April 29.

*(Eva, Avae, Ave, Eve)*

# B

## Bakhita

See Josephina Bakhita

## Balbina

Meaning: Latin "little stammerer"

+ (d.c. 130): Roman martyr. Feast day: March 31.

## Balda

Meaning: unknown

+ (d. late seventh century): Benedictine abbess. Feast day: December 9.

## Barbara

Meaning: Latin "foreign"

+ (d. fourth century): Legendary martyr, patron against sudden death. Feast day: December 4.

*(Babe, Babs, Bobbie, Babette)*

## Barbea

Meaning: unknown

+ (d. 101): Martyr. Feast day: January 29.

## Basilissa

Meaning: Feminine form of Basil

+ (d.c. 68): Martyr and disciple of Sts. Peter and Paul. Feast day: April 15.

+ (d.c. 303): Martyr of Nicomedia. Feast day: September 3.

## Basilla

Meaning: Feminine form of Basil

+ (d. 304): Roman martyr under Emperor Diocletian. Feast day: May 20.

+ (date unknown): Virgin and martyr at Smyrna in modern Turkey. Feast day: August 29.

## Bassa

Meaning: unknown

+ (date unknown): Virgin martyred in Carthage. Feast day: August 10.

+ (d. 304): Martyr, wife of a pagan priest. Feast day: August 21.

## Bathildis

Meaning: Old German "battle maid"

+ (d. 680): Wife of King Clovis II. Feast day: January 30.

## Baya

Meaning: unknown

+ (d. fifth century): Hermitess of Scotland. Feast day: November 2.

## Beatrix

Meaning: Latin "happy"

+ Beatrix da Silva (d. 1490): Portuguese Cistercian abbess. Feast day: August 16.

*(Bea, Beatrice, Beattie, Beatty, Trixie, Trissie)*

## Bega, Begga

Meaning: Greek "the bee's head"

+ Bega (d. seventh century): Irish princess and hermitess. Feast day: October 31.

+ Begga (d. 698): Benedictine nun. Feast day: December 17.

## Belina

Meaning: possibly from Spanish "lovely"

+ (d. 1135): French virgin martyr. Feast day: February 19.

## Belle

See Isabel

## Benedicta

Meaning: feminine form of Benedict

+ (date unknown): Virgin and martyr. Feast day: October 8.

+ (d. sixth century): Mystic and nun. Feast day: May 6.

+ (d. tenth century): French princess and abbess. Feast day: August 17.

## Benildis

Meaning: unknown

+ (d. 853): Spanish martyr. Feast day: June 15.

## Berlinda

Meaning: Latin "good and kind"

+ (d. 702): Flemish hermitess. Feast day: February 3.

## Bernadette

Meaning: feminine form of Bernard

+ Bernadette Soubirous (d. 1879): Visionary of Lourdes. Feast day: April 16.

*(Bernardette, Bernardina, Bernette, Bernie)*

## Bertha

Meaning: Old German "bright"

+ (d. 612): First Christian queen of England.

+ (d. 680): French abbess and martyr. Feast day: May 1.

+ (d.c. 725): Widow and Benedictine abbess. Feast day: July 4.

+ (d.c. 840): Widow. Feast day: May 15.

## Bertilia

Meaning: Latin "kind and shy"

+ (d.c. 687): Virgin and hermitess. Feast day: January 3.

## Bertilla

Meaning: Latin "kind and shy"

+ (d.c. 705): French Benedictine abbess. Feast day: November 5.

+ Bertilla Boscardin (d. 1922): Nun. Feast day: October 20.

## Bess, Beth, Bettina, Betty

See Elizabeth

## Bibiana

Meaning: Latin "lively"

+ (d. fourth century): Martyr. Feast day: December 2.

*(Vivian)*

## Bilhild

Meaning: unknown

+ (d.c. 710): German Benedictine abbess. Feast day: November 27.

## Blaesilla

Meaning: unknown

+ (d. 383): Widow and disciple of St. Jerome. Feast day: January 22.

## Blanche

See Gwen

## Blath

Meaning: unknown

+ (d. 523): Cook in St. Brigid's convent. Feast day: January 29.

*(Flora)*

## Boleslawa

Meaning: unknown

+ Boleslawa Maria Lament, Blessed (d. 1946): Polish woman who worked for unity between Orthodox and Catholics.

## Bolonia

Meaning: unknown

+ (d. 362): Young virgin martyr. Feast day: October 16.

## Breaca

Meaning: unknown

+ (d. fifth or sixth century): Disciple of St. Brigid. Feast day: June 4.

*(Branca, Branka, Breque)*

## Brenda

Meaning: feminine form of Brendan

## Briana

Meaning: feminine form of Brian

## Brigid

Meaning: Gaelic "the high one"

+ (d. fifth century): English princess murdered on pilgrimage. Feast day: January 28.

+ (d. 525): Patroness of Ireland. Feast day: February 1.

+ (d. ninth century): Sister of St. Andrew of Donatus. Feast day: February 1.

+ Brigid of Sweden (d. 1373): Wife and Swedish princess. Patron of Sweden. Feast day: July 23.

*(Biddie, Birdie, Birgit, Birgitta, Bittan, Bridget, Brigida, Bride, Brighde, Bridie, Brighid, Brigitta, Brigitte, Brigit, Brita, Britta, Britt)*

## Brigida
Meaning: Gaelic "the high one"

+ Brigida of Jesus Morello (d. 1679): Mystic, prophet and foundress of the Ursuline Sisters of Mary.

## Buriana
Meaning: unknown

+ (d. sixth century): Irish hermitess. Feast day: June 4.

# C

## Caesarea, Caesaria
Meaning: feminine form of Caesarius

+ Caesarea (date unknown): Virgin recluse. Feast day: May 15.

+ Caesaria (d.c. 530): Abbess. Feast day: January 12.

## Caitlin
See Catherine

## Callinica
Meaning: unknown

+ (d. 250): Martyr of Galatia (now Turkey). Feast day: March 22.

## Camilla
Meaning: Italian "evergreen"

+ (d.c. 437): Italian recluse. Feast day: March 3.

*(Cam, Camelia, Camellia, Camille, Cammie, Cammy)*

## Candida
Meaning: Latin "white"

+ (date unknown): Roman martyr. Feast day: August 29.

+ (date unknown): Martyred virgin under Emperor Maximian. Feast day: September 20.

+ (date unknown): English martyr. Feast day: June 1.

+ Candida the Elder (d.c. 78): Convert of St. Peter. Feast day: September 4.

+ Candida the Younger (d.c. 586): Miracle worker, wife and mother. Feast day: September 10.

+ (d.c. 798): Mother of St. Memerius, hermitess. Feast day: January 27.

+ Cándida Maria of Jesus Cpiitria y Barriola, Blessed (d. 1912): Visionary and foundress of the Daughters of Jesus.

*(Candace, Candice, Candy, Candyce, Kandace, Kandise, Kandy)*

## Cannera
Meaning: unknown

+ (d.c. 530): Irish hermitess. Feast day: January 28.

## Capitolina
Meaning: unknown

+ (d. 304): Martyr under Emperor Diocletian. Feast day: October 27.

# Carissima

Meaning: Latin "most loved"

+ (d. fifth century): French nun. Feast day: September 7.

# Caroline

Meaning: feminine form of Charles

+ Caroline Kozka, Blessed (d. 1914): Virgin, martyr under communism.

# Catherine

Meaning: Greek "pure"

+ Catherine of Alexandria (d.c. 310): Mystical martyr who appeared in a vision to St. Joan of Arc. Invoked against diseases of the head and tongue, assistance in drowning, and harvests. Feast day: November 25.

+ Catherine of Siena (d. 1380): Doctor of the Church, Dominican mystic, and papal advisor. Feast day: April 29.

+ Catherine of Sweden (d. 1381): Cofoundress of the Brigittines and daughter of St. Brigid of Sweden. Feast day: March 24.

+ Catherine of Bologna (d. 1463): Mystic, Poor Clare nun, patron of artists. Feast day: March 9.

+ Catherine of Genoa (d. 1510): Mystic, wife, and hospital director. Feast day: September 15.

+ Catherine Tomas (d. 1574): Augustinian mystic. Feast day: April 5.

+ Catherine dei Ricci (d. 1590): Mystic and counselor to future popes. Feast day: February 2.

+ Catherine, Blessed (d. 1622): Japanese widowed martyr. Feast day: September 10.

+ Catherine Tanaka, Blessed (d. 1626): Martyr of Japan. Feast day: July 12.

+ Catherine Jarrige, Blessed (d. 1836): Saint of the French revolution.

+ Catherine Labouré (d. 1876): Mystic and saint of the Miraculous Medal. Feast day: November 28.

*(Caitlin, Caitrona, Caren, Carin, Caron, Catarine, Catherine, Catherina, Catheryn, Cathleen, Cathrene, Cathrine, Catrine, Catrina, Catherleen, Catrin, Kaitlin, Karen, Kari, Kate, Katharine, Katharyn, Kathilnes, Katheryn, Kathleen, Katrena, Katriona, Katryna, Kattrina, Kerry, Kitty)*

# Cecilia

Meaning: Latin "blind"

+ (d. second or third century): Noble Roman woman, virgin, martyr. Patronness of musicians. Feast day: November 22.

*(Cacelia, Caecilia, Cece, Cecelia, Cecilea, Cecillia, Celia)*

# Ceinwen

See Keyna

# Cera

Meaning: unknown

+ (d. seventh century): Irish abbess. Feast day: January 5.

*(Ceara, Ciar, Cior, Cyra)*

# Charitina

Meaning: English "benevolent"

+ (d.c. 304): Virgin martyr under Emperor Diocletian. Feast day: October 5.

# Charity

Meaning: the virtue of charity

+ Legendary daughter of St. Sophia, martyred with her sisters, Faith and

Hope. Feast day: August 1.

## Charlotte
Meaning: feminine form of Charles

## Chiara
Meaning: Italian "clear"

+ Chiara Bossatta de Pianello, Blessed (d. 1887): Italian nun.

## Chloe
Meaning: Greek "blooding"

+ (biblical): Early Christian leader mentioned by St. Paul. (1 Corinthians 1:11).

## Chelidonia
Meaning: unknown

+ (d. 1152): Benedictine hermitess. Feast day: October 13.

## Christiana
Meaning: feminine form of Christian

+ (d. seventh century): Patron saint of Termonde in Belgium. Feast day: July 24.

## Christina
Meaning: feminine form of Christian

+ (date unknown): Persian martyr. Feast day: March 13.

+ (d. third century): Roman martyr. Feast day: July 24.

+ (d. 1160): English Benedictine recluse. Feast day: December 5.

+ (d. 1224): Mystic, called "the Astonishing." Feast day: July 24.

*(Christiana, Christiann, Christie, Christine, Christen, Christien, Crystal, Kristine, Kristin, Tina)*

## Cilinia
Meaning: unknown

+ (d.c. 458): Mother of Sts. Principius and Remigius. Feast day: October 21.

## Cinnia
Meaning: possibly from the Irish "ancient"

+ (d. fifth century): Irish princess converted by St. Patrick. Feast day: February 1.

## Clare
Meaning: Latin "bright"

+ Clare of Assisi (d. 1253): Foundress of the Franciscan Poor Clares, mystic, and patron of television, the blind, laundry women, embroiderers, gilders, glaziers, and glass painters. Feast day: August 11.

+ Clare of Montefalco (d. 1308): Abbess and mystic, also known as Clare of the Cross. Feast day: August 17.

+ Clare Shamada, Blessed (d. 1622): Japanese martyr. Feast day: September 10.

*(Clara, Claire, Clair, Clarette, Clarina, Clarinda, Clarita)*

## Claudia
Meaning: Feminine form of Claudius

+ (d. first century): Mother of Pope Linus. Feast day: August 7.

*(Claudeen, Claudette)*

## Cleopatra
Meaning: Greek "fame of her father"

+ (d. 319): Widow in ancient Palestine. Feast day: October 19.

*(Cleo, Clio, Cliopatra)*

## Clementina

Meaning: feminine form of Clement

## Clotilde

Meaning: Old German "loud battle"

+ (d. 545): Queen of the Franks and wife of Clovis. Feast day: June 3.

*(Clotilda)*

## Cocca

Meaning: possibly from Spanish "coconut"

+ (date unknown): Irish patroness. Feast day: June 6.

*(Coco, Cocco, Coccoa)*

## Cocha

Meaning: unknown

+ (d. sixth century): Nurse and abbess. Feast day: June 29.

## Cointha

Meaning: Latin "fifth"

+ (d. 249): Martyr of Alexandria, Egypt. Feast day: February 8.

*(Quinta)*

## Colette

Meaning: French feminine form of Nicholas

+ (d. 1447): Poor Clare and friend of St. Vincent Ferrer. Feast day: March 6 or February 7.

## Columba

Meaning: Latin "dove"

+ (date unknown): English martyr. Feast day: November 13.

+ Columba of Sens (d. 273): Spanish martyr of noble descent. Feast day: December 31.

+ (d. 853): Spanish virgin and martyr of Córdoba. Feast day: September 17.

+ Colomba Joanna Gabriel, Blessed (d. 1926): Disciple of Blessed Hyacinth Cormier.

## Connat

Meaning: unknown

+ (d. 590): Abbess of St. Brigid's convent at Kildare, Ireland. Feast day: January 1.

## Crispina

Meaning: feminine form of Crispin

+ (d. 304): Wife, mother, martyr. Feast day: December 5.

## Crystal

See Christina

## Cuthburga

Meaning: possibly Anglo-Saxon "brilliant"

+ (d.c. 725): English princess and abbess. Feast day: August 31.

## Cyra

See Cera

## Cyrenia

Meaning: unknown

+ (d. 306): Martyr under Emperor Galerius. Feast day: November 1.

## Cyriaca

Meaning: unknown

+ (d. 249): Roman widow and martyr. Feast day: August 21.

## Cyrilla

Meaning: feminine form of Cyril

+ (d.c. 270): Martyred virgin. Feast day: October 28.

+ (d.c. 300): Martyred widow of Cyrene (modern Libya). Feast day: July 5.

# D

## Daniela, Danielle

Meaning: feminine form of Daniel

## Darerca

Meaning: unknown

+ (d. fifth century): Sister of St. Patrick. Feast day: March 22.

## Deborah

Meaning: Hebrew "swarm of bees"

+ (biblical): Prophetess and judge of Israel (Judges 4: 4).

*(Debbie, Debbora, Debborah, Debora, Deborrah, Debra)*

## Deidre

See Ita

## Demetria

Meaning: Greek "plentiful"

+ (d. 363): Reportedly the sister of St. Bibiana. Feast day: June 21.

*(Demetra, Demitra)*

## Denise

Meaning: feminine form of Denis

## Devota

Meaning: probably from Latin "devoted"

+ (d. 303): Virgin martyr, patron of Monaco and Corsica. Feast day: January 27.

## Diana

Meaning: Latin "divine"

+ (d.c. 1236): Dominican nun. Feast day: June 10.

*(Deane, Deanna, Deanne, Deann, Dianah, Diane, Dianne, Dianna, Diania, Diandre, Dyan, Dyann, Dyana, Dyanne)*

## Digna

Meaning: unknown

+ (d.c. 259): Roman martyr. Feast day: September 22.

+ (d. fourth century): Italian virgin hermitess. Feast day: August 11.

+ (d. 853): Nun and martyr. Feast day: June 14.

## Dina

Meaning: Hebrew "God has vindicated"

+ Dina Belanger, Blessed (d. 1929): Canadian mystic.

*(Dinah, Dyna, Dynah)*

## Dominica

Meaning: feminine form of Dominic

+ (date unknown): Martyr during the reign of Emperor Diocletian. Feast day: July 6.

+ Dominica Ongata, Blessed (d. 1622): Japanese martyr. Feast day: September 10.

*(Dominique)*

## Domnina

Meaning: unknown

+ (d. 269): Martyred with St. Valentine. Feast day: April 14.

+ (d.c. 310): Martyred with her daughters. Feast day: October 4.

## Dorcas
See Tabetha

## Dorothy
Meaning: Greek "gift of God"

+ (d. early fourth century): Martyr and virgin. Feast day: February 6.

+ Dorothy of Montau (d. 1394): Polish widow and hermitess. Feast day: October 30.

*(Dolly, Doretha, Dorethea, Dorothea, Dorothée, Dorthea, Dorthy, Dot, Dothy, Dotty)*

## Dula
Meaning: unknown

+ (date unknown): Virgin martyr at Nicomedia in Asia Minor. Feast day: March 25.

## Dymphna
Meaning: unknown

+ (d. mid-seventh century): Patron of those suffering insanity, nervous breakdowns, and epilepsy. Feast day: May 15.

# E

## Ebba
Meaning: Hebrew "giving"

+ (d. 683): Scottish princess, foundress of a monastery and a convent. Feast day: August 25.

+ (d.c. 870): English abbess martyred by Danes. Feast day: August 23.

## Edana
Meaning: Irish "ardent flame"

+ (date unknown): Patron of several parishes in western Ireland. Feast day: July 5.

## Edburga
Meaning: unknown

+ (d. seventh century): English Benedictine nun. Feast day: December 13.

+ Edburga of Bicester (d. seventh century): English nun. Feast day: July 18.

+ (d. 751): Benedictine abbess and noted calligrapher. Feast day: December 12.

+ Edburga of Winchester (d. 960): English abbess and granddaughter of Alfred the Great. Feast day: June 15.

## Edith
Meaning: Old English "rich-war"

+ Edith of Polesworth (d.c. 926): Widow, queen, Benedictine abbess. Feast day: July 15.

+ Edith of Wilton (d. 984): Benedictine nun raised in Wilton Abbey from infancy. Feast day: September 16.

+ Edith Stein, (d. 1942): Philosopher, spiritual writer, and convert from Judaism who died at Auschwitz. Also known as Sister Teresa Benedicta of the Cross in Carmel. Feast day: August 9.

*(Edie)*

## Edna
Meaning: Hebrew "delight"

+ (biblical): Mother-in-law of Tobias (Tobit 7).

## Edwen

Meaning: feminine form of Edwin

+ (d. seventh century): Welsh patron. Feast day: November 6.

*(Edweena, Edwina, Edwyn, Edwyna)*

## Eileen

See Helen

## Eiluned

See Almedha

## Elfleda

Meaning: unknown

+ (d. 714): Sister of King Oswy of Northumbria, England. Feast day: February 8.

+ (d.c. 936): Anglo-Saxon princess Feast day: October 23.

+ (d.c. 1000): Benedictine abbess. Feast day: October 29.

*(Edifleda, Elfeda, Elgiva, Ethelfleda)*

## Elgiva

Meaning: unknown

+ (d. 944): Queen and mother of Edgar, King of England. Feast day: May 18.

## Elined

Meaning: unknown

+ (date unknown): Welsh virgin and martyr. Feast day: August 1.

## Elizabeth

Meaning: Hebrew "oath of God"

+ (biblical): Mother of John the Baptist and cousin of Mary, the mother of Jesus (Luke 1). Feast day: November 5.

+ Elizabeth Rose (d. 1130): French Benedictine abbess. Feast day: December 13.

+ Elizabeth of Schönau (d. 1164): Benedictine abbess and mystic. Feast day: June 18.

+ Elizabeth of Hungary (d. 1231): Queen of Hungary, renowned for her charity and deep spirituality. Feast day: November 17.

+ Elizabeth of Portugal (d. 1336): Queen of Portugal and Franciscan tertiary, also called Isabella. Feast day: July 4.

+ Elizabeth of Hungary, the Younger (d. 1338): Daughter of King Andrew III of Hungary. Feast day: May 6.

+ Elizabeth Ann Seton (d. 1821): First American-born saint, founder of the Sisters of Charity. Feast day: January 4.

+ Elizabeth Canori Mora, Blessed (d. 1825): Patroness of abused wives.

+ Elizabeth Rienzi, Blessed (d. 1859): Foundress of the Sisters of Our Lady of Sorrows.

+ Elizabeth Vendramini, Blessed (d. 1860): Foundress of the Franciscan Tertiary Sisters of St. Elizabeth.

+ Elizabeth of the Trinity Catez Rolland (d. 1903): Carmelite nun and mystical writer.

*(Bess, Bessi, Beta, Beth, Bettina, Betty, Elsa, Elise, Eliza, Elsie, Elspeth, Elspet, Ilse, Isabel, Libby, Lisbeth, Lisa, Liz, Liza, Liese, Lisette)*

## Elaine, Ellen

See Helen

## Emiliana

Meaning: Latin "eager"

+ (d.c. 550): Mystic and aunt of Pope St. Gregory the Great. Feast day: January 5.

# Emily

Meaning: German "industrious"

+ Emily de Rodat (d. 1852): Foundress of the Congregation of the Holy Family of Villefranche. Feast day: September 19.

+ Emily de Vialar (d. 1856): Foundress of the Sisters of St. Joseph of the Apparition. Feast day: June 17.

+ Emilie d'Outremont d'Hoogvorst, Blessed (d. 1876): Wife of Belgian nobleman and foundress of the Congregation of St. Mary Reparatrix.

*(Amelia, Emiley, Emile, Emiley, Emilie, Emilly, Emylee)*

# Ermelinda

Meaning: unknown

+ (d. 595): Belgian hermitess. Feast day: October 29.

# Ermenberga

Meaning: unknown

+ (d.c. 700): Wife of an early English king. Feast day: November 19.

# Ermengild

Meaning: unknown

+ (d.c. 700): English queen and Benedictine nun. Feast day: February 13.

# Emma

See Gemma, Imma

# Esther

Meaning: Persian "star"

+ (biblical): Heroine of the story of Purim (Book of Esther).

*(Esta, Estelle, Estella, Hadassah)*

# Ethel

Meaning: Old English "noble"

+ Ethelburga (d.c. 647): Wife of King St. Edwin of Northumbria, England. Feast day: April 5.

+ Ethelburga (d.c. 664): English abbess of Farmoutiers-en-Brie, France. Feast day: July 7.

+ Ethelburga (d. 675): Benedictine abbess. Feast day: October 11.

+ Etheldreda (d. 679): Benedictine abbess and popular Anglo-Saxon saint. Feast day: June 23.

+ Ethelgiva (d. 896): Daughter of King Alfred the Great. Feast day: December 9.

+ Etheldwitha (d. 903): Widowed queen of King Alfred the Great of England. Feast day: July 20.

# Ethenea

Meaning: unknown

+ (d. 433): One of the first converts of St. Patrick. Feast day: January 11.

# Eugenia

Meaning: feminine form of Eugene

+ (d.c. 257): Roman martyr. Feast day: December 25.

+ (d. 735): Benedictine abbess. Feast day: September 16.

+ Eugénie Joubert, Blessed (d. 1904): French nun.

# Eulalia

Meaning: Greek "sweet spoken"

+ (d.c. 304): Martyr of Barcelona, Spain. Feast day: February 12.

+ (d.c. 304): Martyr of Merida, Spain. Feast day: December 10.

*(Aulaire, Aulazie, Ollala)*

## Eunice

Meaning: Greek "fine victory"

+ (biblical): Mother of St. Timothy (Acts 16: 1).

## Euphemia

Meaning: Greek "well spoken"

+ (d.c. 303): Martyred virgin. Feast day: September 16.

*(Ephie, Eufemia, Euphan, Euphen, Euphie, Fanny, Phemi)*

## Euphrasia

Meaning: from the Greek "spoken"

+ (d.c. 420): Noble Roman who became a nun. Feast day: March 13.

+ Euphrasia Pelletier (d. 1868): Disciple of St. John Eudes. Feast day: April 24.

## Eusebia

Meaning: unknown

+ (d. third century): Martyred virgin. Feast day: October 29.

+ (d.c. 680): Benedictine abbess. Feast day: March 16.

+ (d.c. 731): French Benedictine abbess. Feast day: September 20.

## Eustolia

Meaning: unknown

+ (d. seventh century): Daughter of Emperor Maurice of Constantinople (modern Istanbul, Turkey). Feast day: November 9.

## Eutropia

Meaning: unknown

+ (d. fifth century): French widow. Feast day: September 15.

## Eve

Meaning: Hebrew "life"

+ (biblical): First woman, wife of Adam (Genesis 4:1).

*(Eva, Evah, Evie, Hava)*

## Everild

Meaning: Old English "boar-battle"

+ (d. seventh century): English Benedictine abbess. Feast day: July 9.

# F

## Fabiola

Meaning: Latin "woman of good works"

+ (d. 399): Roman widow and friend of St. Jerome. Feast day: December 27.

## Faith

Meaning: the virtue of faith

+ (date unknown) Legendary daughter of St. Sophia, martyred with sisters, Hope and Charity. Feast day: August 1.

+ (d. third century): French virgin martyr. Feast day: October 6.

*(Fay)*

## Fanchea

Meaning: possibly from Old German "independence"

+ (d. 585): Irish abbess. Feast day: January 1.

# Fanny

See Euphemia, Frances

# Fausta

Meaning: Latin "lucky"

+ (d. third century): Mother of St. Anastasia of Sirmium, Serbia. Feast day: December 19.

# Febronia

Meaning: unknown

+ (d. 304): Martyred nun of Nisibis, Mesopotamia (modern Turkey). Feast day: June 25.

# Felicitas

Meaning: Latin "lucky"

+ (d. ninth century): Italian nun. Feast day: March 26.

# Felicity

Meaning: Latin "lucky"

+ (d. 165): Roman slave martyred with St. Perpetua. Mentioned in the first Eucharistic Prayer. Feast day: November 23.

# Filomena

See Philomena

# Flora

Meaning: Latin "flower"

+ (d. 856): Spanish martyr. Feast day: November 24.

*(Fleur, Flo, Florann, Florella, Florette, Florentina, Florie, Florine, Florise, Florrie, Flory, Floss)*

# Florentina

Meaning: Spanish form of Flora

+ (d.c. 636): Spanish abbess. Feast day: June 20.

# Florida

Meaning: Spanish "flowery"

+ Florida Cevoli, Blessed (d. 1767): Noblewoman and mystic.

# Foila

Meaning: unknown

+ (d. sixth century): Sister of St. Colgan, has shrine in Galway, Ireland. Feast day: March 3.

*(Faile)*

# Fortunata

Meaning: Old French "lucky"

+ (d. 303): Virgin martyr in ancient Palestine. Feast day: October 14.

# Franca

Meaning: uncertain, possibly variation of Frances

+ Franca Visalta (d. 1218): Cistercian nun. Feast day: April 26.

# Frances

Meaning: feminine form of Francis

+ Frances of Rome (d. 1440): Mystic and the patroness of motorists. Feast day: March 9.

+ Frances Bizzocca (d. 1627): Martyr of Japan. Feast day: August 17.

+ Frances Brideau, Blessed (d. 1794): Martyr in the French Revolution. Feast day: July 17.

+ Frances de Croissy (d. 1794): Martyr in the French Revolution. Feast day: July 17.

+ Frances Anne Carbonnell, Blessed (d. 1855): Founded religious community when she was 70.

+ Frances Xavier Cabrini (d. 1917): First American citizen to become a saint. Feast day: December 22.

*(Fanny, Fran, Francie, Francine,
Francisca, Frankie, Frannie, Franny)*

## Francisca

Meaning: Italian form of Francis

+ Francisca Salesai Aviat, Blessed (d.
1914): Foundress of Sister Oblates
of St. Francis de Sales.

## Fynifed

See Winifred

# G

## Galla

Meaning: Old Norse "singer"

+ (d.c. 550): Widowed Roman noblewoman. Feast day: October 5.

## Gaudentia

Meaning: unknown

+ (date unknown): Roman virgin martyr. Feast day: August 30.

## Geena, Gena, Gina

See Iphigenia, Regina

## Gemma

Meaning: feminine form of James

+ (d. 1045): Widow and Benedictine
nun. Feast day: June 29.

+ Gemma Galgani (d. 1903): Italian
mystic. Feast day: April 11.

*(Emma, Jemma, Jemima)*

## Geneviève

Meaning: Celtic "woman of the
people"

+ (d.c. 500): Patroness of the city of
Paris, France, Feast day: January 3.

*(Genevieve, Genavieve, Jenavieve)*

## Genoveva

Meaning: probably from French
"juniper tree"

+ Genoveva Torres Morales, Blessed
(d. 1956): Foundress of the Sisters
of the Sacred Heart of Jesus and the
Holy Angels in Valencia.

## Georgia

Meaning: feminine form of George

+ (d.c. 500): French virgin hermitess.
Feast day: February 15.

*(Georgeann, Georgeanna,
Georgeina, Georgena, Georgette,
Georgiana, Georgianna, Georgina)*

## Geraldine

Meaning: feminine form of Gerald

## Germana

Meaning: Latin "German woman"

+ Germana Cousin (d. 1201): Mystic
and daughter of a French farmer.
Feast day: June 15.

*(Germaine)*

## Gertrude

Meaning: Old German "spear-
strength"

+ Gertrude the Elder (d. 649): Widow
and Benedictine nun. Feast day:
December 6.

+ Gertrude of Nivelles (d. 659):
Benedictine abbess and mystic, a
patron of travelers and gardeners.
Feast day: March 17.

+ Gertrude of Remiremont (d.c. 690):
Benedictine abbess. Feast day: November 7.

+ Gertrude the Great of Helfta (d.c. 1302): Benedictine mystic, patron of the West Indies. Feast day: November 16.

+ Gertrude Catarina Comesali (d. 1903): Foundress of the Sisters of the Blessed Sacrament.

*(Gert, Gertie, Gerty, Trudi, Trudie, Trudy)*

## Ginnie
See Virginia

## Gladys
Meaning: Irish "princess"

+ (d. fifth century): Welsh wife of St. Gundleus and mother of St. Cadoc. Feast day: March 29.

*(Gladis, Gladness, Gladwys)*

## Glyceria
Meaning: unknown

+ (d.c. 177): Martyred virgin in Greece. Feast day: May 13.

## Godeleva
Meaning: unknown

+ (d. 1070): Martyred wife, strangled by her husband. Feast day: July 6.

## Gorgonia
Meaning: unknown

+ (d.c. 375): Daughter of St. Gregory Nazianzus the Elder and sister of St. Gregory Nazianzus the Younger. Feast day: December 9.

## Grata
Meaning: possibly English "pearl"

+ (d. fourth or eighth century): Italian holy woman. Feast day: May 1.

*(Greta)*

## Gretchen
See Margaret

## Guadalupe
Meaning: Spanish "from the valley of wolves," used in honor of Our Lady of Guadalupe

*(Guadulupe)*

## Gudelia
+ (d.c. 340): Persian martyr. Feast day: September 29.

## Gudula
Meaning: unknown

+ (d. 712): Patroness of Brussels, Belgium. Feast day: January 8.

## Gundelindis
Meaning: unknown

+ (d.c. 750): Benedictine abbess and daughter of a French duke. Feast day: March 28.

## Guinevra
See Winifred

## Gwen
Meaning: Welsh "fair"

+ (d. fifth century): Aunt of St. David of Wales. Feast day: October 18.

*(Blanche, Wenn)*

## Gwendoline
Meaning: Welsh "blessed ring"

+ (d. sixth century): Welsh saint. Feast day: October 18.

*(Gwen, Gwendolen, Gwendolene, Gwendolin, Gwendollyne, Gwendolyn, Gwendolynn, Gwendolynne, Gwennie)*

# Gwenfrewi
See Winifred

# Hadassah
See Esther

# Hannah
+ (biblical): Mother of Samuel (1 Sam 1: 1)

# Harriet
Meaning: feminine form of Henry

*(Hattie)*

# Hava
See Eve

# Hedwig
Meaning: German "struggle"

+ (d.c. 1243): Duchess and widow. Feast day: October 16.

+ Hedwig, Blessed (d. 1399): Queen of Poland. Feast day: February 28.

*(Hedy, Hedda, Hetta)*

# Heidi
See Adelaide

# Helen
Meaning: Greek "the bright one"

+ (d.c. 418): Martyred virgin. Feast day: May 22.

+ Helen of Skövde (d.c. 1160): Martyred noblewoman of Sweden. Feast day: July 31.

*(Elaine, Eileen, Ellen, Halina, Haleena, Halena, Helena, Hélène, Hellen, Lena, Pamela)*

# Helena
Meaning: Greek "the bright one"

+ (d. 330): Empress mother of Constantine the Great and discoverer of the true Cross. Feast day: August 18.

+ (d.c. 750): German Benedictine abbess. Feast day: June 20.

# Hereswitha
Meaning: unknown

+ (d.c. 690): Benedictine nun and English princess. Feast day: September 3.

# Herlindis
Meaning: unknown

+ (d.c. 745): Benedictine abbess in Belgium. Feast day: October 12.

# Hermione
Meaning: Greek derivative of Hermes "messenger of the gods"

+ (d.c. 117): Martyr of Ephesus (modern Turkey), daughter of Philip, the deacon, mentioned in Acts 21:9. Feast day: September 4.

*(Hermia)*

# Hia
See Ia

# Hieu
Meaning: unknown

+ (d.c. 657): English abbess. Feast day: September 2.

# Hilaria
Meaning: Latin "cheerful"

+ (d.c. 304): Martyr and mother of St. Afra. Feast day: August 12.

*(Hilary, Hillary)*

## Hilda

Meaning: Old German "battle"

+ (d. 680): Benedictine abbess, daughter of an English king. Feast day: November 16.

*(Hilde, Hildy)*

## Hildegard

Meaning: Old German "war stronghold"

+ Hildegard of Bingen (d. 1179): Benedictine abbess and mystic called "the Sybil of the Rhine." Feast day: September 17.

*(Hildagard, Hildagarde)*

## Hildegund

Meaning: Old German derivative of "battle"

+ (d. 1183): Widow and nun. Feast day: February 6.

## Honorata

Meaning: Latin "woman of honor"

+ (d.c. 500): Italian nun. Feast day: January 11.

*(Honarah, Honner, Honnor, Honnour, Honoure, Honora, Honorina, Honorine, Honoure)*

## Honorina

Meaning: Latin "woman of honor"

+ (date unknown): French virgin. Feast day: February 27.

## Hope

Meaning: the virtue of hope.

+ (date unknown): Legendary daughter of St. Sophia, martyred with sisters, Faith and Charity. Feast day: August 1.

## Humbeline

Meaning: unknown

+ (d. 1135): Benedictine abbess and younger sister of St. Bernard of Clairvaux. Feast day: February 12.

## Humilitas

Meaning: Latin "humble"

+ (d. 1310): Mother and nun. Feast day: May 22.

## Hunegund

Meaning: unknown

+ (d.c. 690): Benedictine nun. Feast day: August 25.

## Hunna

Meaning: unknown

+ (d. 679): "The Holy Washerwoman" of France. Feast day: April 15.

## Hyacinth

Meaning: the "hyacinth" flower

+ (d. 1640): Franciscan tertiary. Feast day: January 30.

# I

## Ia

Meaning: unknown

+ (d. 360): Persian martyr. Feast day: August 4.

*(Hia)*

## Ida

Meaning: "youthful"

+ Ida of Herzfeld (d.c. 813): Widow and nun. Feast day: September 4.

*(Idaleena, Idarina)*

## Illuminata

Meaning: Latin "illuminated"

+ (d. 320): Italian virgin. Feast day: November 29.

## Ilse

See Elizabeth

## Imma

Meaning: Old German "all-embracing"

+ (d. mid-eighth century): Abbess. Feast day: November 25.

*(Emma, Ima)*

## Inez

See Agnes

## Iphigenia

Meaning: unknown

+ (d. first century): Ethiopian virgin. Feast day: September 21.

*(Geena, Gena)*

## Irais

Meaning: unknown

+ (d.c. 300): Egyptian martyr. Feast day: September 22.

*(Rhais)*

## Irene

Meaning: Greek "peace"

+ (d. 304): Martyred virgin. Feast day: April 5.

*(Irena, Iryna)*

## Irmina

Meaning: Old German "whole" or "universal"

+ (d. 708): Benedictine abbess. Feast day: December 24.

## Isabel

Meaning: Spanish form of Elizabeth

+ Isabel Fernandez, Blessed (d. 1622): Martyr of Japan. Feast day: September 10.

*(Belle, Ibbie, Isa, Isabell, Isabella, Isabelle, Isobel, Isobell, Isobelle, Izabelle, Izabel, Tibby)*

## Isberga

Meaning: unknown

+ (d.c. 800): Benedictine nun and traditionally considered a sister of Charlemagne. Feast day: May 21.

## Isidora

Meaning: Feminine form of Isidore

+ (d. 365): Nun and hermitess of Egypt. Feast day: May 1.

## Ita

Meaning: Old Irish "thirst"

+ (d.c. 570): Born of royal lineage, established school for young boys, including St. Brendan. Feast day: January 15.

*(Deidre, Mida, Ytha)*

# J

## Jacqueline

Meaning: feminine form of French Jacques (James)

# Jane

Meaning: feminine form of John

+ Jane de Lestonnac (d. 1640): Foundress of the Sisters of Notre Dame of Bordeaux. Feast day: February 2.

+ Jane Frances de Chantal (d. 1641): Foundress of the Order of the Visitation and close friend of St. Francis de Sales. Feast day: December 12.

+ Jane Delanoue (d. 1732): Foundress of the Sisters of St. Anne. Feast day: August 16.

+ Jane Gerard, Blessed (d. 1794): French nun and martyr. Feast day: June 26.

+ Jane-Louise Barré and Jane-Reiné Prin, Blesseds (d. 1794): Ursuline nuns and martyrs. Feast day: October 17.

+ Jane Antide Thouret (d. 1828): Foundress of the Institute of the Daughters of Charity. Feast day: August 24.

+ Jane-Elizabeth Bichier des Ages (d. 1832): Foundress of the Congregation of the Daughters of the Cross. Feast day: August 26.

*(Jaine, Janell, Janelle, Janene, Janessa, Janet, Janetta, Janice, Janina, Janine, Janis, Janise, Janita, Janna, Jayne, Jennette, Jennie, Jenny, Jonet, Jess, Jessica, Jessie)*

# Jemma

See Gemma

# Jemina

Meaning: Hebrew "dove"

+ (biblical): Daughter of Job (Job 42:14).

# Jenavieve

See Genevieve, Gemma

# Jessica, Jessie

See Jane

# Joan

Meaning: feminine form of John

+ Joan of Arc (d. 1431): French peasant girl who heard voices that told her to lead the French army to resist the English. Also called the Maid of Orléans, she is the patron of France. Feast day: May 30.

+ Joan of Valois (d. 1504): French queen. Feast day: February 4.

*(Joana, Joanelle, Jo-Ann, JoAnna, Joanne, Joeanne, Johanna, Joni, Joey, Jo)*

# Joanna

Meaning: feminine form of John

+ (biblical): Wife of Chuza, steward of King Herod Antipas of Galilee (Luke 24:10). Feast day: May 24.

+ Joanna Bereta Molla, Blessed (d. 1962): Native of Brazil, physician, wife, mother.

# Joaquina

Meaning: Portugese "God is my salvation"

+ Joaquina de Mas Vedruna (d. 1854): Widow and mystic. Feast day: May 19.

*(Joaquin, Jocquin, Juquin)*

# Josepha

Meaning: feminine form of Joseph

+ Josepha Naval Girbes, Blessed (d. 1893): Third Order Carmelite and mystic.

*(Josephine, Jo, Joey, Josee, Joselle, Josephina, Josetta, Josey, Josie)*

## Josephina

Meaning: feminine form of Joseph

+ Josephina Bakhita, Blessed (d. 1947): Save from Sudan, became a Canassian Sister.

+ Josephine Gabriella Bonino, Blessed (d. 1906): Foundress of Sisters of the Holy Family.

+ Josephine Vannini (d. 1911): Foundress of Daughters of St. Camillus.

## Jucunda

Meaning: unknown

+ (d. 466): Italian virgin. Feast day: November 25.

## Judith

Meaning: Hebrew "praise"

+ (biblical): Heroine who beheaded Holofernes and saved the Israelites (Book of Judith).

+ (d. ninth century): Benedictine anchoress. Feast day: June 29.

*(Judy, Judi, Judie)*

## Julia

Meaning: feminine form of Julius

+ (biblical): Woman mentioned among the "saints" of Rome by St. Paul (Romans 16:15).

+ Julia of Troyes (d.c. 272): French martyr. Feast day: July 21.

+ (d.c. 300): Martyr. Feast day: October 7.

+ Julia of Mérida (d.c. 304): Spanish martyr. Feast day: December 10.

+ (d. fifth century): Virgin and martyr. Feast day: May 22.

+ Julia of Billiart (d. 1816): Foundress of the Sisters of Notre Dame. Feast day: April 8.

*(Julee, Juleen, Jullette, Juli, Julliana, Jullianna, Juliane, Juliann, Julie, Juliet, Julieta, Juliette, Julilla, Julina, Juline, Julisa, Julissa)*

## Juliana

Meaning: feminine form of Julius

+ Juliana of Cumae (d.c. 305): Italian virgin martyr. Feast day: February 16.

+ Juliana of Bologna (d. 435): Single mother. Feast day: February 7.

+ Juliana of Pavilly (d.c. 750): French Benedictine abbess. Feast day: October 11.

+ Juliana Falconieri (d. 1341): Foundress of the Servite Nuns, also called the Mantellates. Feast day: June 19.

+ Juliana of Norwich, Blessed (d.c. 1423): Benedictine English mystic, usually called Julian. Feast day: May 13.

## Juliette

Meaning: Italian form of Julia

+ Juliette Verolot, Blessed (d. 1794): French Carmelite martyr. Feast day: July 17.

## Julitta

Meaning: diminute form of Julia

+ (d.c. 303): Martyr in Cappadocia, in modern Turkey. Feast day: July 30.

## Justa

Meaning: feminine form of Justus

+ (d. 287): Potter, martyr, patron of Seville, Spain. Feast day: July 19.

## Justina

Meaning: feminine form of Justus

+ (date unknown): Martyr in

Constantinople. Feast day: November 30.

+ (d.c. 300): Virgin martyr. Feast day: October 7.

## Juthware

Meaning: unknown

+ (d. seventh century): English virgin and martyr. Feast day: July 1.

## Jutta

Meaning: Latin "spiritual friend"

+ (d.c. 1260): German widow and noblewoman. Feast day: May 5.

*(Juta)*

# K

## Kahenta

See Kateri

## Kandace

See Candida

## Kateri

Meaning: Native American form of Katherine

+ Kateri Tekakwitha, Blessed (d. 1680): Native American mystic, called "The Lily of the Mohawks." Feast day: April 17.

*(Kahenta)*

## Kathleen

See Catherine

## Katherine

Meaning: Greek "pure"

+ Katherine Marie Drexel, (d. 1955): Foundress of the Sisters of the Blessed Sacrament and Xavier University, New Orleans. Missionary to Native Americans and Blacks in North America. Feast day: March 3.

## Kennera

Meaning: unknown

+ (d. fourth century): Scottish virgin martyr. Feast day: October 29.

## Kennocha

Meaning: unknown

+ (d. 1007): Scottish nun. Feast day: March 25.

## Kentigerna

Meaning: unknown

+ (d. 734): Widow and hermitess. Feast day: January 7.

## Keyna

Meaning: unknown

+ (d. fifth century): Welsh virgin. Feast day: October 18.

*(Ceinwen)*

## Kiara

Meaning: unknown

+ (d.c. 680): Irish virgin, became a religious under St. Fintan. Feast day: January 5 and October 16.

## Kigwe

Meaning: unknown

+ (date unknown): Welsh saint. Feast day: February 8.

## Kinga

Meaning: unknown

+ (d. 1292): Polish princess, wife. Feast day: July 24.

## Kinnia

Meaning: unknown

+ (d. fifth century): Irish convert of St. Patrick. Feast day: February 1.

## Kioga

See Kinga

## Kitty

See Catherine

## Kristin

See Christina

## Kummernis

See Wilgefortis

## Kyneburga

Meaning: Gaelic "intelligence"

+ (d.c. 680): English abbess. Feast day: March 6.

## Kyneswide

Meaning: Gaelic "intelligence"

+ (d.c. 680): English abbess. Feast day: March 6.

# L

## Landrada

Meaning: unknown

+ (d.c. 690): Benedictine abbess. Feast day: July 8.

## Lasar

Meaning: unknown

+ (d. sixth century): Irish virgin. Feast day: March 29.

## Laura

Meaning: Latin "laurel"

+ (d. 864): Spanish martyr. Feast day: October 19.

+ Laura Vicuña (d. 1904): Chilean martyr for chastity.

*(Laurel, Laureen, Laurentia, Lauricia, Laurina, Laurine, Lorah, Lori, Lora, Lorene, Loretta)*

## Leah

Meaning: Hebrew "weariness" or Latin "lion"

+ (biblical): Jacob's first wife (Genesis 29:16).

+ (d. 384): Roman widow. Feast day: March 22.

*(Lea, Lee, Leigh, Lia, Leia, Leeah)*

## Leilia

Meaning: possibly from Arabic "dark as night"

+ (date unknown): Irish virgin. Feast day: August 11.

*(Laila, Layla, Leilah, Lila, Lilah)*

## Lena

See Helen

## Leocadia

Meaning: unknown

+ (d.c. 303): Spanish martyr. Feast day: December 9.

## Leocrita

Meaning: unknown

+ (d. 859): Spanish virgin martyr. Feast day: March 15.

## Lewina

Meaning: Old English "beloved friend"

+ (d. fifth century): English virgin and martyr. Feast day: July 24.

## Libby

See Helen

## Liberata

Meaning: Latin "free"

+ (d. fifth century): Virgin sister of St. Honorata. Feast day: January 16.

## Limbania

Meaning: unknown

+ (d. 1294): Italian Benedictine nun and hermitess. Feast day: August 15.

## Lioba

Meaning: unknown

+ (d.c. 781): Benedictine abbess. Feast day: September 22.

## Lisa, Lisbeth, Lisette, Liz, Liza

See Elizabeth

## Lois

Meaning: Greek "good"

+ (biblical): Grandmother of Timothy (2 Timothy 1:5).

## Lori, Loretta

See Laura

## Louise

Meaning: feminine form of Louis

+ Louise de Marillac (d. 1660): Widow and patron of social workers. Feast day: March 15.

+ Louise of Omura (d. 1628): Native-born Japanese martyr. Feast day: September 8.

*(Louisa, Louiza)*

## Louisa

Meaning: feminine form of Louis

+ Louisa Montaignac de Chauvance (d. 1885): Foundress of the Oblates of the Sacred Heart of Jesus.

## Lucilla

Meaning: Latin "light"

+ (d.c. 260): Martyr. Feast day: July 29.

*(Luci, Lucia, Lucile, Lucille, Lucina, Lucy, Lucinda)*

## Lucretia

Meaning: Latin "riches"

+ (d. 306): Spanish virgin martyr. Feast day: November 22.

*(Lacresha, Lacreshia, Lacretia, Lakreska, Lakreshia, Leocrita, Lucresha, Lucreshia)*

## Lucy

Meaning: Latin "light"

+ Lucy of Syracuse (d. 304): Virgin martyr, mentioned in the first Eucharistic Prayer. Patron of the blind. Feast day: December 13.

+ Lucy Chakichi, Blessed (d. 1622): Martyr of Japan. Feast day: October 2.

+ Lucy de Freitas, Blessed (d. 1622): Native-born Japanese martyr. Feast day: September 10.

+ Lucy Filippini (d. 1732): Co-foundress of the Pontifical Institute of Religious Teachers, the Filippini Sisters. Feast day: March 25.

+ Lucy, Blessed (d. 1862): Martyr of China. Feast day: February 19.

## Ludmilla

Meaning: unknown

+ (d. 921): Slav princess, martyred

duchess of Bohemia (in present-day Czech Republic). Feast day: September 16.

## Lutgard
Meaning: unknown

+ (d. 1246): Mystic nun. Feast day: June 16.

## Lybe
Meaning: unknown

+ (d. 303): Virgin martyr. Feast day: June 15.

## Lydia
Meaning: "woman from Lydia"

+ (biblical): St. Paul's first convert in Macedonia, also called Lydia Purpuraria (Lydia of the purple cloth). (Acts 16:12-15). Feast day: August 3.

*(Lidi, Lidia, Lidiya, Liddiya, Liddy, Liddie)*

# M

## Mabyn
Meaning: Gaelic "joy"

+ (d. sixth century): Welsh and Cornish saint. Feast day: September 21.

## Macra
Meaning: unknown

+ (d. 287): French virgin martyr. Feast day: January 6.

## Macrina
Meaning: unknown

+ Macrina the Elder (d.c. 340): Grandmother of Sts. Basil and Gregory of Nyssa. Feast day: January 14.

+ Macrina the Younger (d. 379): Granddaughter of St. Macrina the Elder and daughter of Sts. Basil and Emmelia. Feast day: July 19.

## Madalberta
Meaning: Greek "elevated"

+ (d. 706): Benedictine abbess. Feast day: September 7.

## Madeleine
Meaning: French form of Magdalene

+ Madeleine Brideau (d. 1794): Martyr in the French Revolution. Feast day: July 17.

+ Madeleine Lidoine (d. 1794): Martyr in the French Revolution. Feast day: July 17.

+ Madeleine Sophie Barat (d. 1865): Foundress of the Society of the Sacred Heart of Jesus. Feast day: May 25.

*(Madalaina, Madaline, Madalyn, Madalyne, Maddaline, Maddelena, Maddy, Madelain, Madelaine, Madelene, Madeliene, Madelin, Madelina, Madellen, Madelyn, Madilyn, Madlyn, Madolline, Madylon, Maudlin, Modlen)*

## Madge
See Margaret

## Madrun
Meaning: unknown

+ (d. fifth century): Welsh or Cornish widow. Feast day: April 9.

## Mafalda
Meaning: unknown

+ (d. 1252): Cistercian nun and Portuguese princess. Feast day: May 2.

## Magdalene

Meaning: Greek "from Magdala" or "high fortress"

+ Mary Magdalene (biblical): Early supporter of Jesus' ministry and first witness to the Resurrection (John 20:11-18). Feast day: July 22.

*(Magda, Magdaline, Magdelene, Magdlen, Magdelena, Magdalena, Magdelina, Maggie)*

## Manechildis

Meaning: unknown

+ (d.c. 490): Hermitess and French nun. Feast day: October 14.

## Marana

Meaning: probably from Hebrew "bitter"

+ (d. fifth century): Virgin martyr. Feast day: August 3.

*(Mara, Marah)*

## Marcella

Meaning: feminine form of Mark

+ (d. 410): Widowed Roman noblewoman. Feast day: January 31.

## Marcellina

Meaning: diminutive feminine form of Mark

+ (d. 398): Consecrated virgin. Feast day: July 17.

## Marcia

Meaning: feminine form of Mark

+ (d. first century): Martyr. Feast day: June 5.

+ (d.c. 284): Martyred with St. Ariston. Feast day: July 2.

*(Maciann, Marcean, Macianna, Marciana, Marcie, Marci, Marcilyn, Marcene, Marcine, Marcina, Marcy, Marsha)*

## Marciana

Meaning: feminine form of Mark

+ (d.c. 303): Virgin martyr. Feast day: January 9.

## Margaret

Meaning: Greek "pearl"

+ (date unknown): Martyr of Antioch who spoke in a vision to St. Joan of Arc. Feast day: July 20.

+ Margaret of Scotland (d. 1093): Queen of Scotland and model of charity. Feast day: November 16.

+ Margaret of England (d. 1270): Cistercian nun. Feast day: February 3.

+ Margaret of Hungary (d. 1270): Dominican nun. Feast day: January 18.

+ Margaret of Cortona (d. 1297): Franciscan tertiary and miracle worker. Feast day: February 22.

+ Margaret Ebner, Blessed (d. 1351): Dominican nun and mystic.

+ Margaret the Barefooted (d. 1395): Wife. Feast day: August 27.

+ Margaret Pole, Blessed (d. 1541): Martyr in England. Feast day: May 28.

+ Margaret Clitherow (d. 1586): One of the Forty Martyrs of England and Wales. Feast day: October 21.

+ Margaret Ward (d. 1588): One of the Forty Martyrs of England and Wales. Feast day: August 30.

+ Margaret Mary Alacoque (d. 1690): Mystic and promoter of the devotion to the Sacred Heart. Feast day: October 16.

+ Margaret Bays, Blessed (d. 1879): Swiss mystic and stigmatic.

*(Gretchen, Madge, Maggie, Maise, Margarita, Margat, Marguerite, Marget, Margret, Margrett, Margareta, Margarete, Margaretha, Maragrethe, Margeretta, Margot, Margretta, Margietam, Marjorie, Marjory, Margery, Meaghen, Meg, Megan, Mysie, Peg, Peggie, Peggy)*

## Margarita

See Margaret, Rita

## Margot

See Margaret

## Marguerite

Meaning: French form of Margaret

+ Marguerite Bourgeoys (d. 1700): Foundress of the Sisters of Notre Dame de Montreal, Canada. Feast day: January 19.

## Maria, Marie

Meaning: Latin form of Mary

+ Maria de Cerevellon (d. 1290): Superior of the Mercedarians, the Order of Our Lady of Ransom. Feast day: September 19.

+ Maria Magdalen dei Pazzi (d. 1607): Discalced Carmelite mystic and healer. Feast day: May 25.

+ Maria Angela Astorch, Blessed (d. 1665): Poor Clare nun.

+ Marie of the Incarnation Guyart (d. 1672): Foundress of the Ursuline Sisters in Quebec, Canada.

+ Maria Francesca Gallo (d. 1791): Mystic and stigmatic. Feast day: October 6.

+ Marie Claude Brard (d. 1794): French Carmelite martyr. Feast day: July 17.

+ Marie Croissy (d. 1794): Martyr in the French Revolution. Feast day: July 17.

+ Marie Dufour (d. 1794): French Carmelite martyr. Feast day: July 17.

+ Marie Hanisset (d. 1794): French Carmelite martyr. Feast day: July 17.

+ Marie Magdalen Desjardin, Blessed (d. 1794): French Carmelite martyr. Feast day: October 17.

+ Marie Magdalen Fontaine, Blessed (d. 1794): French Carmelite martyr. Feast day: June 26.

+ Marie Meunier (d. 1794): Carmelite nun. Feast day: July 17.

+ Marie St. Henry (d. 1794): Martyr. Feast day: July 16.

+ Marie Trezelle (d. 1794): French Carmelite martyr. Feast day: July 17.

+ Maria Magdalen of Canossa (d. 1835): Foundress of the Daughters of Charity at Verona, Italy. Feast day: May 8.

+ Marie Rose Durocher, Blessed (d. 1849): Foundress of the Order of the Names of Jesus and Mary (Holy Names Sisters). Given name was Melanie.

+ Maria Michaela (d. 1865): Foundress of the Institute of the Handmaids of the Blessed Sacrament and of Charity. Feast day: August 24.

+ Maria Domenica Brun Barbantini, Blessed (d. 1868): Foundress of the Pious Union of the Sisters of Charity and Servants of the Sick of St. Camillus.

+ Maria of Jesus Crucified Bouardy, Blessed (d. 1878): Carmelite nun, called "the little Arab."

+ Maria Theresa of Jesus Gerhardinger, Blessed (d. 1879): Foundress of the School Sisters of Notre Dame.

+ Maria Dominic Mazzarello (d. 1881): Co-foundress of the Daughters of Mary Auxiliatrix or Our Lady Help of Christians. Disciple of St. John Bosco. Feast day: May 14.

+ Maria Crucifixa di Rosa (d. 1885): Foundress of the Handmaids of Charity of Brescia, also called the Servants of Charity. Feast day: December 15.

+ Marie Teresa Couderc (d. 1885): Foundress of the Society of Our lady of the Cenacle at La Louvesc, France. Feast day: September 26.

+ Maria Anna Mogas Fontcuberta (d. 1886): Foundress of the Capuchins of the Divine Shepherdess.

+ Maria Encarnación Rosal, Blessed (d. 1886): Mystic from Guatemala.

+ Maria Soledad Torres-Acosta (d. 1887): Foundress of the Handmaids of Mary. Feast day: October 11.

+ Maria Catherine of St. Rose Troiani, Blessed (d. 1887): Missionary to Egypt.

+ Maria Giuseppe Rossello (d. 1888): Foundress of the Daughters of Our Lady of Mercy. Feast day: December 7.

+ Maria Theresa Scherer, Blessed (d. 1888): Swiss woman known as the "Mother of the Poor."

+ Maria Goretti (d. 1902): Virgin, martyred for her chastity. Feast day: July 6.

+ Maria of Jesus Siedliska, Blessed (d. 1902): Foundress of the Sisters of the Holy Family of Nazareth.

+ Maria of Mount Carmel Sallés y Baranqueras, Blessed (d. 1911): Foundress of the Congregation of the Missionary Teaching Sisters of the Immaculate Conception.

+ Maria Marcellina Darowska, Blessed (d. 1911): Widow and foundress of the Congregation of the Sisters of the Immaculate Conception of the Blessed Virgin Mary.

+ Maria Antonia Bandres y Elósequi, Blessed (d. 1919): Spanish nun.

+ Maria Margaret Caiani, Blessed (d. 1921): Foundress of the Franciscan Minims of the Sacred Heart.

+ Maria Bernarda Butler, Blessed (d. 1924): Missionary to South America.

+ Maria Pilar Martinez Garcia, Blessed (d. 1936): Carmelite nun and martyr. Feast day: July 24.

+ Maria Sagrario Cantero, Blessed (d. 1936): Carmelite nun and martyr.

+ Maria Mercedes Prat y Prat, Blessed (d. 1936): Martyr in the Spanish Civil War.

+ Maria Faustina Kowalska, Blessed (d. 1938): Promoter of the Divine Mercy meditations.

+ Maria Restituta Kafka, Blessed (d. 1943): Martyred by the Nazis.

+ Maria Raffaela Cimatti, Blessed (d. 1945): Minister to the wounded of World War II.

+ Maria Teresa Fasce, Blessed (d. 1947): Augustinian nun.

+ Maria Vicenta of St. Dorothy Chavez Orozco, Blessed (d. 1949): Foundress of Mexican Servants of the Holy Trinity and the Poor.

+ Maria Clementine Anuarite Nengapete, Blessed (d. 1964): Martyr in Zaire, Africa.

+ Maria Alvarado Cardozo, Blessed (d. 1967): Foundress of the Augustinian Recollects of the Heart of Jesus.

+ Maria Maravillas de Jesús Pidal y Chico de Guzmán, Blessed (d. 1974): Carmelite nun.

*(Marea, Mariae, Mariah)*

## Marina

Meaning: Latin "of the sea"

+ (date unknown): Virgin martyr. Feast day: June 18 and July 17.

+ (date unknown): Spanish martyr. Feast day: July 18.

## Marian, Marion

See Mary, Modwenna

## Mariana

Meaning: form of Mary

+ Mariana de Paredes (d. 1645): Ecuadorian holy woman. Feast day: May 26.

## Marjorie, Marjory

See Margaret

## Merryn

See Modwenna

## Martha

Meaning: Aramaic "mistress of the house"

+ (biblical): Sister of Mary and Lazarus, among first to profess faith in Jesus as the Messiah (John 11:17-27). Patron of cooks and housewives. Feast day: July 29.

+ (date unknown): German virgin and martyr. Feast day: October 20.

+ (d. 251): Spanish virgin and martyr. Feast day: February 23.

+ Martha Wang, Blessed (d. 1861): Martyr in, Vietnam. Feast day: July 29.

*(Marta, Marthe, Marti, Martie)*

## Martina

Meaning: feminine form of Martin

+ (d. 228): Virgin martyr in Rome. Feast day: January 30.

## Mary

Meaning: possibly from Hebrew "sea of bitterness"

+ (biblical): Mary, the mother of Jesus (Luke 2:1-8). Also called the Blessed Virgin and numerous other titles. Feast days: January 1 (Mary Mother of God), March 25 (Annunciation), August 15 (Assumption), December 8 (Immaculate Conception) and many others.

+ Mary Magdalene (biblical): Early supporter of Jesus' ministry and first witness to the Resurrection (John 20:11-18). Feast day: July 22.

+ (biblical): Sister of Martha and Lazarus, Jesus said she chose the "better part" by listening to him (Luke 10:38-42). Feast day: July 29.

+ (biblical): Mother of John Mark (Acts 12:12). Feast day: June 29.

+ Mary Clophas (biblical): One of the "Three Marys" present at the Crucifixion (John 19:25) and companion of Mary Magdalene to the tomb (Mark 16:1). Feast day: April 9.

+ Mary Salome (biblical): Mother of Sts. James the Great and John, wife of Zebedee (Matthew 27:56). Feast day: October 22.

+ Mary the Slave (d.c. 300): Roman martyr and slave. Feast day: November 1.

+ Mary of Egypt (d. fifth century): Egyptian hermitess and former prostitute. Feast day: April 2.

+ Mary Choun, Blessed (d. 1619): Martyr of Japan.

+ Mary Tokuan, Blessed (d. 1619): Martyr of Japan. Feast day: September 10.

+ Mary Guengoro, Blessed (d. 1620): Martyr of Japan. Feast day: August 18.

+ Mary Magdalen Kiota, Blessed (d. 1620): Native-born Japanese martyr. Feast day: August 16.

+ Mary Tanaura, Blessed (d. 1622): Martyr of Japan. Feast day: September 10.

+ Mary Vaz, Blessed (d. 1627): Martyr of Japan. Feast day: August 17.

+ Mary Margaret d'Youville (d. 1771): Foundress of the Sisters of Charity, the Grey Nuns of Canada. Feast day: April 11.

+ Mary MacKillop, Blessed (d. 1909): First native Australian to be beatified. Feast day: August 8.

*(Mara, Maria, Marian, Marie, Mari, Marietta, Marion, Meri, Merry)*

## Matilda

Meaning: Old German "mighty in battle"

+ (d. 968): Queen, wife, mother. Feast day: March 14.

## Matrona

+ (d.c. 350): Greek virgin martyr, patroness of victims of dysentery. Feast day: March 15.

## Maura

Meaning: Irish form of "Moira" or "Mary"

+ (date unknown): Virgin martyr. Feast day: November 30.

+ (d. fourth century): Virgin. Feast day: January 15.

+ (d. 850): French virgin. Feast day: September 21.

## Maxellendis

Meaning: unknown

+ (d.c. 670): Virgin martyr. Feast day: November 13.

## Maxentia

Meaning: unknown

+ Maxentia of Beauvais (date unknown): Irish or Scottish virgin and martyr. Feast day: November 20.

## Maxima

Meaning: Latin "maximum"

+ (date unknown): Virgin. Feast day: May 16.

+ (d. 304): Martyred under Emperor Diocletian. Feast day: July 30.

+ (d. 304): Martyred Roman slave. Feast day: September 2.

## Mazota

Meaning: unknown

+ (d. eighth century): Irish virgin. Feast day: December 23.

## Mechtildis

Meaning: unknown

+ (d. 1160): Benedictine abbess, mystic and miracle worker. Feast day: May 31.

+ Mechtildis of Helfta (d. 1298): Benedictine nun who trained St. Gertrude the Great. Feast day: November 19.

## Meda

See Ita

## Medana

Meaning: possible form of Madonna

+ (d. eighth century): Irish virgin. Feast day: November 19.

## Megan, Meaghen

See Margaret

# Melangell

Meaning: unknown

+ (d.c. 590): Welsh virgin. Feast day: May 27.

# Melania

Meaning: Greek "black"

+ Melania the Elder (d.c. 410): Roman noblewoman, one of the first to make a pilgrimage to the Holy Land. Feast day: June 8.

+ Melania the Younger (d. 438): Granddaughter of Melania the Elder. Feast day: December 31.

*(Melanee, Melaney, Melani, Melanie, Mellanie, Melaniya, Mellanney, Melanya)*

# Melitina

Meaning: Greek "black" or "sweetened with honey"

+ (d. second century): Greek virgin martyr. Feast day: September 15.

# Mella

+ (d.c.780): Widow and abbess. Feast day: April 25.

# Menna

Meaning: (unknown)

+ (d.c. 395): French virgin. Feast day: October 3.

# Menodora

Meaning: unknown

+ (d. 306): Martyr. Feast day: September 10.

# Merewenna

Meaning: unknown

+ (d.c. 970): English abbess. Feast day: May 13.

*(Merwenna, Merwinna)*

# Messalina

Meaning: unknown

+ (d. 251): Virgin martyr. Feast day: January 19.

# Micheala, Michelle

Meaning: feminine form of Michael

# Mida

See Ita

# Milburga

Meaning: unknown

+ (d.c. 715): English Benedictine abbess. Feast day: February 23.

# Mildred

Meaning: Old English "mild strength"

+ (d.c. 700): English Benedictine abbess. Feast day: July 13.

*(Millie, Milley, Milly)*

# Miriam

Meaning: Hebrew "sorrow"

+ (biblical): Sister of Moses (Exodus 15:20).

*(Mindy, Minna, Mira, Mollie)*

# Modesta

Meaning: Latin "modest"

+ (d.c. 680): Benedictine abbess. Feast day: November 4.

# Modwenna

Meaning: unknown

+ (d. seventh century): English hermitess. Feast day: July 5.

*(Marian, Merryn)*

# Monegundis

Meaning: unknown

+ (d. 570): French wife and hermitess. Feast day: July 2.

+ (d.c. 251): Greek martyr. Feast day: July 13.

## Monennaa

Meaning: unknown

+ (d. 518): Irish abbess. Feast day: July 6.

## Monessa

Meaning: unknown

+ (d. 456): Virgin, convert of St. Patrick. Feast day: September 4.

## Monica

Meaning: Greek "alone"

+ (d. 387): Mother of St. Augustine of Hippo. Patron of married women. Feast day: August 27.

+ Monica Naisen, Blessed (d. 1626): Native-born Japanese martyr. Feast day: July 12.

*(Moni, Monika, Monique)*

## Morwenna

Meaning: unknown

+ (d. fifth century): Cornish virgin. Feast day: July 8.

## Musa

Meaning: unknown

+ (d. sixth century): Roman mystic and virgin. Feast day: April 2.

## Myra

Meaning: feminine form of Myron

## Mysie

See Margaret

## Myrope

Meaning: derived from Greek "wonderful"

# N

## Namadia

Meaning: unknown

+ (d.c. 700): Widow and nun. Feast day: August 19.

## Nancy

See Anne

## Naomi

Meaning: Hebrew "pleasant"

+ (biblical): Mother-in-law of Ruth (Book of Ruth).

## Natalia

Meaning: Latin "Christmas Child"

+ (d.c. 311): Martyr in Nicomedia (in present-day Turkey). Feast day: December 1.

*(Natalee, Natali, Natalya, Natasha, Natelie, Nathalie, Nattalia)*

## Nennoc

Meaning: unknown

+ (d.c. 467): British virgin. Feast day: June 4.

## Nessie

See Agnes

## Nicarete

Meaning: unknown

+ (d.c. 405): Virgin, supporter of St. John Chrysostom. Feast day: December 27.

## Nicolle, Nicolette

Meaning: feminine version of Nicholas

## Nina

See Anne

## Nino

Meaning: English "grace of God"

+ (d.c. 320): Virgin and hermitess. Feast day: December 15.

*(Christina, Neena, Nina, Ninah)*

## Non

Meaning: Latin "ninth"

+ (d. sixth century): Mother of St. David of Wales. Feast day: March 3.

## Nonna

Meaning: Latin "ninth"

+ (d. 374): Wife of St. Gregory Nazianzus the Elder. Feast day: August 5.

*(Nona, Nonah, Noni, Nonie, Nony, Nonya)*

## Notburga

Meaning: unknown

+ (d.c. 714): German Benedictine nun. Feast day: October 31.

+ (d.c. 1313): Tyrolian servant, patron of peasants and servants. Feast day: September 14.

## Noyala

Meaning: unknown

+ (date unknown): Virgin martyr. Feast day: July 6.

# O

## Obdulia

Meaning: unknown

+ (date unknown): Spanish virgin. Feast day: September 5.

## Oda

Meaning: unknown

+ (d.c. 723): French widow. Feast day: October 23.

## Odilia

Meaning: Hebrew "I will praise God"

+ (d.c. 720): Abbess. Feast day: December 13.

*(Odeleya)*

## Olga

Meaning: Scandinavian "holy"

+ (d.c. 969): Ruler of Kiev, Russia. Feast day: July 11.

*(Olya, Ollya)*

## Oliva

Meaning: Latin "olive"

+ (date unknown): Mystic nun. Feast day: June 3.

+ (d. 138): Martyr. Feast day: March 5.

+ (d.c. 850): Virgin and martyr. Feast day: June 10.

*(Olive, Olivia, Olivette, Olivea)*

## Ollalla

See Eulalia

## Olympias

Meaning: Greek "heavenly"

+ (d.c. 408): Friend of St. John Chrysostom. Feast day: December 17.

*(Olympia, Olympa)*

## Opportuna

Meaning: Latin "good"

+ (d.c. 770): Benedictine abbess. Feast day: April 22.

## Oriel

See Aurea

## Osburga

Meaning: unknown

+ (d.c. 1018): English abbess. Feast day: March 30.

## Osmanna

Meaning: Hebrew "save us"

+ (d.c. 650): Benedictine nun. Feast day: September 9.

*(Osanna)*

## Osyth

Meaning: Anglo-Saxon "woman of Essex"

+ (d.c. 700): Martyred English nun. Feast day: October 7.

*(Osith)*

# P

## Pamela

See Helen

## Panacea

Meaning: Latin "remedy"

+ (d. 1383): Child martyr. Feast day: May 1.

## Paschasia

Meaning: possibly from Hebrew "Passover"

+ (d. late second century): Virgin and martyr. Feast day: January 9.

## Patricia

Meaning: Latin "noble"

+ (d.c. 665): Legendary figure who gave her wealth to the poor, reportedly related to the imperial family at Constantinople (Istanbul in present-day Turkey). Patron of Naples, Italy. Feast day: August 25.

*(Pat, Patrice, Patsi, Patsy, Patti, Pattrice, Pattriece, Patty)*

## Paula

Meaning: feminine form of Paul

+ (d.c. 273): Martyr and virgin. Feast day: June 3.

+ (d. 404): Roman noblewoman, friend of St. Jerome, helped translate the Bible into the vernacular. Patron saint of widows. Feast day: January 26.

+ (d. 1368): Camaldolesean nun. Feast day: January 5.

+ Paula Frasinetti (d. 1882): Foundress of the Congregation of St. Dorothy. Feast day: June 11.

+ Paula Montral, Blessed (d. 1889): Foundress of the Daughters of Mary.

*(Paula, Paule, Pauleen, Paulene, Paulette, Paulina, Pauline, Paulyne, Paulann, Paola)*

## Paulina

Meaning: feminine form of Paul

+ (date unknown): Roman martyr. Feast day: December 31.

+ Pauline von Mallinckrodt, Blessed (d. 1881): German aristocrat and foundress of Sisters of Christian Charity.

+ Pauline Amabilis Visenteiner, Blessed (d. 1942): First saint who grew up in Brazil.

## Pega

Meaning: Greek "joined together"

+ (d.c. 719): English hermitess. Feast day: January 8.

## Peggy

See Margaret

## Pelagia

Meaning: Latin "sorrow of the sea"

+ Pelagia the Penitent (date unknown): Actress who converted and became a hermitess. Feast day: October 8.

+ Pelagia of Antioch (d.c. 311): Roman martyred virgin. Feast day: June 9.

## Perpetua

Meaning: Latin "eternal"

+ (d.c. 80): Roman matron, converted by St. Peter. Feast day: August 4.

+ (d. 203): Martyred with her servant, St. Felicity, mentioned in the first Eucharistic Prayer. Feast day: March 7.

## Perseveranda

Meaning: Latin "persistence"

+ (d.c. 726): Spanish virgin. Feast day: June 26.

*(Pezaine)*

## Petra

Meaning: feminine form of Peter
Greek "rock"

+ Petra of St. Joseph Perez Florida, Blessed (d.. 1906): Spanish nun called "Mother of the Helpless."

## Petrina

Meaning: feminine form of Peter

+ Petrina Morosini (d. 1957): Martyred for her chastity.

## Pezaine

See Perseveranda

## Pharäildis

Meaning: unknown

+ (d.c. 740): Legendary Belgian saint, also called Varelde, Verylde or Veerle in Flanders. Patron of Ghent, Belgium. Feast day: January 4.

*(Varelde, Variede, Veerle, Verylde)*

## Phemi

See Euphemia

## Philippa

Meaning: feminine form of Philip
Greek

+ (d. 220): Roman martyred with her son St. Theodore. Feast day: September 20.

## Philomena

Meaning: Greek "be loved"

+ (d.c. 500): Italian virgin. Feast day: July 5.

*(Philomene, Philomina, Filomena)*

## Phoebe

Meaning: Greek "pure and bright"

+ (biblical): Benefactor of St. Paul and

deaconess in the church at Cenchreae (Romans 16:1). Feast day: September 3.

*(Pheabe, Pheaby, Pheba, Pheby, Pheobe, Pheoby, Phobe, Phoeboe, Pheoby)*

## Photina
Meaning: Latin "friend of the Lord"

+ (biblical): Samaritan martyr, traditional name of the woman at the well (John 4:7-42). Feast day: March 20.

## Placide, Placidia
Meaning: Latin "calm"

+ Placidia (d. 460): Virgin. Feast day: October 11.

+ Placide Viel, Blessed (d. 1877): Nun and superior of order. Feast day: March 4.

## Platonides
Meaning: unknown

+ (d.c. 308): Deaconess. Feast day: April 6.

## Plautilla
Meaning: unknown

+ (d.c. 67): Roman widow, reputedly the wife of Emperor Vespasian. Feast day: May 20.

## Pomposa
Meaning: unknown

+ (d. 835): Martyred Spanish nun. Feast day: September 19.

## Praxedes
Meaning: unknown

+ (d. mid-second century): Virgin, probably a martyr. Feast day: July 21.

## Primitiva
Meaning: unknown

+ (d. first century): Roman martyr. Feast day: February 24.

+ (d. first century): Roman martyr. Feast day: July 23.

## Principia
Meaning: unknown

+ (d.c. 420): Roman virgin. Feast day: May 11.

## Prisca
Meaning: Latin "primitive"

+ (d. third century): Virgin martyr. Feast day: January 18.

## Priscilla
Meaning: Latin "primitive"

+ (biblical): Wife of Aquila, convert of St. Paul in Corinth. (Acts 18:2).

+ (d. first century): Martyr of Rome. Feast day: January 16.

*(Precilla, Prescilla, Pricilla, Prisca, Priscella, Prissilla)*

## Publia
Meaning: feminine form of Publias

+ (d.c. 362): Syrian widow. Feast day: October 9.

## Pulcheria
Meaning: Latin "beautiful"

+ Pulcheria Augusta (d. 453): Daughter of Emperor Arcadius. Feast day: September 10.

# Q

## Quinta
See Cointha

## Quiteria
Meaning: Latin "vital"

+ (date unknown): Spanish virgin and martyr. Feast day: May 22.

# R

## Rachel
Meaning: Hebrew "ewe"

+ (biblical): Wife of Jacob (Genesis 29:16).

*(Rachael, Racheal, Rachelle, Rachele, Rachele, Raquel, Rachal, Riquelle)*

## Rachildis
Meaning: unknown

+ (d.c. 946): Benedictine hermitess. Feast day: November 23.

## Radegund
Meaning: unknown

+ (d. 587): Wife of King Clotaire I. One of the first Merovingian saints. Feast day: August 13.

+ (d.c. 1300): German virgin slain by a pack of wolves. Feast day: August 13.

## Raphaela
Meaning: feminine form of Raphael

+ Raphaela Mary Porras (d. 1925): Spanish nun. Feast day: January 6.

*(Rafael, Rafaela, Rafaell, Rafaelle, Rafalea)*

## Rebecca
Meaning: Hebrew "to tie"

+ (biblical): Mother of Jacob and Esau (Genesis 24:15).

+ Rebecca de Himlay, Blessed (d. 1914): Maronite saint.

*(Beckie, Becky, Rebbecca, Rebeca, Rebeccah, Rebecka, Rebeckah, Rebekah, Rebehak, Rebekka, Rivhak)*

## Regina
Meaning: Latin "queen"

+ (d. second century): Virgin martyr. Feast day: September 7.

*(Geena, Gena, Gina, Regena, Regiena, Reginia, Reginna, Reine, Reinee)*

## Reineldis
Meaning: unknown

+ (d. 680): French martyr. Feast day July 16.

*(Raineldis, Reinildis)*

## Relindis
Meaning: unknown

+ (d.c. 750): Benedictine abbess. Feast day: February 6.

## Reparata
Meaning: unknown

+ (d. mid-third century): Virgin martyr of Caesarea (in present-day Palestine). Feast day: October 8.

## Restituta

Meaning: unknown

+ (d. 255): Virgin martyr from Africa. Feast day: May 17.

+ Restituta of Sora (d.c. 270): Roman virgin martyr. Feast day: May 27.

## Reyne

See Regina

## Rhais

See Irais

## Rhipsime

Meaning: unknown

+ (d.c. 290): Virgin martyr from Armenia. Feast day: September 29.

## Rhoda

Meaning: Hebrew "rose"

+ (biblical): Maid who answered the door for Peter when he escaped from prison (Acts 12:13-15).

## Richardis

Meaning: probably female form of Richard

+ (d.c. 895): Empress and wife of Emperor Charles the Fat. Feast day: September 18.

## Rictrudis

Meaning: unknown

+ (d.c. 688): Benedictine abbess. Feast day: May 12.

## Rita

Meaning: Spanish "pearl"

+ Rita of Cascia (d. 1457): Augustinian nun, patron, with St. Jude, of hopeless causes. Feast day: May 22.

*(Margareta, Reta, Reeta, Rheta)*

## Roberta

Meaning: feminine form of Robert

## Romana

Meaning: Latin "from Rome"

+ (d. 324): Roman virgin. Feast day: February 23.

## Romula

Meaning: Latin "feminine citizen"

+ (d. sixth century): Virgin and hermitess. Feast day: July 23.

## Rosalia

Meaning: Latin "rose"

+ (d. 1160): Virgin and hermit. Feast day: September 4 and July 15.

*(Rosalie, Rosella, Rosalea, Rosalee, Rosalina, Roselia)*

## Rose

Meaning: Latin "rose"

+ Rose Chretien, Blessed (d. 1794): Martyr in the French Revolution. Feast day: July 17.

+ Rose of Lima (d. 1617): Patron of South America and the first saint of the Americas. Feast day: August 23.

+ Rose of Viterbo (d. 1252): Virgin and preacher. Feast day: September 4.

+ Rose-Philippine Duchesne (d. 1852): Foundress of the Society of the Sacred Heart and American missionary. Feast day: November 17.

*(Rosa, Rosie, Rosemarie, Rosemary)*

## Rotrudis

Meaning: unknown

+ (d.c. 869): Virgin, traditionally thought to be the sister or daughter of Charlemagne. Feast day: June 22.

## Rufina

Meaning: Latin "girl with bright-red hair"

+ (d. 257): Roman martyr. Feast day: July 10.

+ (d. early fourth century): Martyr. Feast day: April 6.

## Ruth

Meaning: Hebrew "friend"

+ (biblical): Daughter-in-law of Naomi, ancestor of Jesus (Book of Ruth).

# S

## Sabina

Meaning: Latin "vine-planter"

+ (d.c. 119): Roman noblewoman and martyr. Feast day: August 29.

+ (d.c. 275): Martyr, sister of St. Sabinian of Troyes, Gaul (modern France). Feast day: August 29.

*(Sabine, Sebinah, Sabinna, Sabrina)*

## Saethryth

Meaning: unknown

+ (d.c. 660): Benedictine abbess. Feast day: January 10.

## Salaberga

Meaning: unknown

+ (d.c. 665): Widow, abbess. Feast day: September 22.

## Sally

See Sarah

## Salome

Meaning: Hebrew "peace"

+ Mary Salome (biblical): Mother of Sts. James the Great and John, wife of Zebedee (Matthew 27:56). Feast day: April 9

+ (d. ninth century): Anglo-Saxon princess, Benedictine nun. Feast day: June 29.

*(Saloma, Salomea)*

## Salomea

Meaning: Hebrew "peace"

+ Salomea, Blessed (d. 1268): Poor Clare abbess. Feast day: November 17.

## Samthan

Meaning: unknown

+ (d. sixth century): Irish abbess noted for her culture. Feast day: December 18.

## Sandra

Meaning: feminine form of Alexander

## Sapientia

See Sophia

## Sarah

Meaning: Hebrew "princess"

+ (biblical): Wife of Abraham and mother of Isaac (Genesis 17:15).

*(Sally, Sara, Sahra, Sarai, Sarra, Sharai, Sharaya, Sharayah, Zara)*

## Savina

Meaning: Latin "vine-planter"

+ (d. 311): Martyred under Emperor Diocletian. Feast day: January 30.

+ Savina Petrilli, Blessed (d. 1923): Foundress of Sisters of the Poor.

## Scholastica

Meaning: Latin "scholar"

+ (d.c. 543): Benedictine abbess, twin sister of St. Benedict. Feast day: February 10.

## Secundina

Meaning: Latin "little second-born"

+ (d.c. 250): Martyred virgin. Feast day: January 15.

## Senorina

Meaning: unknown

+ (d. 982): Italian Benedictine abbess. Feast day: April 22.

## Segna

See Agnes

## Seraphina

Meaning: Hebrew "to burn"

+ (d. 1253): Virgin. Feast day: March 12.

*(Sarafina, Serafina, Seraphia, Serapia, Syrafina)*

## Seraphia

Meaning: Hebrew "to burn"

+ (d.c. 119): Slave and martyr. Feast day: July 29.

## Serena

Meaning: Latin "calm"

+ (d.c. 290): Early Christian lay leader. Feast day: August 16.

*(Serina, Sereena, Serenah, Sarina, Sereenah, Serenity)*

## Sethrida

See Saethryth

## Severa

Meaning: unknown

+ (d.c. 680): Virgin and abbess. Feast day: July 20.

+ (d.c. 750): German Benedictine abbess. Feast day: July 20.

## Sharon

Meaning: Hebrew "flat country"

+ (biblical): area of ancient Palestine (Song of Songs 2:1).

*(Shaara, Shaaron, Sharen, Sharona, Sharone, Sharron, Sharyn, Sherryn)*

## Sidwell

Meaning: Anglo-Saxon "of the sea"

+ (date unknown): Virgin martyr. Feast day: August 1 and 2.

## Sigolena

Meaning: unknown

+ (d.c. 769): French Benedictine abbess. Feast day: July 24.

*(Segouléme)*

## Sigrada

Meaning: unknown

+ (d.c. 678): Mother. Feast day: August 8.

## Solangia

Meaning: Latin "good shepherdess"

+ (d.c. 880): Shepherdess, virgin and martyr. Feast day: May 10.

## Solina

Meaning: unknown

+ (d.c. 290): French virgin and martyr. Feast day: October 17.

## Sophia

Meaning: Greek "wisdom"

+ (date unknown): Legendary mother of daughters Faith, Hope, and Charity. She died while praying at their tombs. Feast day: September 30.

+ (d.c. 249): Virgin and martyr under Emperor Trajanus Decius. Feast day: April 30.

+ (d. early third century): Martyr in Egypt. Feast day: September 18.

*(Sofi, Soffi, Sofia, Sofiya, Sonia, Sonya, Sophey, Sophi, Sophie)*

## Soteris

Meaning: unknown

+ (d. 304): Virgin and martyr. Feast day: February 10.

## Sperandea

Meaning: unknown

+ (d. 1276): Benedictine abbess. Feast day: September 11.

## Stacey, Stacy

Meaning: feminine form of Eustace

## Stephanie

Meaning: feminine form of Stephen

*(Stephie, Stephca)*

## Sunniva

Meaning: unknown

+ (d. tenth century): Virgin, known through old Norse legend. Feast day: July 8.

## Susanna

Meaning: Hebrew "lily"

+ (biblical): Woman unjustly accused (Daniel 13).

+ (biblical): Early follower of Jesus. (Luke 8:3).

+ (d. second century): Martyr. Feast day: May 24.

+ (d. 295): Virgin and martyr. Feast day: August 11.

+ (d. 362): Virgin and martyr, daughter of pagan priest and Jewish mother.

+ Susanna, Blessed (d. 1628): Japanese martyr. Feast day: July 12.

*(Shushana, Shoshanna, Sue, Susan, Susann, Suson, Susannah, Susanne, Susette, Suzan, Suzanne, Suzette)*

## Sylvia

Meaning: Latin "wood"

+ (d. 572): Mother of Pope St. Gregory I. Feast day: November 3.

*(Silvia, Silva, Silvana, Silvanna, Sylvanna, Sylvanya, Sylvya)*

## Syra

Meaning: unknown

+ (d.c. 660): French Benedictine abbess. Feast day: October 23.

+ (d. seventh century): Virgin sister of St. Fiacre. Feast day: June 8.

## Sytha

See Osyth

# T

## Tabitha

Meaning: Aramaic "gazelle"

+ (biblical): Widow, also known as

Dorcas, raised from dead by St. Peter (Acts 9:36-42). Feast day: October 25.

*(Tabatha, Tabathia, Tabby, Tabytha)*

# Talida
Meaning: unknown

+ (d. fourth century): Egyptian abbess. Feast day: January 5.

# Tanca
Meaning: unknown

+ (d.c. 637): French virgin and martyr. Feast day: October 10.

# Tarbula
Meaning: unknown

+ (d. 345): Virgin and martyr. Feast day: April 22.

# Tarsicia
Meaning: unknown

+ (d.c. 600): Virgin and hermit. Feast day: January 15.

# Tarsilla
Meaning: unknown

+ (d.c. 581): Aunt of Pope St. Gregory I and niece of Pope St. Felix IV. Feast day: December 24.

# Tatiana
Meaning: Slavic "queen"

+ (d.c. 230): Roman martyr. Feast day: January 12.

*(Taitiana, Taitianna, Tatia, Tatiania, Tatianya, Tatjana, Tatyanan, Tatyanna)*

# Teresa
Meaning: Greek "harvester"

+ Teresa of Portugal (d. 1250): Portuguese princess and Cistercian nun. Feast day: June 17.

+ Teresa of Ávila (d. 1582): Discalced Carmelite mystic and Doctor of the Church. Feast day: October 15.

+ Teresa Margaret Redi (d. 1770): Carmelite nun. Feast day: March 11.

+ Teresa Fantou, Blessed (d. 1794): Martyr in the French revolution. Feast day: June 26.

+ Teresa Couderc (d. 1885): Foundress of the Religious of Our Lady of the Retreat in the Cenacle. Feast day: August 26.

+ Teresa of Jesus Jornet Ibars (d. 1897): Foundress of the Little Sisters of the Poor. Feast day: August 26.

+ Teresa de los Andes (d. 1920): Carmelite mystic and first Chilean to be beatified or canonized. Feast day: July 13.

+ Teresa Bracco, Blessed (d. 1944): Martyred by the Nazis.

+ Teresa Grillo Michel, Blessed (d. 1944): Widow and missionary to Argentina.

*(Taresa, Tarisa, Tarise, Tarissa, Teree, Terese, Teri, Theresa, Therese, Theressa, Thereza, Tresa, Trescha, Tresha, Treshana, Tressa, Treysa, Treyssa)*

# Tetta
Meaning: unknown

+ (d.c. 772): English Benedictine abbess. Feast day: September 28.

# Thais
Meaning: Greek "giving joy"

+ (d. fourth century): Egyptian and former courtesan. Feast day: October 8.

# Thecla

Meaning: Greek "divinely famous"

+ (d. first century): Virgin and martyr. Feast day: September 23.

+ Thecla of Kitzingen (d.c. 790): Benedictine abbess. Feast day: October 15.

+ Thecla Nangashi, Blessed (d. 1622): Japanese martyr. Feast day: September 10.

# Theodora

Meaning: Greek "divine gift"

+ (d.c. 120): Roman martyr. Feast day: April 1.

+ (d. 304): Virgin and martyr. Feast day: April 28.

+ (d.c. 305): Roman martyr. Feast day: September 17.

+ (d. 491): Egyptian penitent. Feast day: September 11.

+ (d. 867): Byzantine empress. Feast day: February 11.

# Theodosia

Meaning: Greek "divine gift"

+ (d.c. 308): Virgin and martyr. Feast day: April 2.

+ (d. 745): Nun and martyr. Feast day: May 29.

# Theodota

Meaning: probably a form of Theodora

+ (d. 304): Martyred with her three sons. Feast day: August 2.

+ (d.c. 318): Former prostitute and martyr. Feast day: September 29.

+ (d. 735): Byzantine martyr. Feast day: July 17.

# Thérèse

Meaning: French form of Teresa

+ Thérèse of Lisieux (d. 1897): Discalced Carmelite mystic, Doctor of the Church, often called "The Little Flower." Feast day: October 1.

# Thomais

Meaning: unknown

+ (d. 476): Egyptian martyr, wife of a fisherman. Feast day: April 14.

# Tibby

See Isabel

# Tigridia

Meaning: unknown

+ (d.c. 925): Benedictine abbess. Feast day: November 22.

# Tina

See Christina

# Tochmura

Meaning: unknown

+ (date unknown): Irish virgin. Feast day: June 11.

# Trea

Meaning: unknown

+ (d. fifth century): Irish hermitess. Feast day: August 3.

# Triphina

Meaning: unknown

+ (d. sixth century): Mother. Feast day: July 5.

# Trissie, Trixie

See Beatrix

## Trudi, Trudy
See Aldetrudis, Gertrude

## Tudy
Meaning: unknown
+ (d. fifth century): Welsh virgin. Feast day: January 30.

*(Uda)*

# U

## Uda
See Tudy

## Ulphia
Meaning: unknown
+ (d.c. 750): Hermitess. Feast day: January 31.

## Ulricha
Meaning: feminine form of Ulric
+ Ulricha Nisch, Blessed (d. 1913): German nun and mystic.

*(Ulrica, Ulricka, Ulrika)*

## Ursula
Meaning: Latin "bear"
+ (d. fourth or fifth century): Tradition calls her the daughter of a Christian king in Britain, believed to have been martyred by the Huns in Cologne, France. Feast day: October 21.

+ Ursula Ledochowska, Blessed (d. 1939): Sister of St. Theresa Ledochowsha.

*(Ursa, Ursella)*

## Ursulina
Meaning: Latin "little bear"
+ Ursulina, Blessed (d. 1410): Virgin and visionary. Feast day: April 7.

# V

## Valentina
Meaning: feminine form of Valentine
+ (d. 308): Virgin, martyred with St. Thea. Feast day: July 25.

## Valeria
Meaning: Latin "to be strong"
+ (d. first century): Mother. Feast day: December 9.

+ (d.c. second century): Martyr, wife of St. Vitalis. Feast day: April 28.

*(Valarie, Valerey, Valerie, Valery, Valeri, Valeree, Vallory)*

## Varelde, Variede, Veerle
See Pharäildis

## Veneranda
Meaning: unknown
+ (d. second century): French virgin and martyr. Feast day: November 14.

## Verena
Meaning: Latin "true"
+ (d. third century): Egyptian hermitess. Feast day: September 1.

*(Verasha, Verasia, Vereena, Verina, Verity)*

## Veridiana

Meaning: unknown

+ (d. 1242): Italian virgin and recluse. Feast day: February 1.

## Veronica

Meaning: Latin "true image"

+ (biblical): Name of woman who tradition says wiped Jesus' face with her veil (one of the "stations of the cross"). Feast day: July 12.

+ Veronica Giuliani (d. 1727): Nun and mystic. Feast day: July 9.

*(Vernice, Veronice, Veronika, Veronique, Vonnie, Vonny, Vronica)*

## Verylde

See Pharaildis

## Victoria

Meaning: Latin "victory"

+ (d. 250): Virgin and martyr. Feast day: December 23.

+ Victoria Rasoamanarivo, Blessed (d. 1894): Saint from Madagascar (Malagasy Republic) off the African coast.

+ Victoria Diez Bustos de Molina, Blessed (d. 1936): Martyr of the Spanish Civil War.

*(Vicci, Vickee, Vicki, Vickie, Vicky, Victori, Victorianna, Vikkie, Viktori, Viktorina, Viktorya)*

## Virginia

Meaning: Latin clan name

+ Virginia Centurione Brocelli, Blessed (d. 1651): Italian widow, nun.

*(Ginnie, Virg, Virgenia, Virgenie)*

## Vissia

Meaning: unknown

+ (d.c. 250): Virgin and martyr. Feast day: April 12.

## Vivian

See Bibiana

## Vivina

See Wivina

# W

## Walburga

Meaning: Old German "power protector"

+ (d. 779): German abbess. Feast day: February 25.

## Waldetrudis

Meaning: unknown

+ (d.c. 688): French abbess. Feast day: April 9.

## Waldrada

Meaning: unknown

+ (d.c. 620): French abbess. Feast day: May 5.

## Wastrada

Meaning: unknown

+ (d.c. 760): Widow. Feast day: July 21.

## Wenn

See Gwen

## Werburg

Meaning: unknown

+ (d.c. 785): Widow and abbess. Feast day: February 3.

## Werburga
Meaning: unknown

+ (d.c. 699): Benedictine nun, patron of Chester, England. Feast day: February 3.

## Wiborada
Meaning: unknown

+ (d. 926): Nun and martyr. Feast day: May 2.

## Wilfretrudis
Meaning: unknown

+ (d. 670): Benedictine abbess, niece of St. Gertrude. Feast day: November 23.

## Wilfrida
Meaning: unknown

+ (d.c. 988): Benedictine abbess. Feast day: September 9.

## Wilgefortis
Meaning: unknown

+ (date unknown): Martyr and virgin. Feast day: July 20.

## Wiltrudis
Meaning: unknown

+ (d.c. 986): Widow and Benedictine nun. Feast day: January 6.

## Winifred
Meaning: Welsh "blessed reconciliation"

+ (d.c. 650): Virgin and martyr. Feast day: November 3.

*(Fynifed, Guinevra, Gwenfrewi, Winefred, Winefride, Winefriede,*
*Winfred, Winifreda, Winifrid, Winn, Winnifed, Winnie)*

## Withburga
Meaning: unknown

+ (d.c. 743): Virgin and Benedictine nun. Feast day: July 8.

## Wivina
Meaning: unknown

+ (d.c. 1170): Flemish Benedictine abbess. Feast day: December 17.

*(Vivina)*

## Wulfhilda
Meaning: unknown

+ (d.c. 1000): Benedictine abbess. Feast day: September 9.

# X

## Xantippa
Meaning: unknown

+ (d. late first century)  Virgin. Feast day: September 23.

# Y

## Ytha
See Ita

# Z

## Zara

See Sarah

## Zenobia

Meaning: Greek "force of Zeus"

+ (d.c. 310): Martyred with her brother, St. Zenobius. Feast day: October 30.

## Zita

Meaning: Greek "to seek"

+ (d. 1272): Italian servant, patron of domestic workers. Feast day: April 27.

## Zoë

Meaning: Greek "life"

+ (d.c. 286): Roman noblewoman and martyr. Feast day: July 5.

*(Zoee, Zöe, Zoey, Zoie, Zowie)*

# SELECTED PATRON SAINTS

Accountants: Matthew
Actors: Genesius
Adopted children: Clotilde,
  Thomas More
Alcoholism: Monica
Altar Servers: John Berchmans
Anesthetists: Rene' Goupil
Architects: Thomas the Apostle
Artists: Catherine of Bologna, Luke
Athletes: Sebastian
Authors: Francis de Sales
Aviators: Joseph of Cupertino,
  Our Lady of Loretto
Bakers: Elizabeth of Hungary
Bankers: Matthew
Blindness: Raphael
Booksellers: John of God
Boy Scouts: George
Brewers: Augustine, Nicholas
Brides: Nicholas of Myra
Builders: Vincent Ferrer
Business Women: Margaret Clitherow
Butchers: Anthony of Egypt
Cabdrivers: Fiacre
Cancer: Peregrinus Laziosi
Carpenters: Joseph
Catechists: Charles Borromeo,
  Robert Bellarmine
Charity Workers: Vincent de Paul
Children: Nicholas of Myra
Cooks: Lawrence, Martha
Dancers: Philemon
Deaf: Francis de Sales
Dentists: Apollonia
Desperate Situations: Jude
Dietitians: Martha
Divorced: Fabiola, Helena
Doctors: Luke
Dying: Joseph
Ecologists: Francis of Assisi
Editors: John Bosco
Emigrants: Frances Xavier Cabrini
Engineers: Ferdinand III
Expectant Mothers: Gerard Majella
Eye Diseases: Lucy
Falsely Accused: Gerard Majella
Farmers: Isidore
Firefighters: Florian
Fishers: Andrew

Florists: Dorothy, Therese of Lisieux
Forest Workers: John Gualbert
Funeral Directors: Dismas,
  Joseph of Arimathea
Gardeners: Dorothy, Fiacre
Girl Scouts: Agnes
Grocers: Michael
Hairdressers: Martin de Porres,
  Pierre Troussaint
Headaches: Teresa of Ávila
Homemakers: Anne
Hospital Administrators: Frances
  Xavier Cabrini
Hospital Workers: Camillus de Lellis,
  John of God
Hotelkeepers: Amandus, Martha
Invalids: Roch
Jealousy: Elizabeth of Portugal
Jewelers: Dunstan
Journalists: Francis de Sales
Laborers: Isidore
Lawyers: Ivo, Thomas More
Librarians: Jerome
Lost Items: Anthony of Padua
Lovers: Raphael
Maids: Zita
Mariners: Michael
Medical Records: Raymond of
  Penafort
Mental Illness: Benedict Joseph Labre
Merchants: Francis of Assisi,
  Nicholas of Myra
Midwives: Margaret of Cortona,
  Raymond Nonnatus
Military Chaplains: John of
  Capistrano
Miners: Barbara
Missions: Francis Xavier
Mothers: Monica
Musicians: Cecilia
Nurses: Agatha
Orphans: Jerome Emiliani
Painters: Luke
Paratroopers: Michael
Pharmacists: Cosmas and Damian,
  Gemma Galgani
Philosophers: Catherine of Siena,
  Justin Martyr

Physicians: Cosmas and Damian, Luke
Poets: Cecilia, David
Police: Michael
Poor: Cuthbert, Julia, Lawrence, Macrina the Elder
Postal Workers: Gabriel
Priests: John Baptist Vianney
Printers: Augustine, John of God
Radiologists: Michael
Rheumatism: James the Greater
Runaways: Dymphna
Sailors: Brendan
Schools: Thomas Aquinas
Scientists: Albert the Great
Second Marriages: Adelaide, Matilda
Secretaries: Genesius
Seminarians: Charles Borromeo
Separated Spouses: Edward the Confessor, Philip Howard
Servants: Martha, Zita
Sick: Camillus de Lellis

Singers: Gregory the Great
Skiers: Bernard of Montjoux
Social Workers: Louise de Marillac
Soldiers: George, Joan of Arc, Sebastian
Stepparents: Adelaide, Thomas More
Students: Thomas Aquinas
Surgeons: Cosmas and Damian, Luke
Tax Collectors: Matthew
Teachers: Gregory the Great
Telecommunication Workers: Gabriel
Theologians: Alphonsus Liguori, Augustine
Throat Disease: Blaise
Travelers: Anthony of Padua, Christopher
Victims of Abuse: Fabiola, Monica
Victims of Rape: Maria Goretti
Workers: Joseph
Writers: Francis de Sales
Youth: Agnes, Aloysius Gonzaga

# SELECTED BOYS' BIBLICAL NAMES

| | | |
|---|---|---|
| Aaron | Ichabod | Nathanael |
| Abel | Isaac | Nathaniel |
| Abraham | Isaiah | Nicanor |
| Absalom | Ismael | Nicodemus |
| Adam | Israel | Noah |
| Amos | Jacob | Obediah |
| Andrew | James | Oren |
| Apollo | Jason | Paul |
| Aquila | Jedediah | Peter |
| Balthasar | Jeremiah | Philemon |
| Barnabus | Jesse | Philip |
| Bartholomew | Joachim | Raphael |
| Benjamin | Job | Reuben |
| Caleb | Joel | Rufus |
| Caspar | John | Samson |
| Claudius | Jonah | Samuel |
| Cornelius | Jonathan | Saul |
| Daniel | Joseph | Seth |
| Darius | Joshua | Silas |
| David | Jude | Simeon |
| Dionysius | Lazarus | Simon |
| Dismas | Lucius | Solomon |
| Elias | Luke | Stephen |
| Elijah | Malachai | Thaddeus |
| Ethan | Mark | Thomas |
| Ezekiel | Matthew | Timon |
| Ezra | Matthias | Timothy |
| Gabriel | Melchior | Titus |
| Gamaliel | Micah | Zachariah |
| Gideon | Michael | Zechariah |
| Haran | Moses | Zebadiah |
| Hiram | Nathan | |

# SELECTED GIRLS' BIBLICAL NAMES

Abigail

Ada

Ann

Anna

Chloe

Deborah

Edna

Elizabeth

Esther

Eunice

Eve

Hannah

Jemina

Joanna

Judith

Julia

Leah

Lois

Lydia

Magdalene

Maria

Martha

Mary

Miriam

Naomi

Phoebe

Photina

Priscilla

Rachel

Rebecca

Rhoda

Ruth

Salome

Sarah

Sharon

Susanna

Tabitha

Veronica

# OUR FAVORITE NAMES

### Boys' Names

### Girls' Names

# ALSO AVAILABLE

## The Gift of Baptism
## A Handbook for Parents
Tom Sheridan

Here is a welcoming, affirming approach to baptismal preparation that helps parents celebrate this blessed event, understand the meaning of the sacrament for their child, recognize their important role as parents in their child's spiritual development, and appreciate the support they receive from their parish faith community. This practical, easy-to understand book explains the sacrament of Baptism's history and symbols and answers often-asked questions. (64-page paperback, $3.95)

## The Gift of Godparents
## For Those Chosen with Love and Trust to Be Godparents
Tom Sheridan

An upbeat, down-to-earth explanation of the whats, whys and hows of being a godparent. Information about the sacrament of Baptism and the responsibilities of godparenting are blended with touching stories of real-life godparents and suggestions about how to help a godchild grow in faith from Baptism to adulthood. This little book answers dozens of practical questions that godparents ask and provides simple prayers and reflections to help them understand the importance of being a godparent. A great gift from parents to godparents. (96-page paperback, $4.95)

## Daily Meditations (with Scripture) for Busy Moms
Patricia Robertson
## Daily Meditations (with Scripture) for Busy Dads
Patrick Reardon

Companion books for Mom and Dad, each containing 366 thoughtful, down-to-earth reflections on the spirituality of parenting. Daily meditations are followed by carefully chosen Scripture quotes. (366-page paperbacks, $9.95 each)

## For Our Children's Children
## Reflections on Being a Grandparent
Carole Kastigar

Brief reflections, practical wisdom, and everyday anecdotes sure to touch the heart of every grandparent. Over one hundred single-page meditations encourage grandparents to celebrate both the responsibilities and rewards of grandparenting. (120-page paperback, $5.95)

**Available from Christian book sellers or call 800-397-2282.**